The Hartnett Guitar Method

The Guitar Method for Complete Technique

By Joe Hartnett

The Hartnett Guitar Method

The Guitar Method for Complete Technique

Written and Edited by Joe Hartnett

Published by Joe Hartnett Guitar Editions

Copyright © 2016 Joe Hartnett
All rights reserved.

www.joehartnettguitar.com

Preface

The Hartnett Guitar Method is a compendium of plectrum and finger plucking guitar techniques. This method provides the guitarist with a variety of advanced guitar techniques as well as developmental studies for composition, improvisation and the interpretation of music on the guitar. This method contains transcriptions, arrangements and compositions of advanced solo guitar works as well as compositional études for both the electric guitar and the classical guitar. The material provided showcases the guitar as a compositional, improvisational and interpretative instrument. The Hartnett Guitar Method displays the transcendental and expressive nature of the guitar as a lyrical, melodic, harmonic, polyphonic, percussive and textural instrument. The musical examples and compositions are presented in standard notation as well as the modern adaption of guitar tablature.

In memory of my brother, Paul Hartnett

Contents

I. Finger Indications 10
II. Fretting Hand 11
III. Improvisation 12
IV. The Electric Guitar 13-99
V. The Classical Guitar 100-123
VI. Transcriptions, Arrangements, and Compositions 124-241
VII. Author Biography 243

I. Finger Indications

Fingering notation is very important and useful in that it can provide immediate physical solutions to a given musical situation. The suggested fingerings are in fact suggestions, and you should always investigate further to discover a more suitable fingering if required. Many difficult situations on the guitar can be alleviated by creating an economical and consistent fingering.

<u>Left Hand (Fretting Hand)</u>

1 - First Finger (Index)

2 - 2nd Finger (Middle)

3 - 3rd Finger (Ring)

4 - 4th Finger (Pinky)

<u>Right Hand (Plucking and Plectrum Hand)</u>

p – (Thumb)

i – (Index)

m – (Middle)

a – (Ring)

c – (Pinky)

<u>Picking Direction</u>

Alternate Picking involves the subtle, relaxed motion of articulating Down and Up strokes, with all movement deriving from the wrist, as arm movement is contained to a minimum.

Alternate Picking movement, and picking in general can also come from a combination of the metacarpophalangeal joint in the thumb and the index finger. This is very effective with Sweep Picking as it can grant subtle movement alterations that are required for a more fluid and relaxed motion.

II. Fretting Hand

The thumb of the fretting hand should always remain straightened and never ascend beyond the middle of the back of the neck. The thumb should be behind the first finger (with minor deviations) and never lead the second finger. The lower your thumb descends the mid-way point of the neck, the easier it will be to stretch and remain on your fingertips.

You must stay on your absolute fingertips (with minor deviations), as notes are to be performed with either the left side or center of the active finger. Your elbow should be close to your body, pushed forward slightly, as it will create an athletic and natural angle to your wrist, much like that of a violinist.

Pressing the strings onto the fretboard should involve minimal pressure, utilizing light pressure between the thumb (supporting) and 1st finger. You will be able to create a clean sound with the finger existing next to the fret, not on, as much as possible. In some musical scenarios, it will not be possible to be directly next to the fret.

Nails on the fretting hand can greatly interfere with playing and should be trimmed at all times (unlike the classical guitar technique of the plucking hand as it is advantageous to have nails).

You should stay as close to the strings as possible, both before playing and directly after. This will allow you to be more efficient at any given tempo.

It is essential to commit yourself to a planned fingering system. Choosing designated fingers to perform certain, if not all passages will lead to less physical trouble (although you may feel uncomfortable due to lack of finger-independence) and a more accurate performance. There are many useful suggested fingerings for recurring, idiomatic situations throughout this guitar method.

Classical guitarists commonly rest their guitar at an elevated position to create an optimal, relaxed and athletic fretting hand. Every player has a preferred comfort zone for playing and there are many variations of seating and neck elevation techniques to be explored.

III. Improvisation

Learning scales and modes in recurring patterns will give you a memorable road map of the guitar and its creative landscape. You will develop faster and eventual automatic results for your improvisations based on this knowledge and programming.

On the guitar, scale and modal patterns can be moved around to be easily transposed from one key or chord to another. For example, moving the first pattern and 1st Mode of C Major (Ionian) up a whole-step will give D Major (Ionian). Moving the 2nd pattern and Mode of C major, D Dorian up a whole-step will lead to E Dorian.

For every initial composed scale, there is a mode (scale) for every note in the initial composed scale. A 7-note scale has 7 modes; a 5-note scale has 5 modes. A modal scale is created by starting on any given note in the parent scale and cadencing on the initial note only now at its higher unison. The unique sound of each scale and mode is based on its series of half-steps, whole-steps, and any other creative configuration of distance from one note to another.

Intervals are the distance from one note to any note higher or lower than the initial note. Subtle alterations to the common intervals of composed scales can lead to interesting improvisational ideas.

IV. The Electric Guitar

Practice and Perform all of the examples including alternate picking, sweep picking and slurs with a palm muted technique. This will give you an ideal position to develop a versatile picking technique with dynamic control. This is especially important when playing with distortion as it eliminates unnecessary noise. You should feel a slight and subtle vibration when muting, with the pitch and quality of each note clearly heard without the existence of a dead note. To release the mute, simply lift up the portion of your hand corresponding to the string the performed note falls under. Remain as close to the guitar as possible when relieving the mute.

Your hand will travel vertically to and from each string, and you should never extend your wrist to reach (with minor deviations) beyond a normal resting state. As stated earlier in this method, the thumb and first finger (holding the pick) can be used to extend your reach for a more subtle and precise attack.

Slurs must be performed with a quick and even attack onto each note, and have a rhythmically even pull-off when leaving. The string must be pulled down swiftly without creating an altered pitch (bend) to produce a quality slur. I suggest on notes above the 1st string, to rest on the string below after a pull-off (slur) to produce a strong and even tone that does not betray volume or pitch. You must remain on the absolute fingertips to produce a well-balanced slur, giving the slur its well-deserved and adequately configured rhythm.

The Electric Guitar

1. Sweep Picking 15-16
2. Alternate Picking 17-20
3. Fretting 21-26
4. Glissando 27-28
5. Left-Hand Independence 29
6. Slurs 30-32
7. Scales and Modes 33-35
8. Expanding the Range of the C Scale and Modes 36-38
9. The Scale on Single Strings 39-40
10. 2 String Arpeggios 41-42
11. 3 String Arpeggios 43-44
12. 4 String Arpeggios 45-46
13. 5 String Arpeggios 47-48
14. 6 String Arpeggios 49-50
15. Learning the Scale and its Modes in Memorable Blocks 51-62
16. Various Ways to Perform the Scale 63-69
17. Creating Melodic Lines 70-71
18. The Pentatonic Scale and Modes 72-74
19. The Pentatonic Scale on Single Strings 75-76
20. The Pentatonic Scale and its Modes in Memorable Blocks 77-80
21. Performing the Pentatonic Scale with Various Melodic and Rhythmic Alterations 81-82
22. The Chromatic Scale 83
23. The A Minor Pentatonic Scale with Chromatic Alterations 85
24. The C Major Scale with Chromatic Alterations 87
25. The Whole Tone Scale 88
26. Whole Tone Arpeggios 89
27. Diminished Arpeggio étude Performed with Alternate Picking 90-93
28. Melodic Development with Scales 94-96
29. Vibrato and Bending 97-98
30. Vibrato and Bending in a Melodic Solo 99

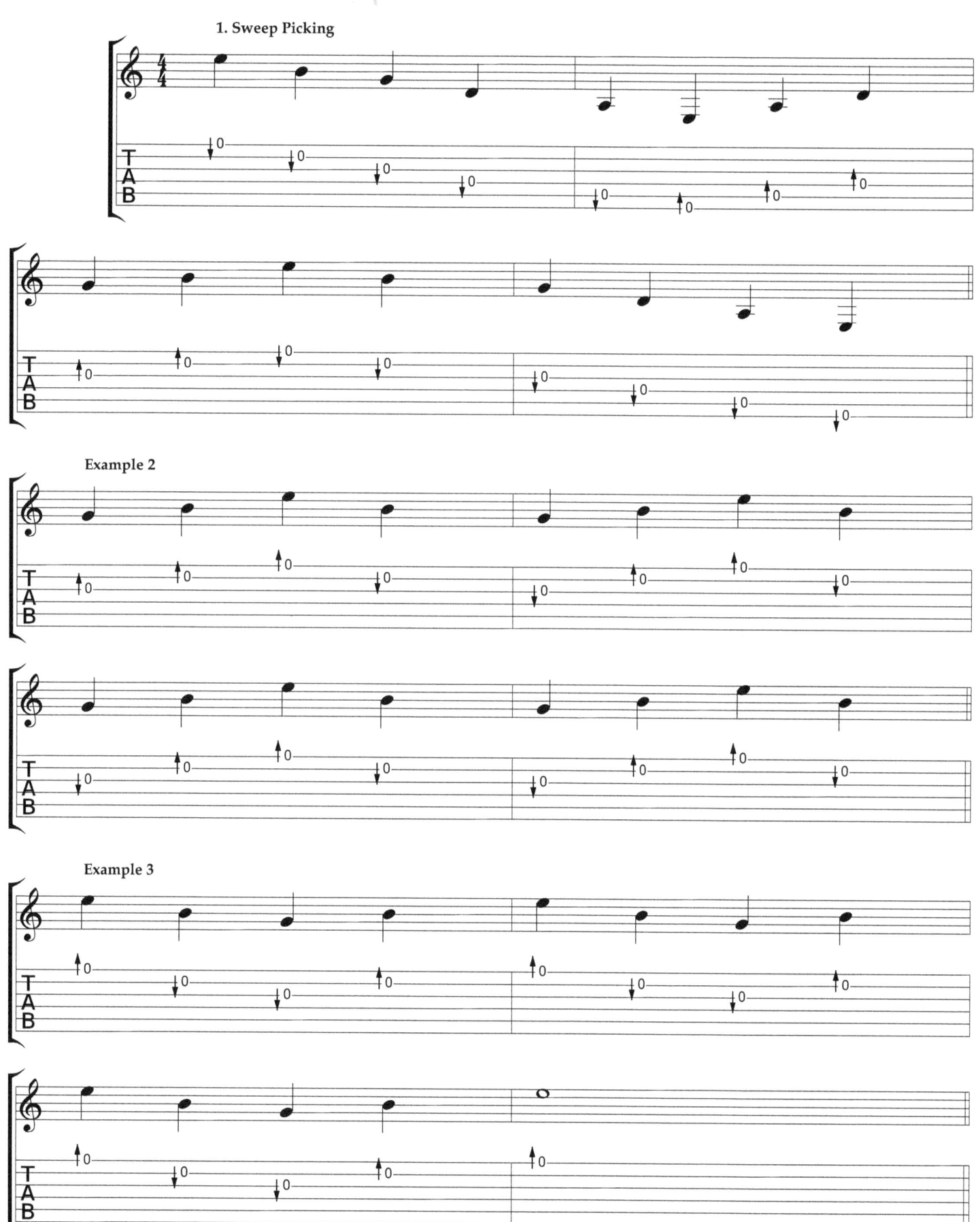

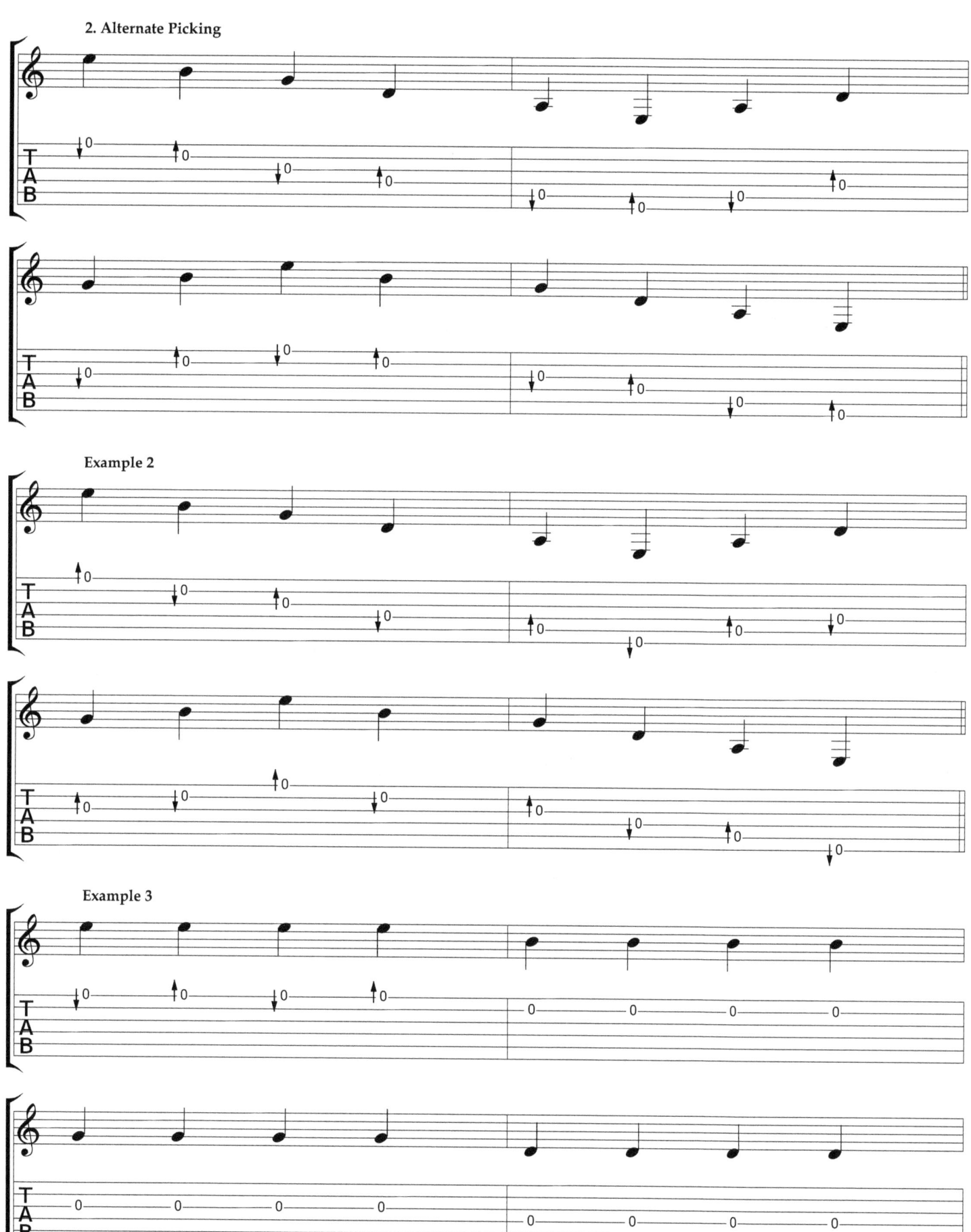

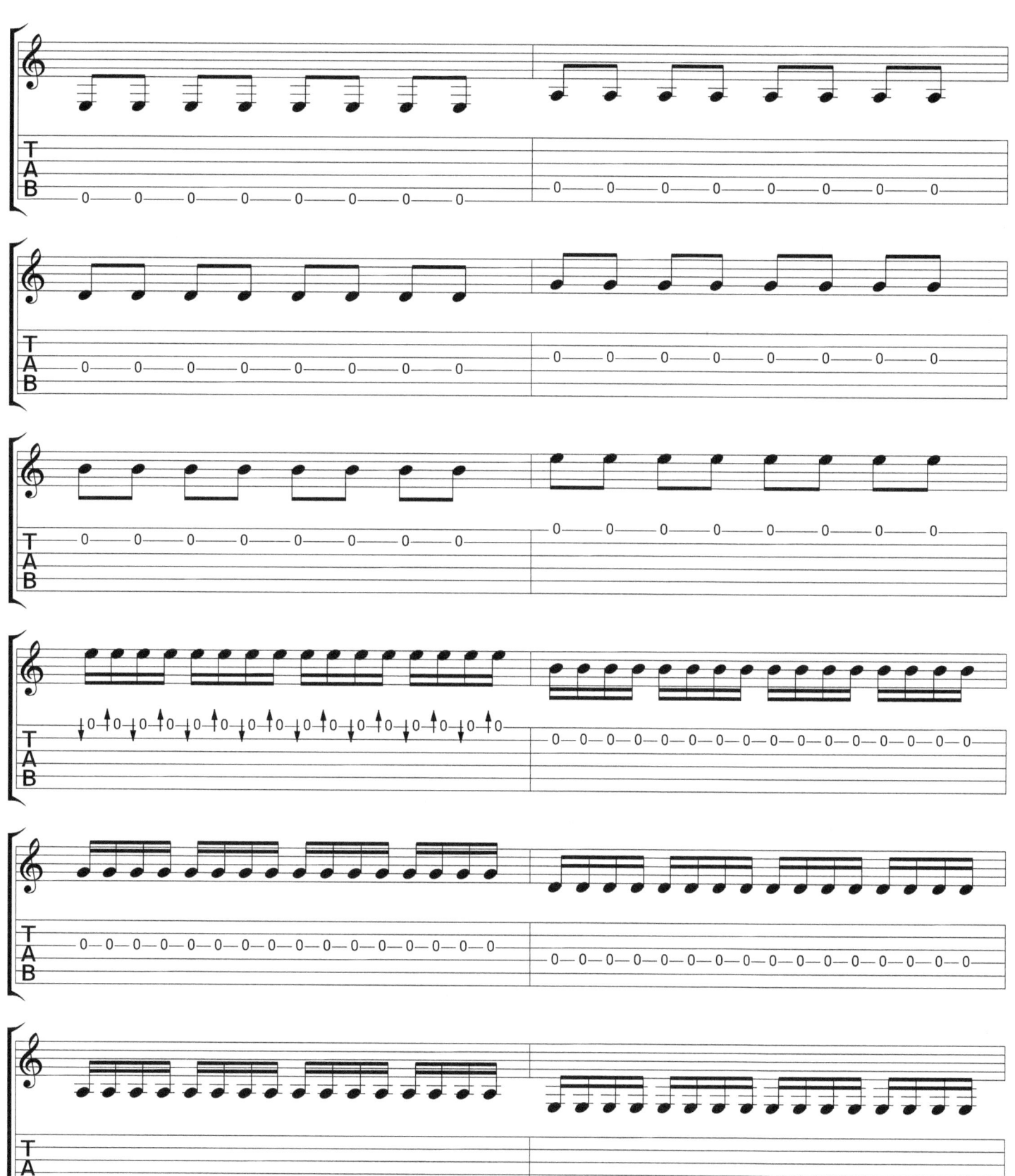

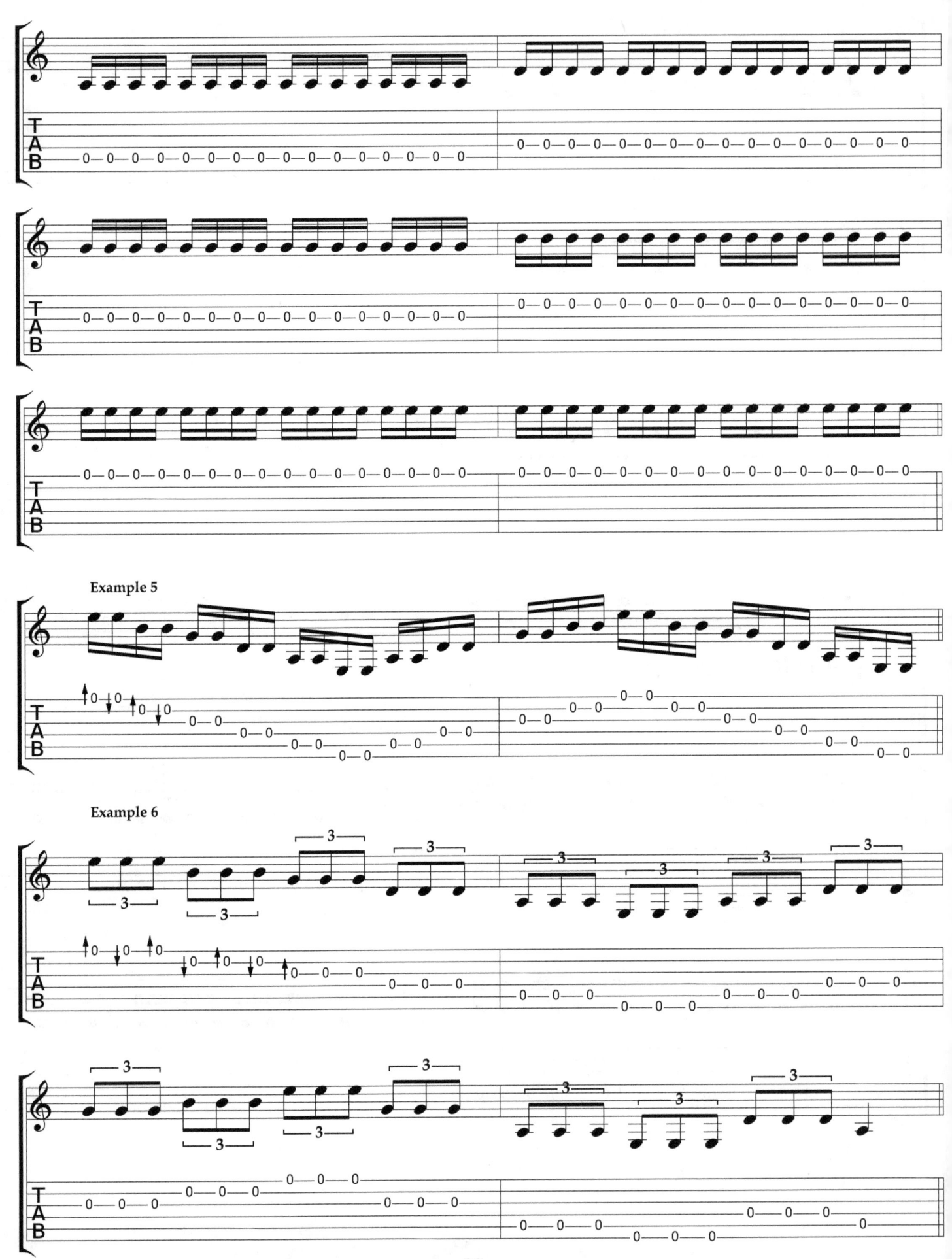

3. Fretting

Example 2

Example 3

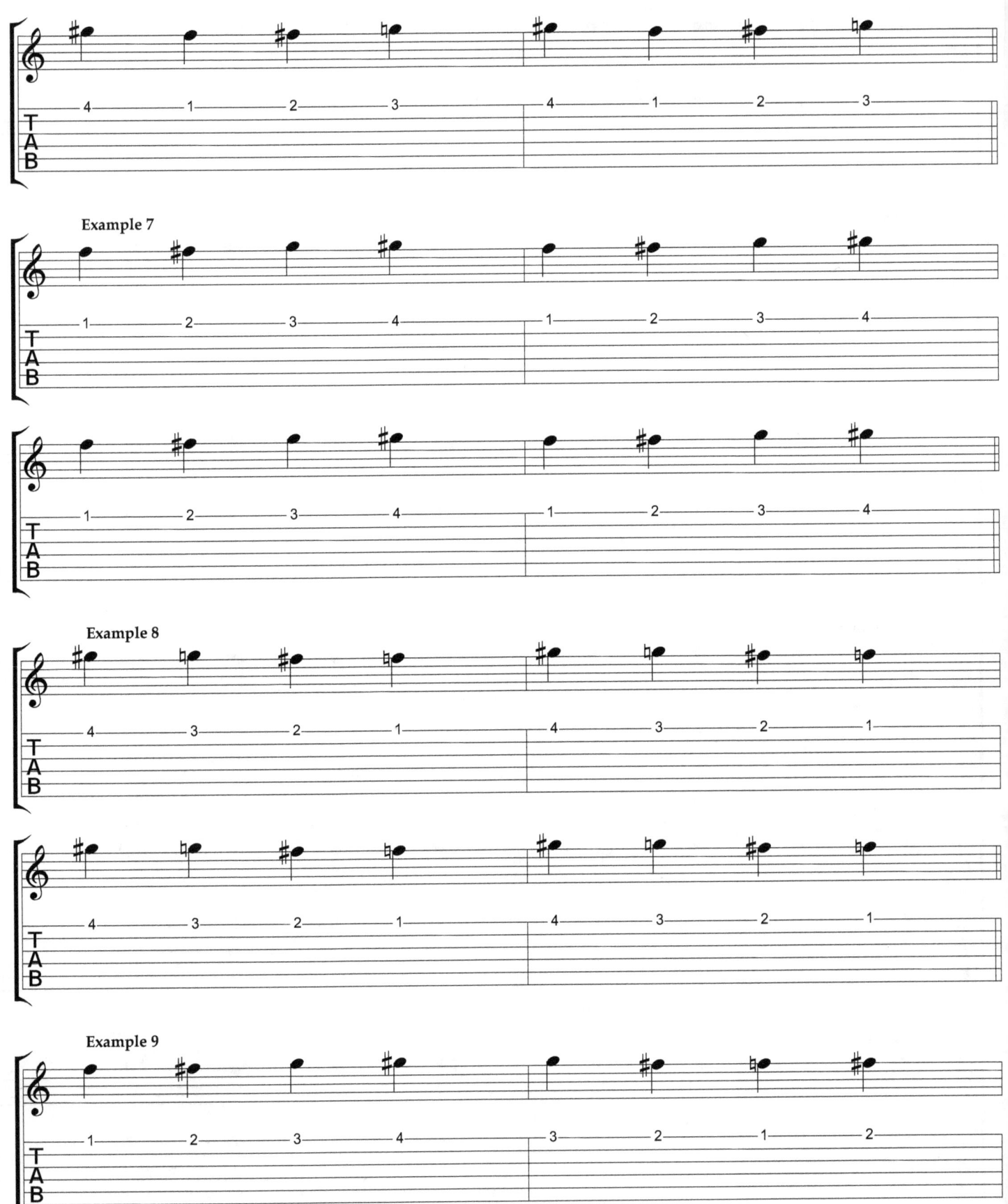

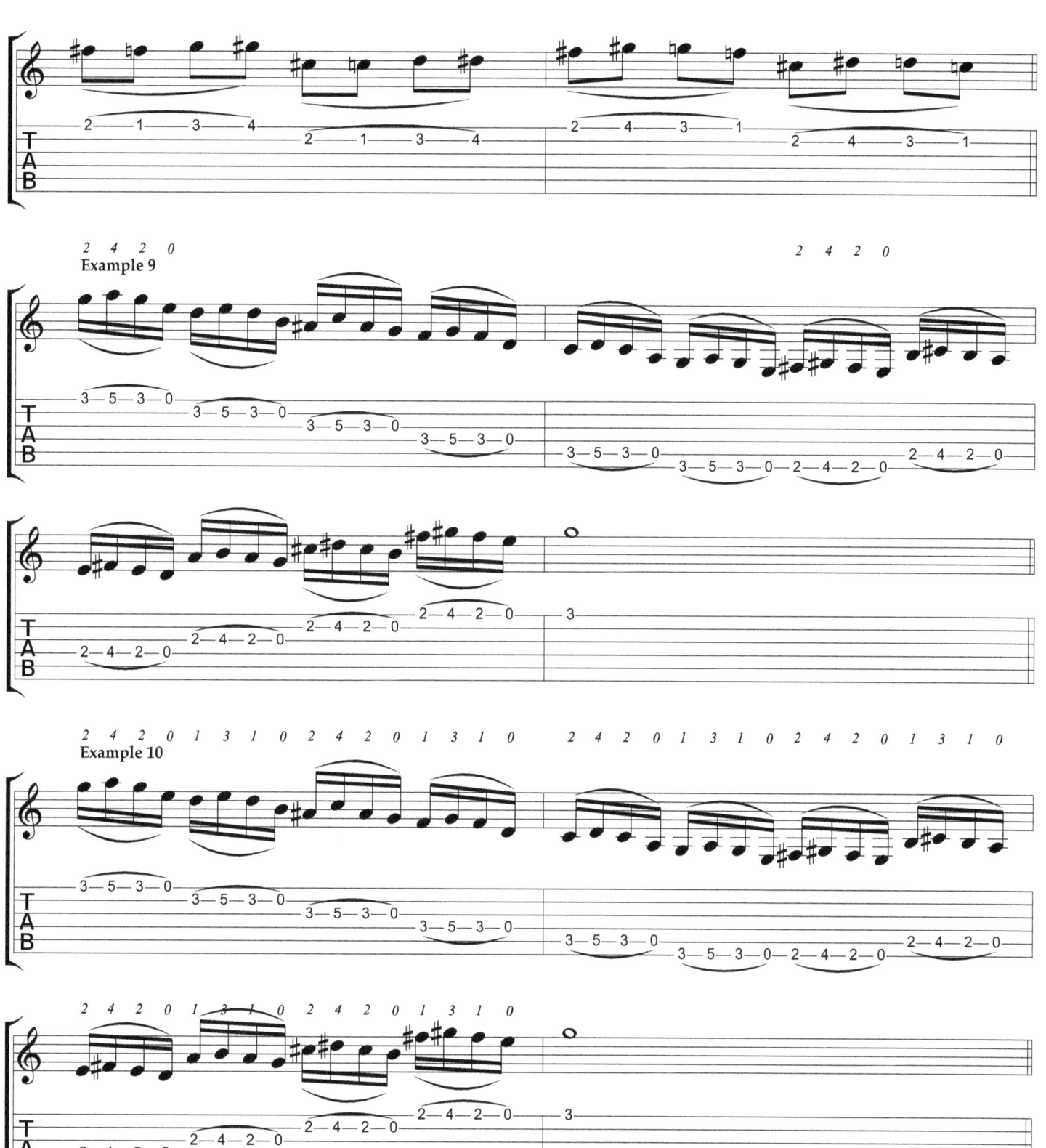

7. Scales and Modes - C Ionian, D Dorian, E Phrygian, F Lydian, G Mixolydian, A Aeolian, B Locrian

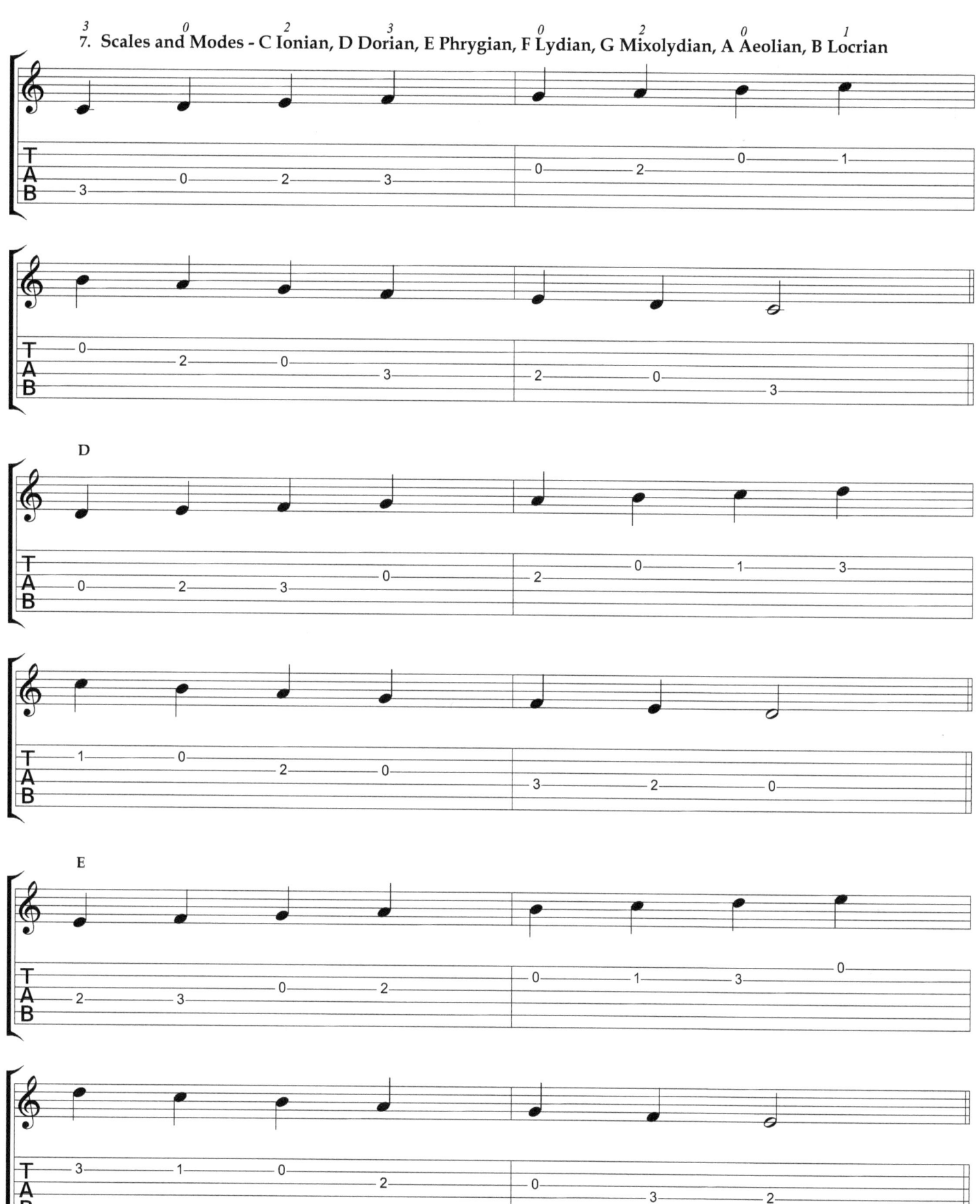

33

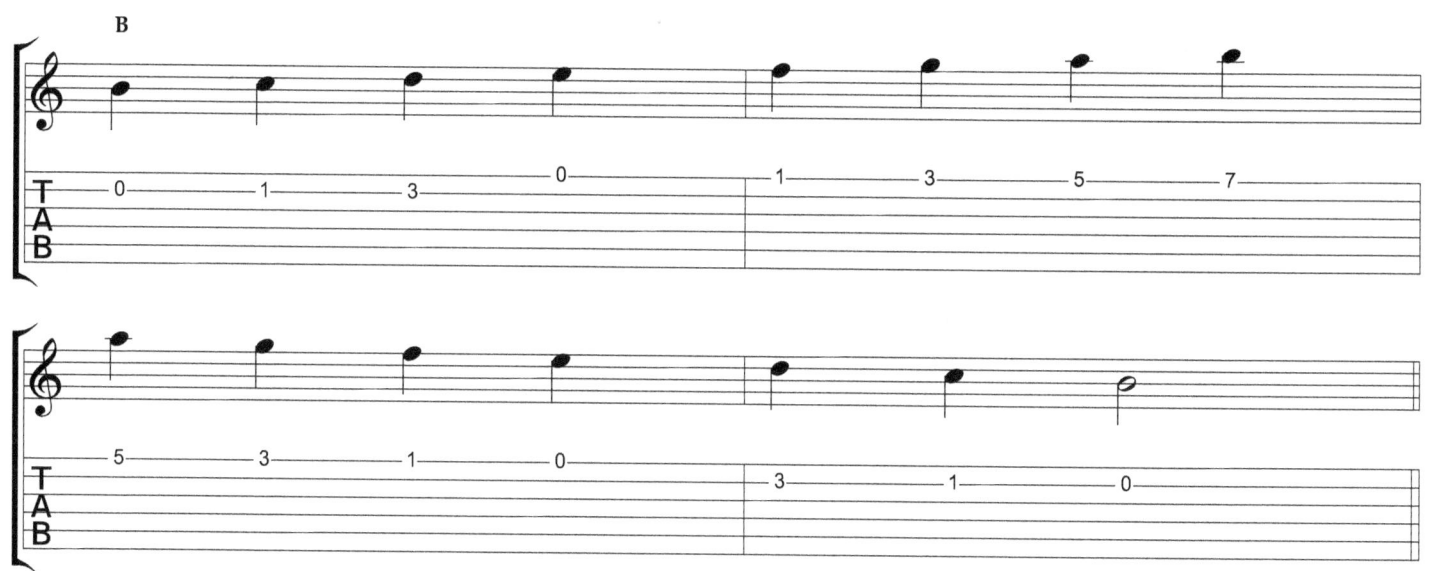

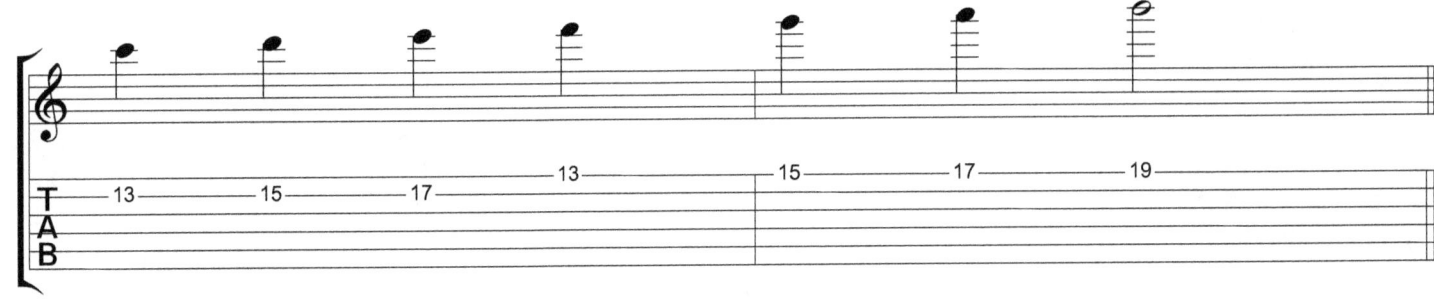

9. The Scale on Single Strings

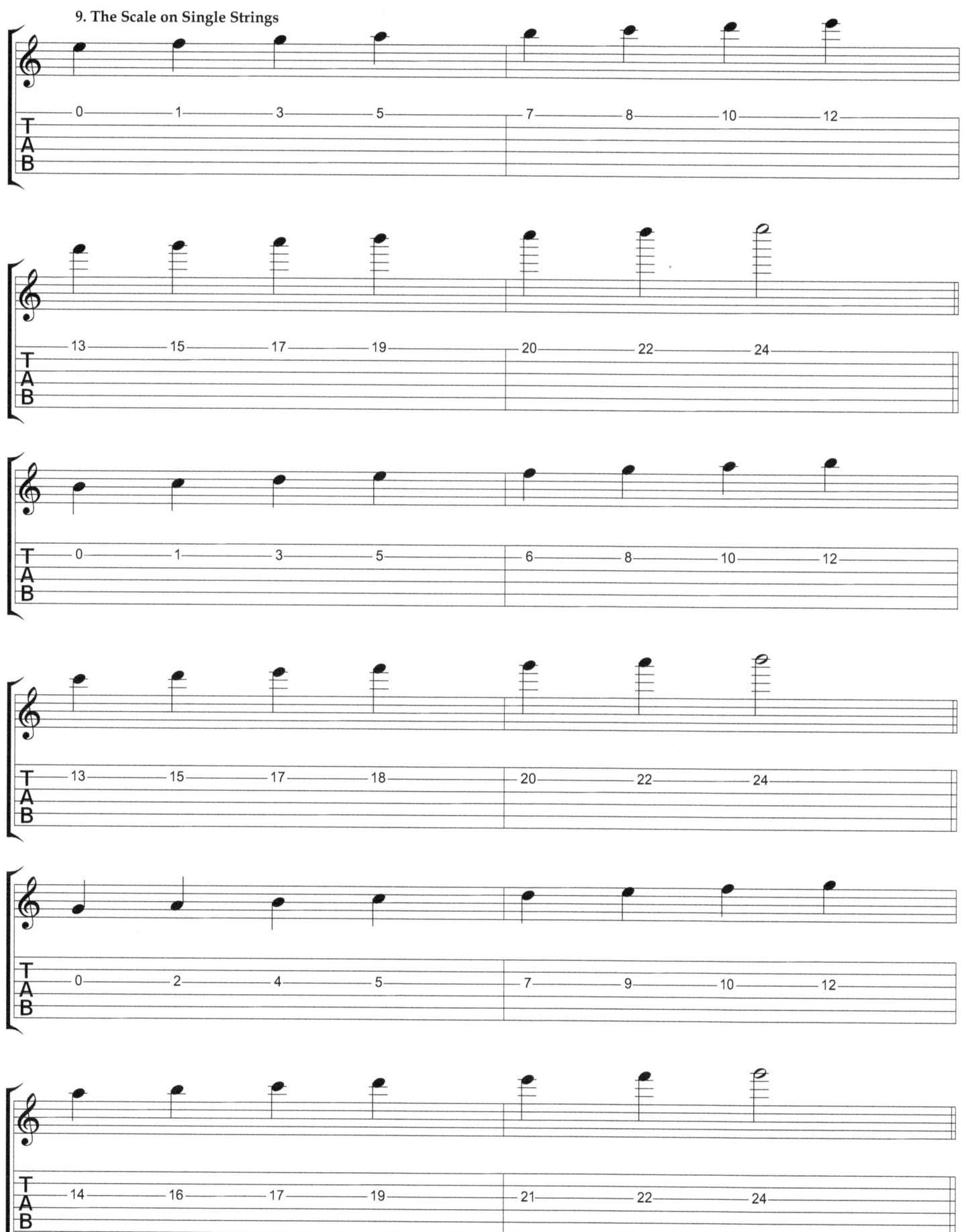

10. 2 String Arpeggios

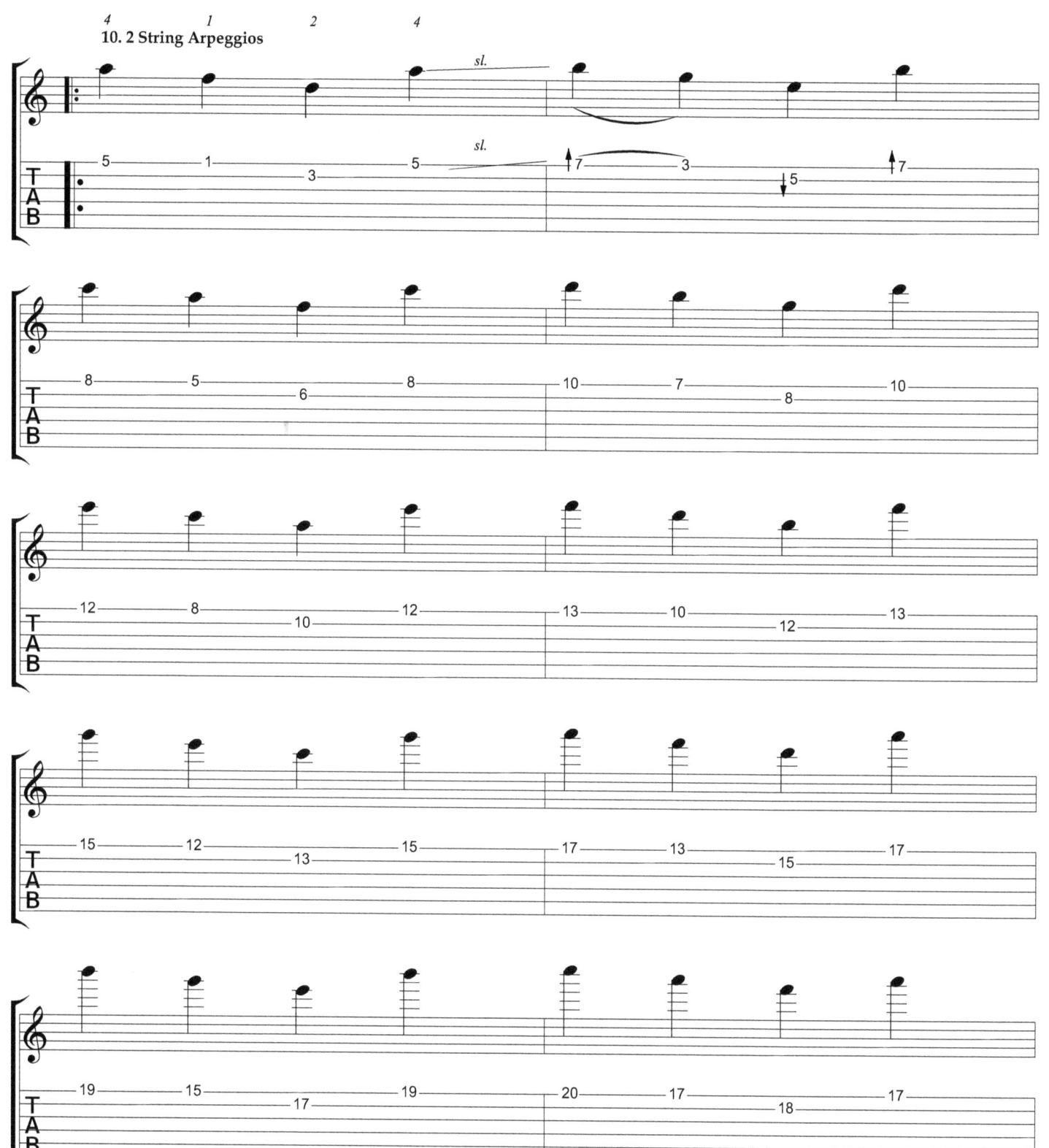

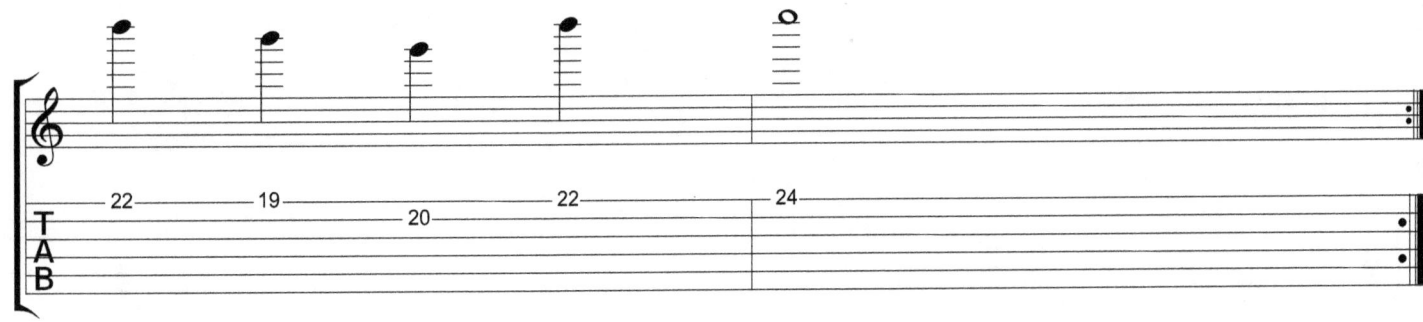

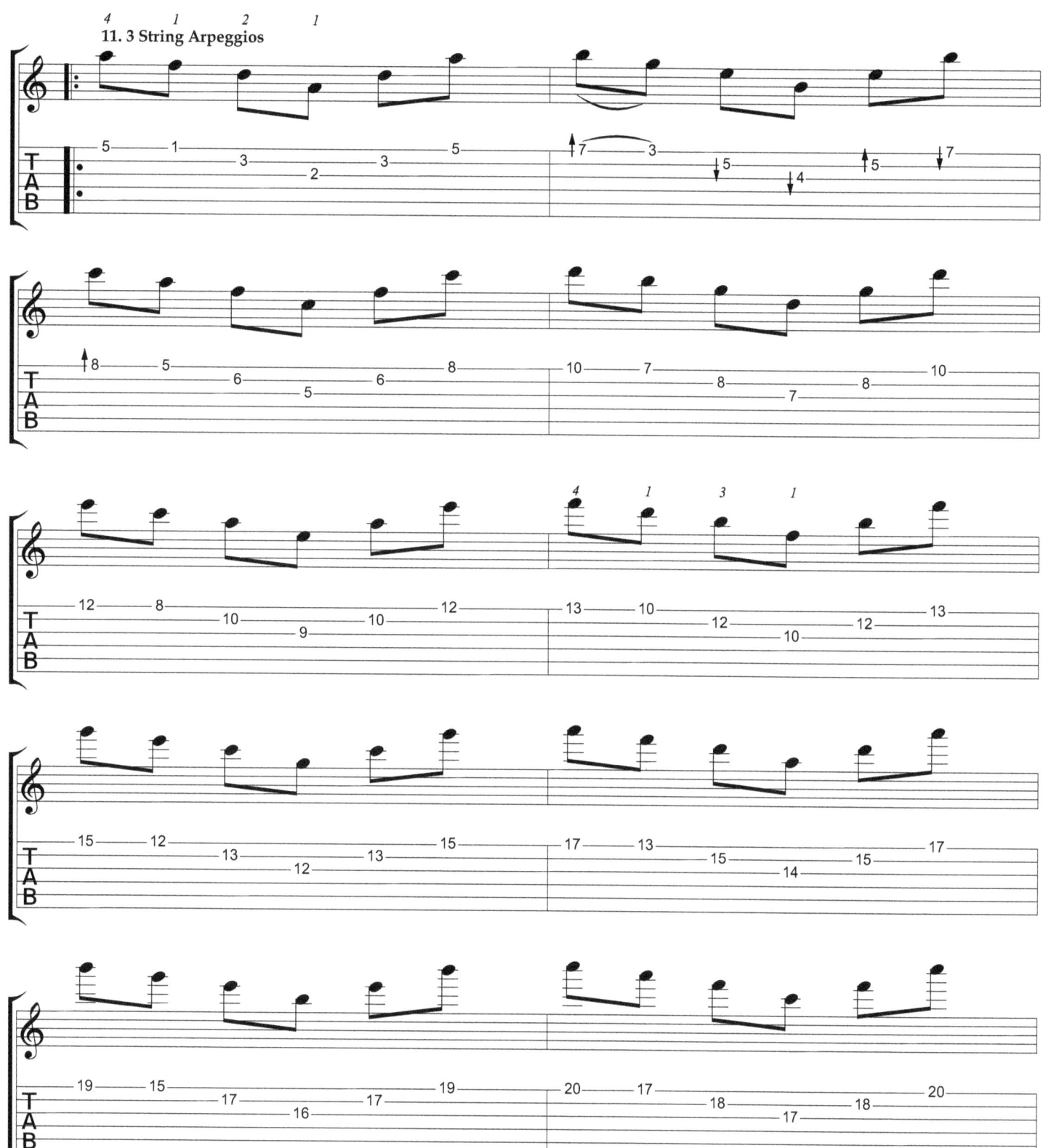

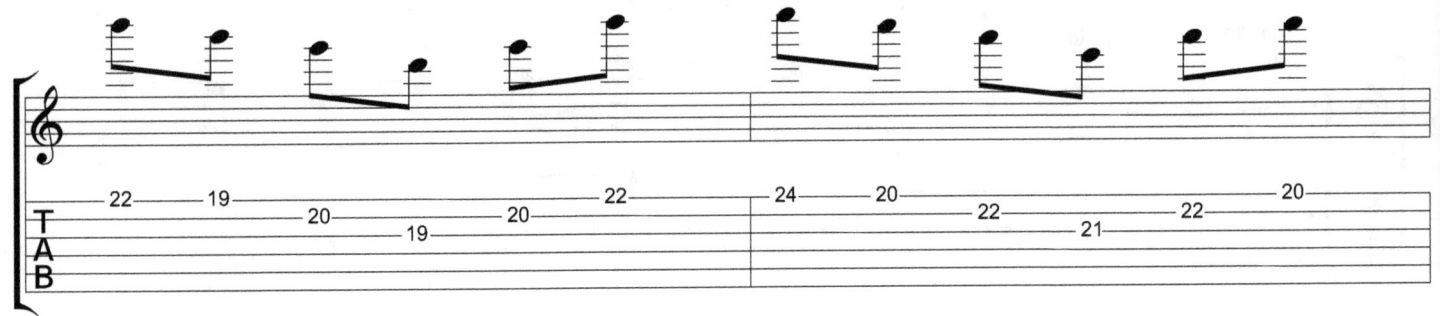

12. 4 String Arpeggios

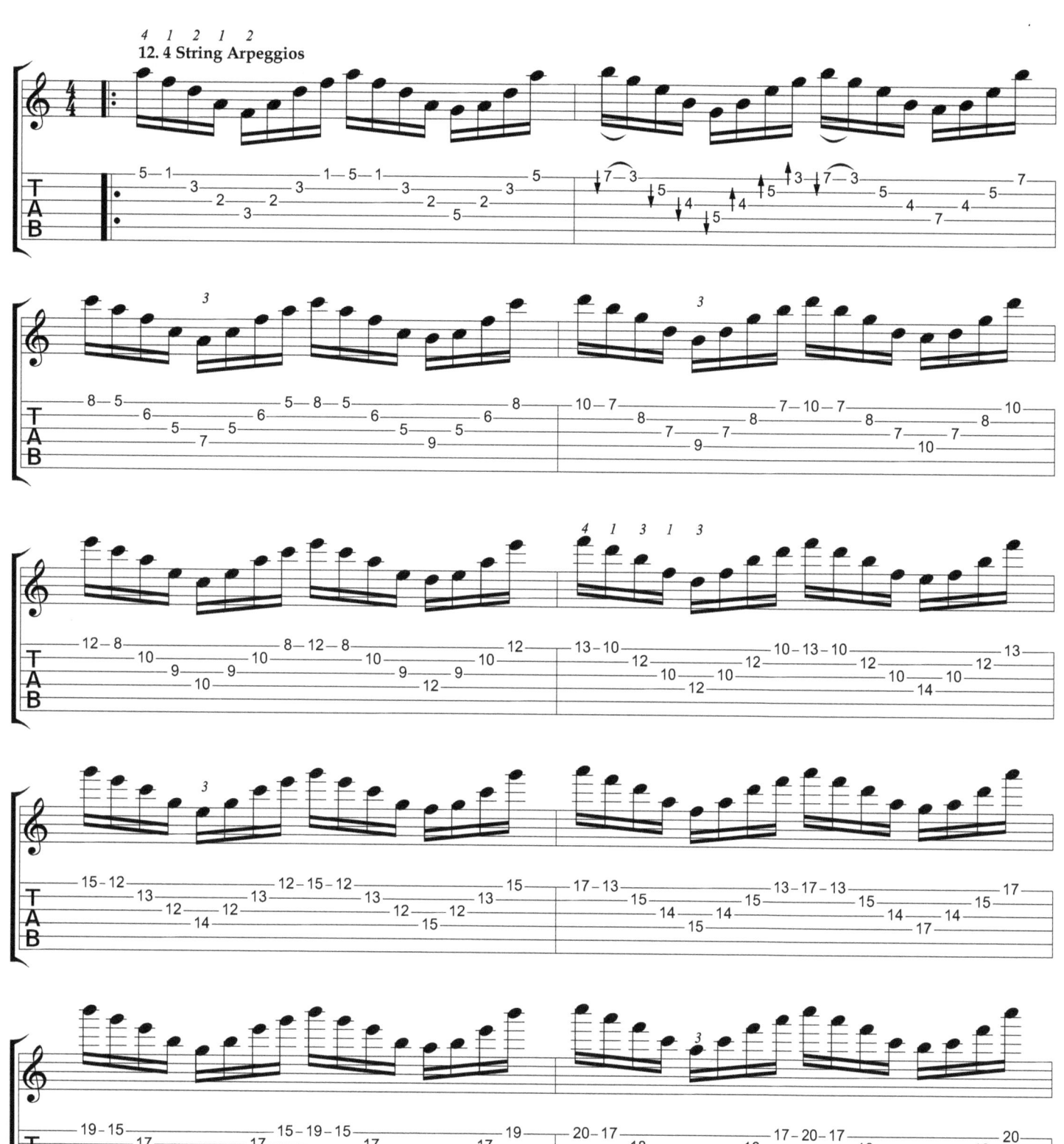

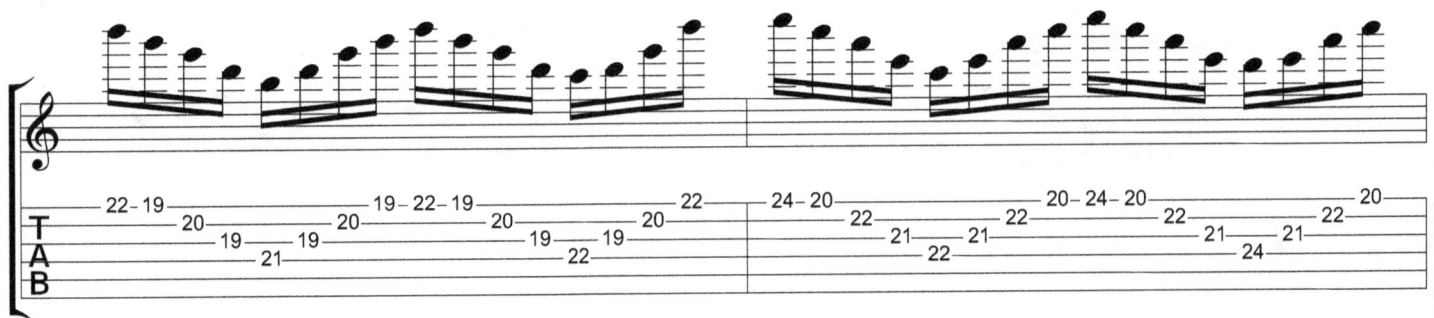

46

13. 5 String Arpeggios

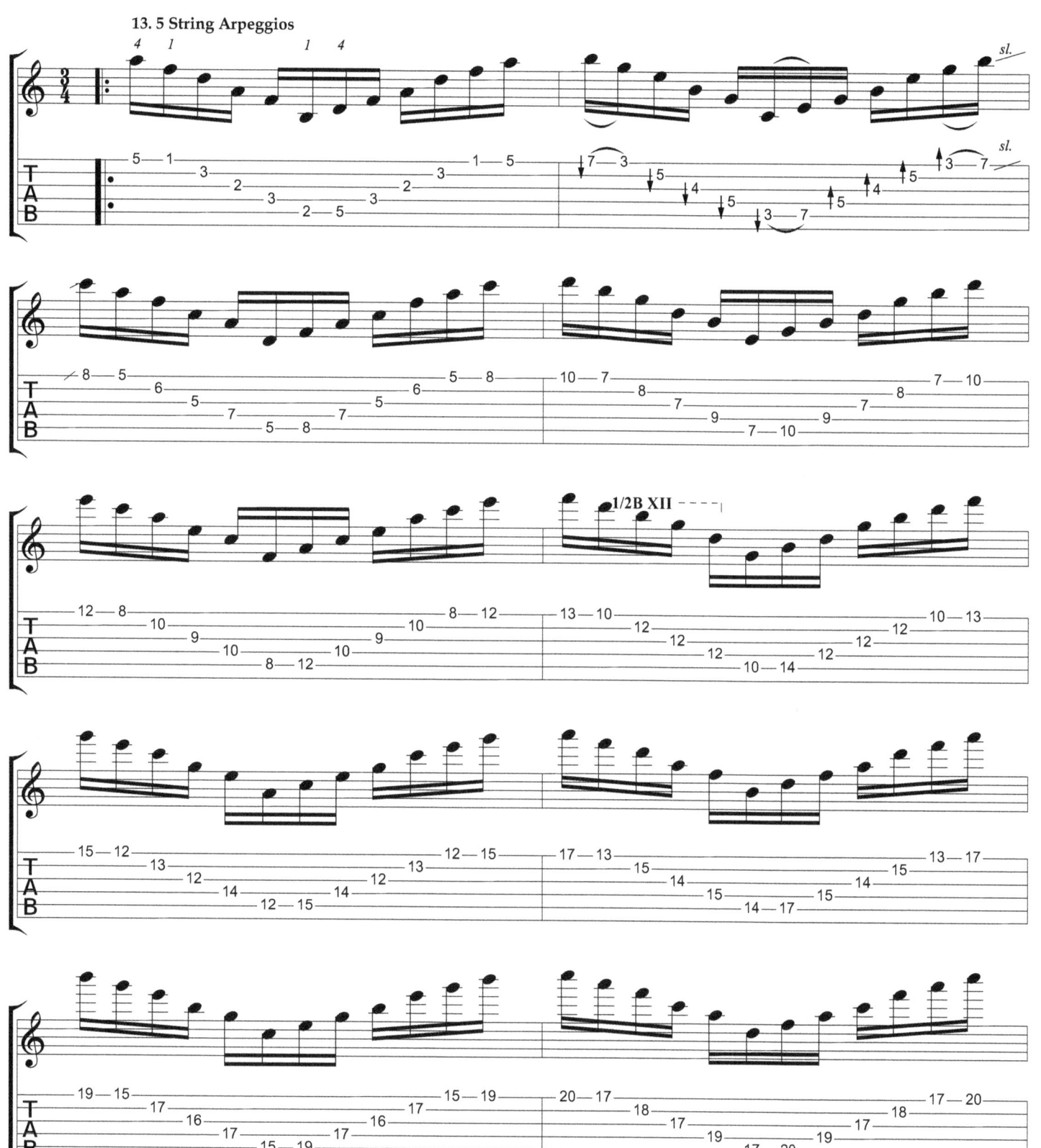

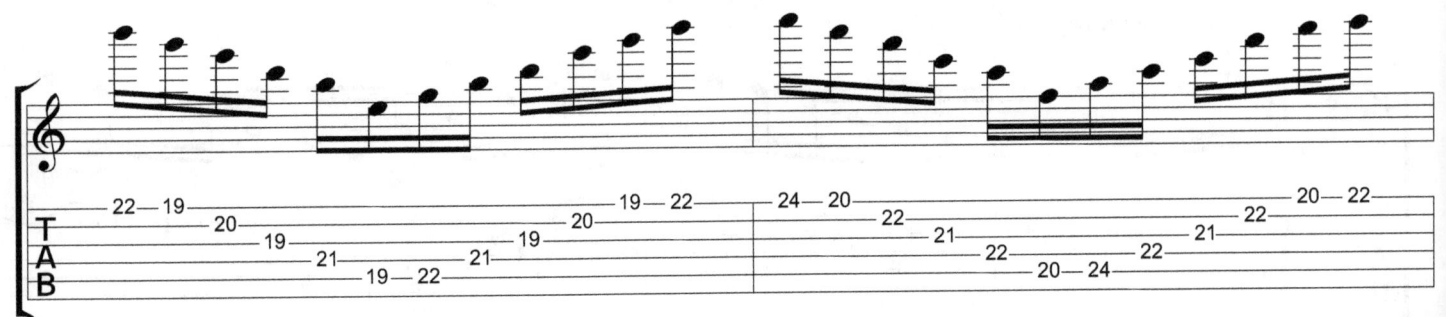

14. 6 String Arpeggios

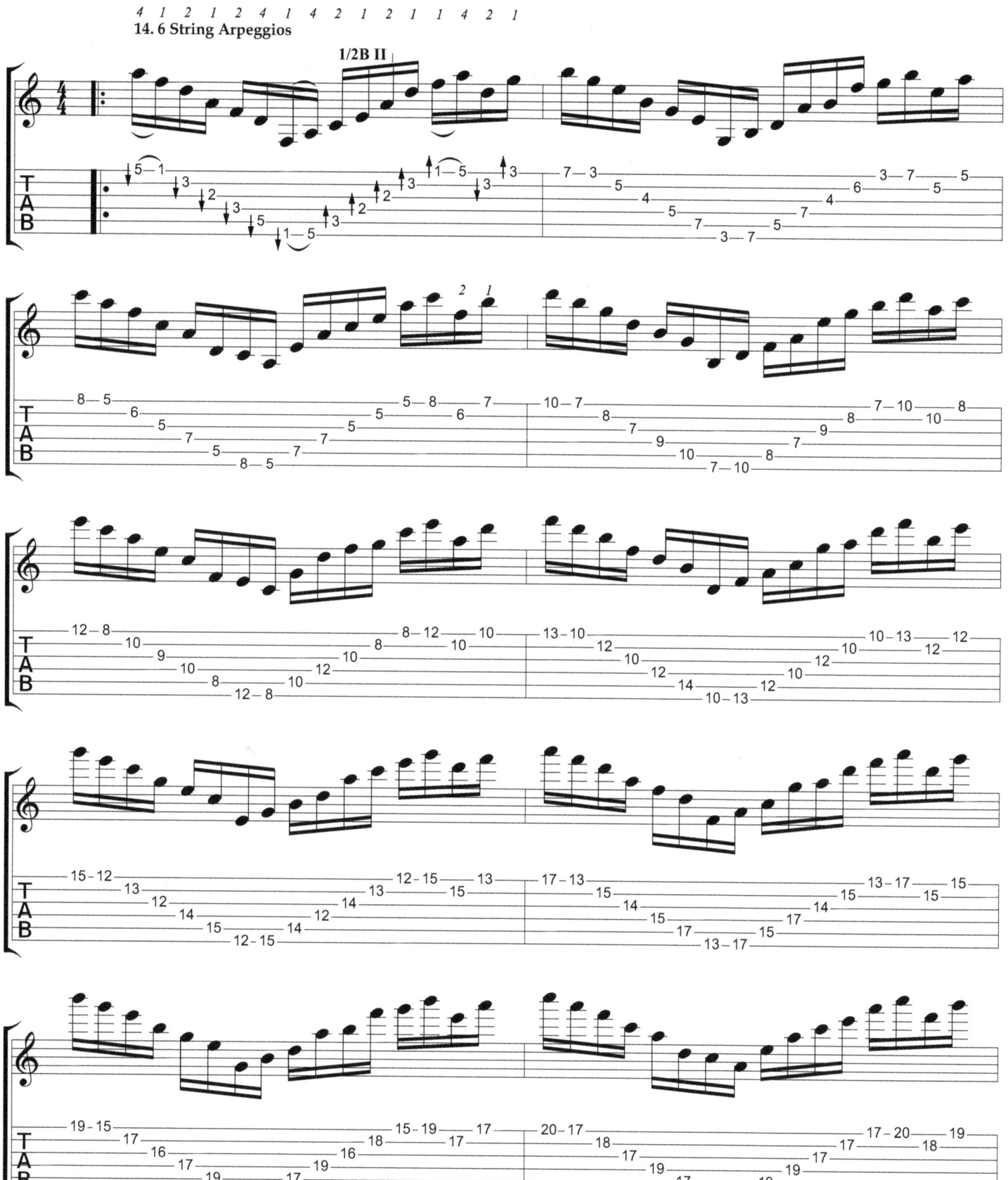

49

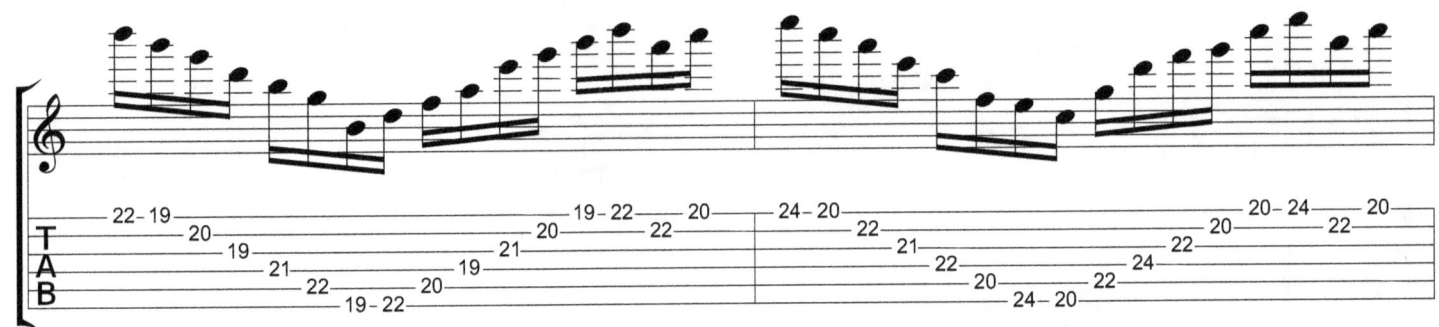

15. Learning the Scale and its Modes in Memorable Blocks

F Lydian

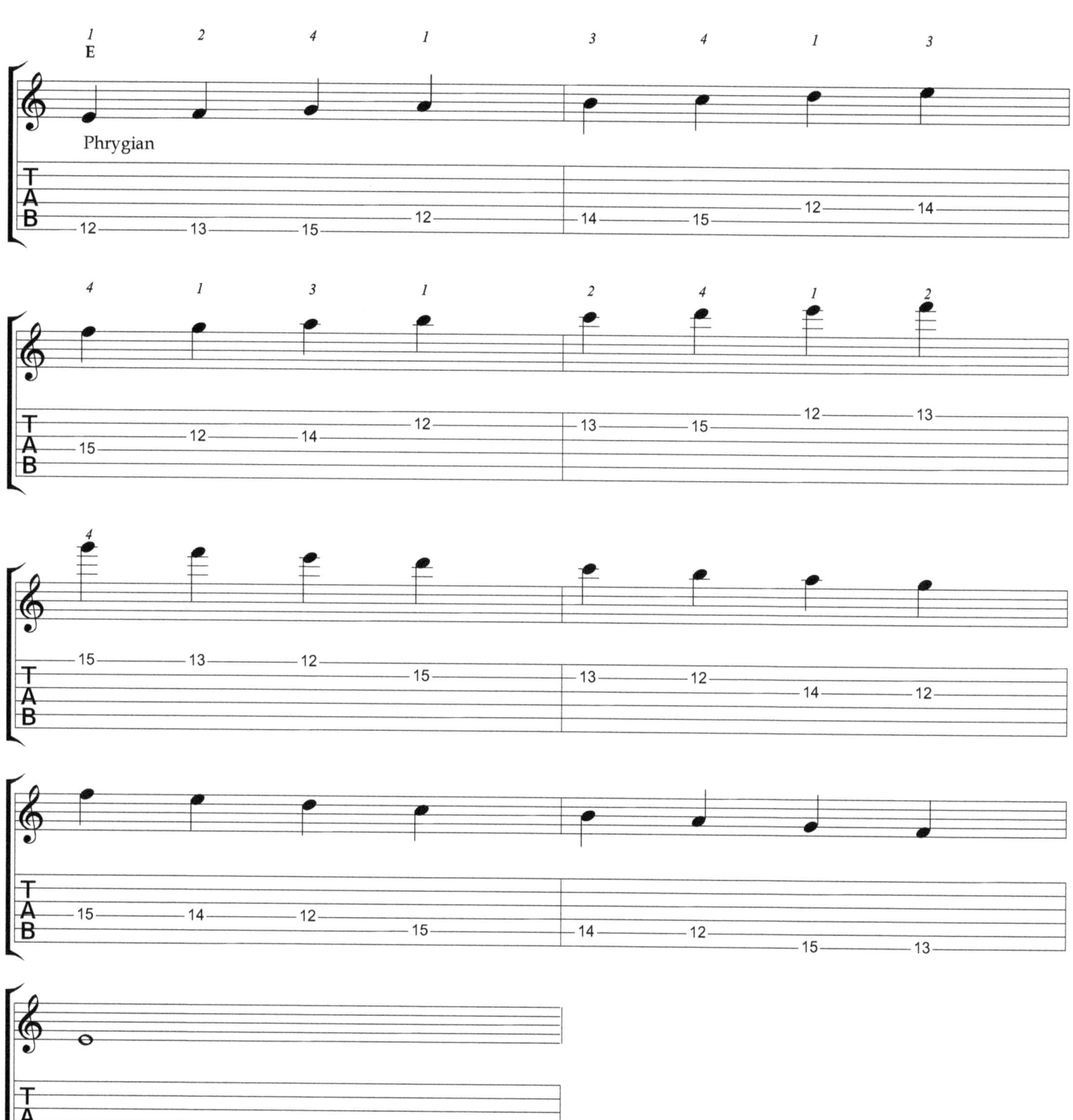

16. Various Ways to Perform the Scale

Example 3

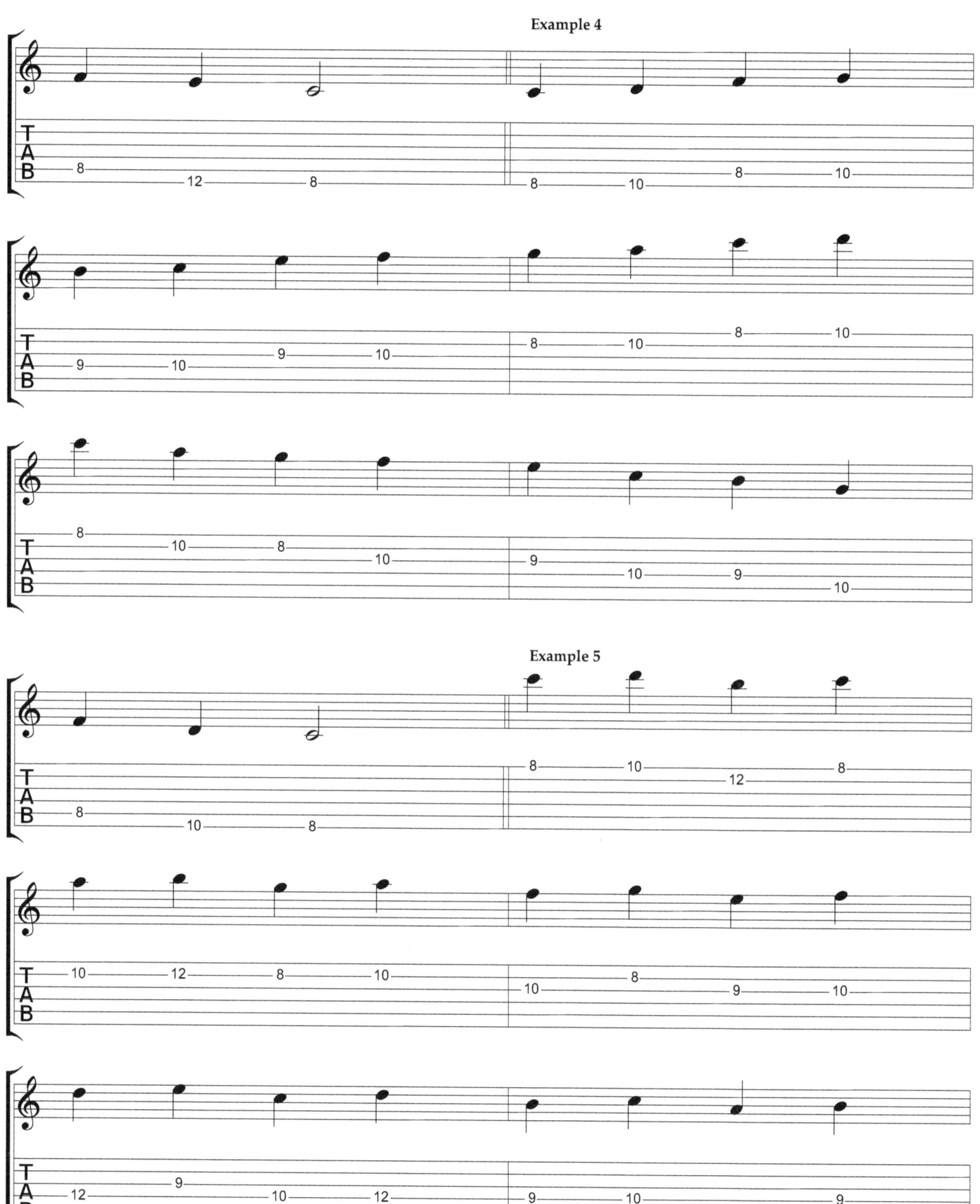

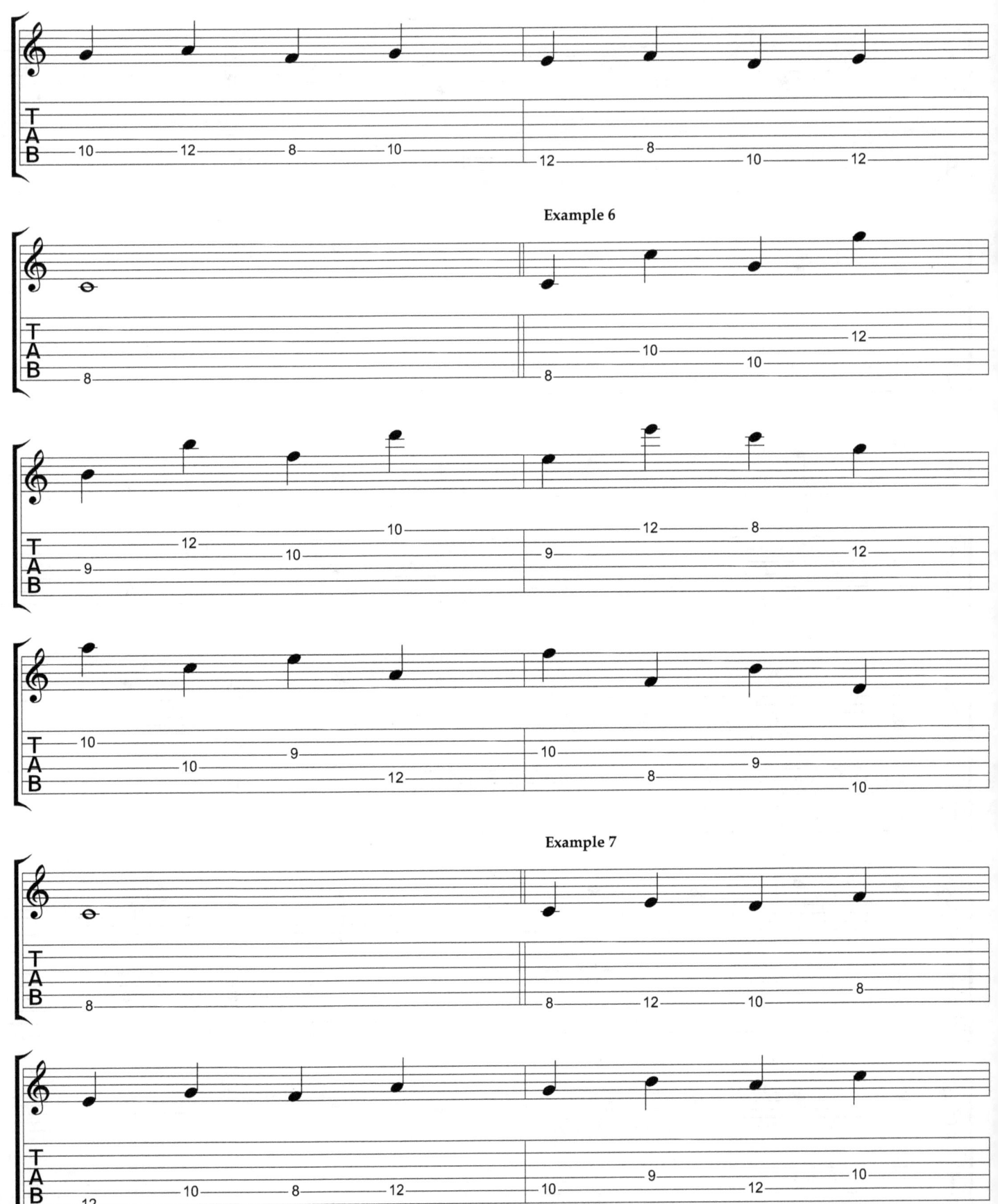

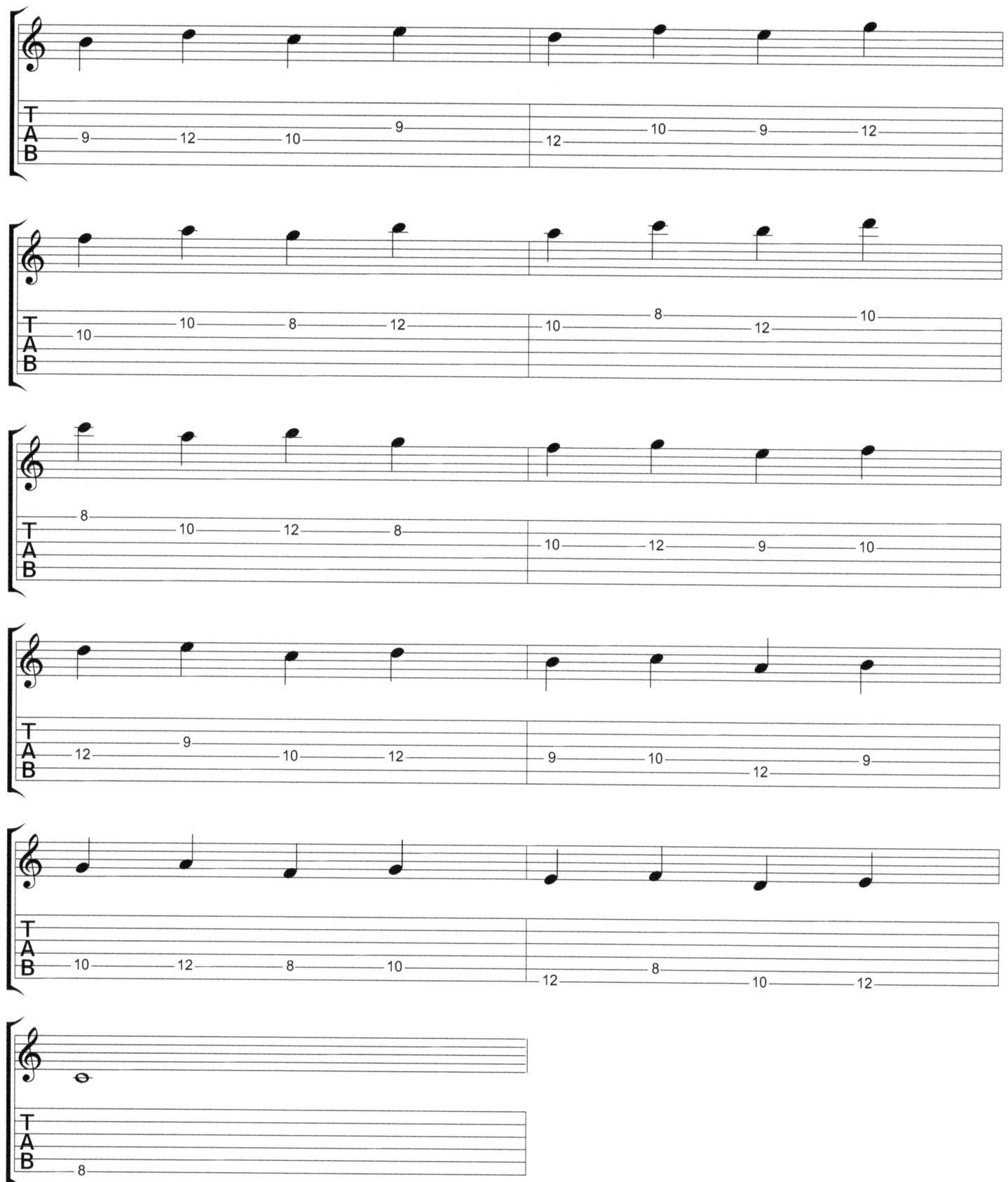

Example 3

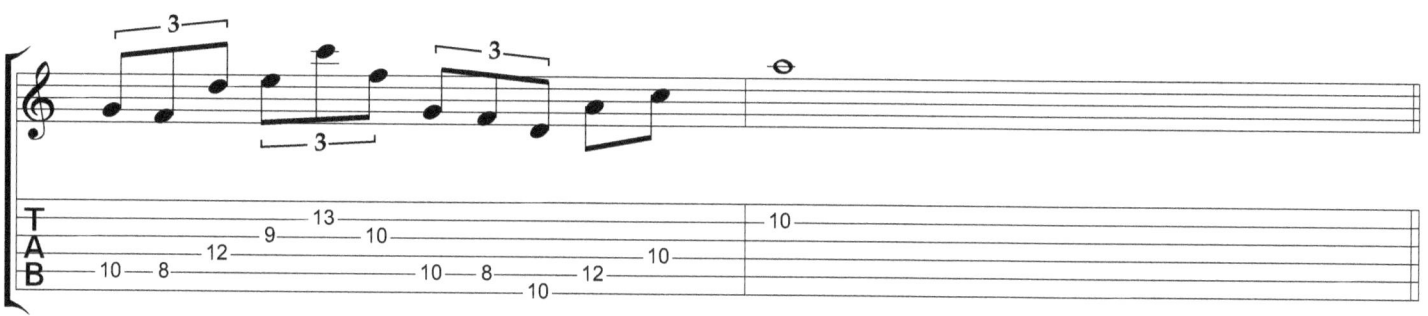

18. The Pentatonic Scale and Modes

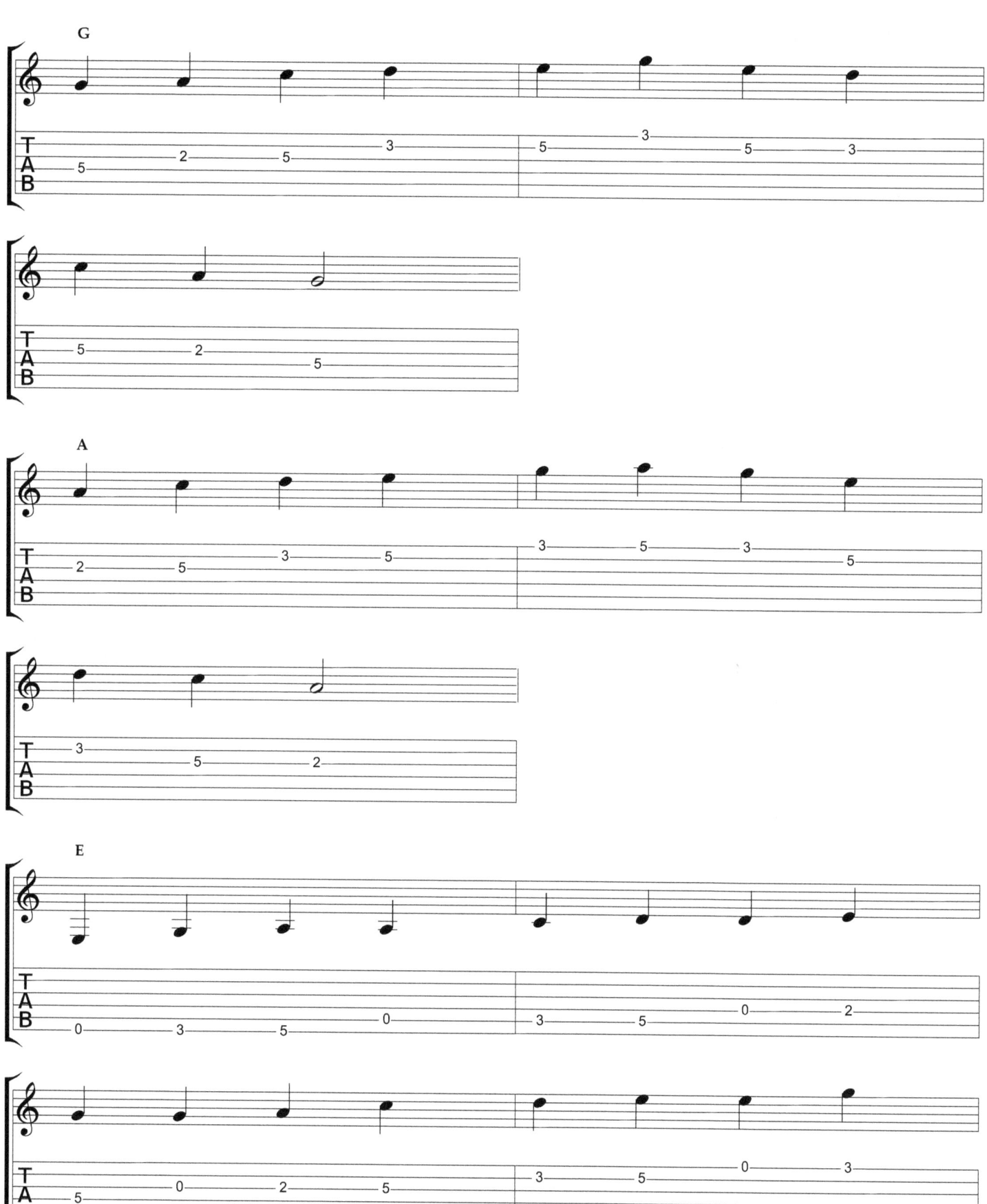

19. The Pentatonic Scale on Single Strings

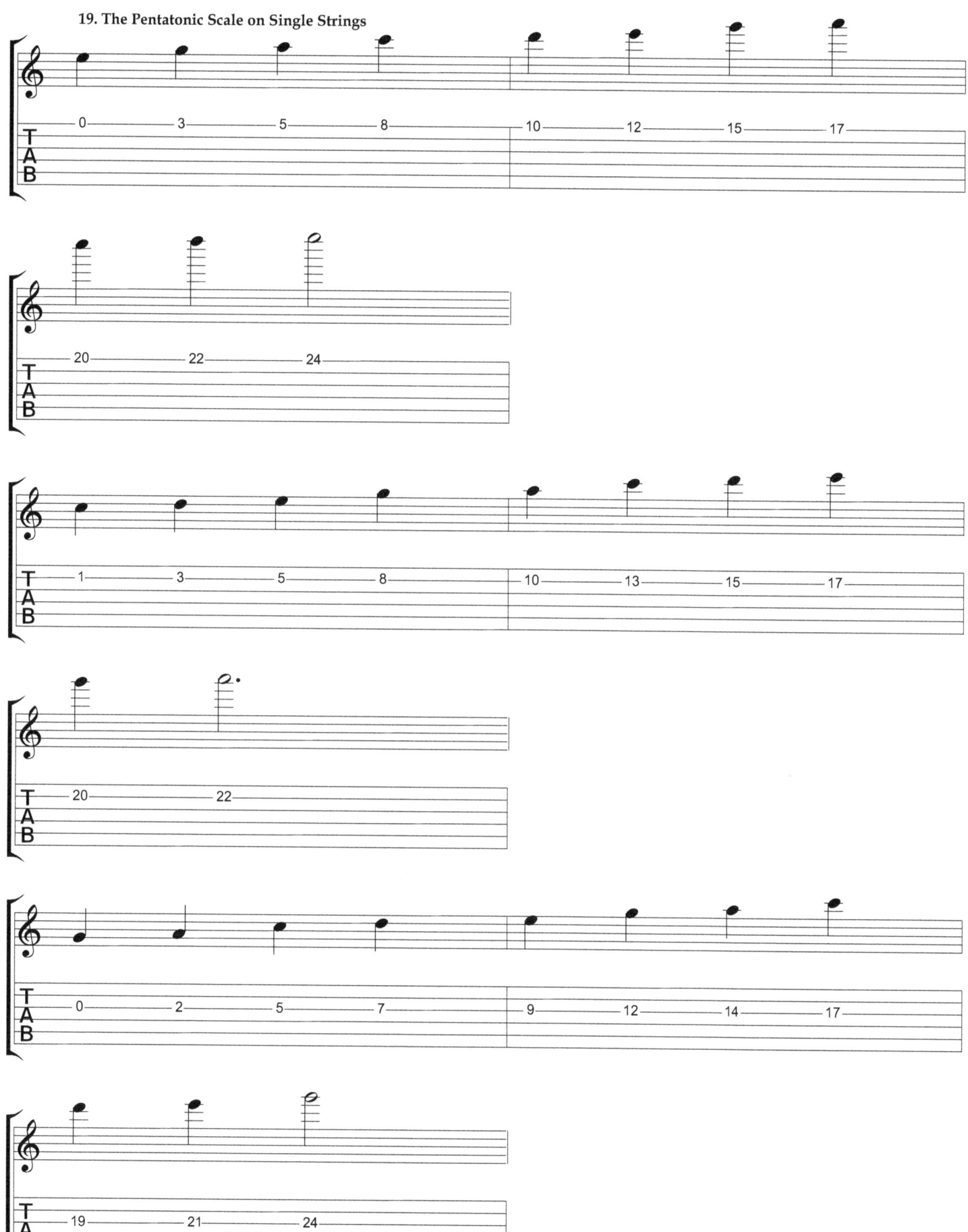

20. The Pentatonic Scale and its Modes in Memorable Blocks (a minor)

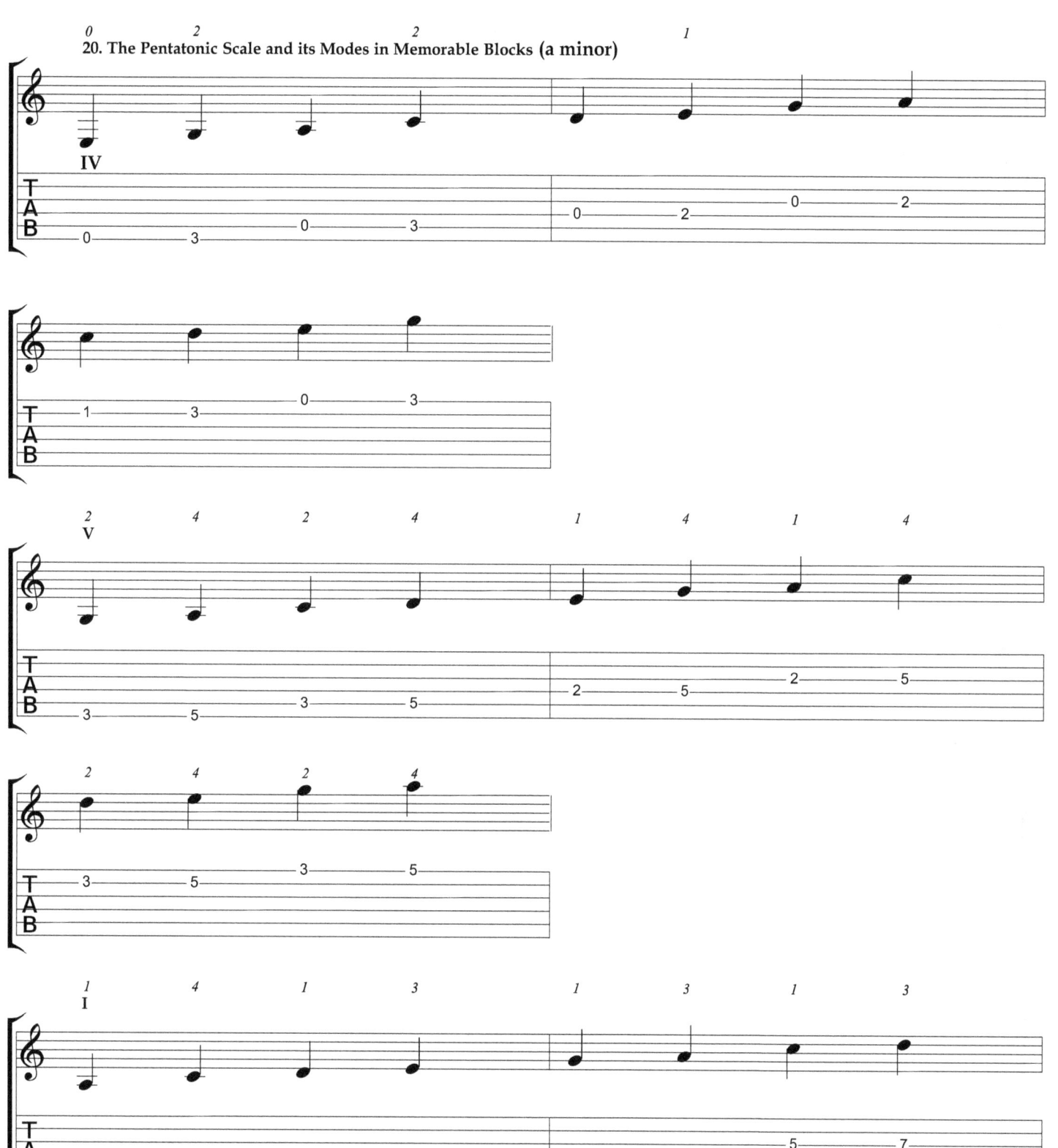

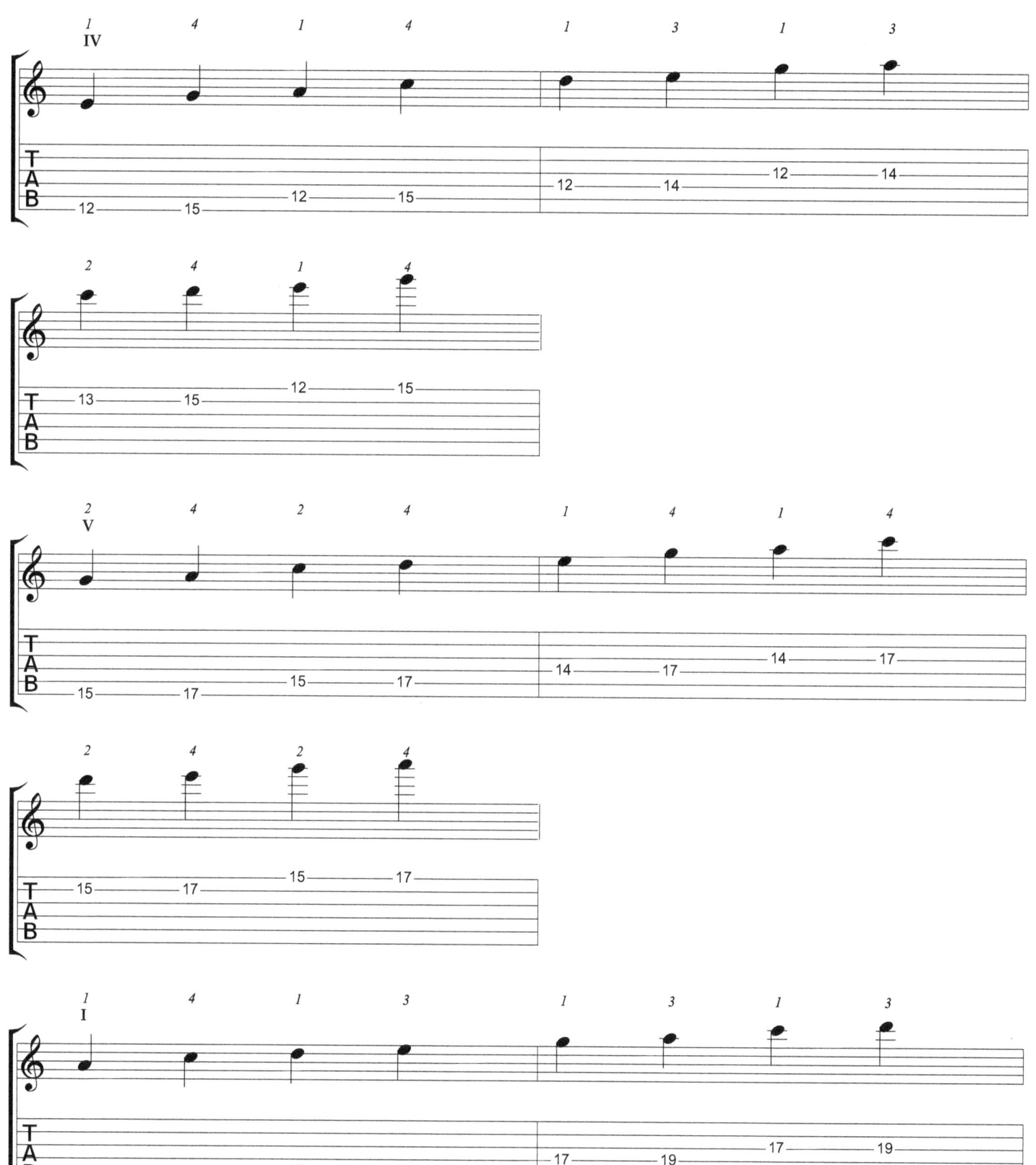

21. Performing the Pentatonic Scale with Various Melodic and Rhythmic Alterations

Example 3

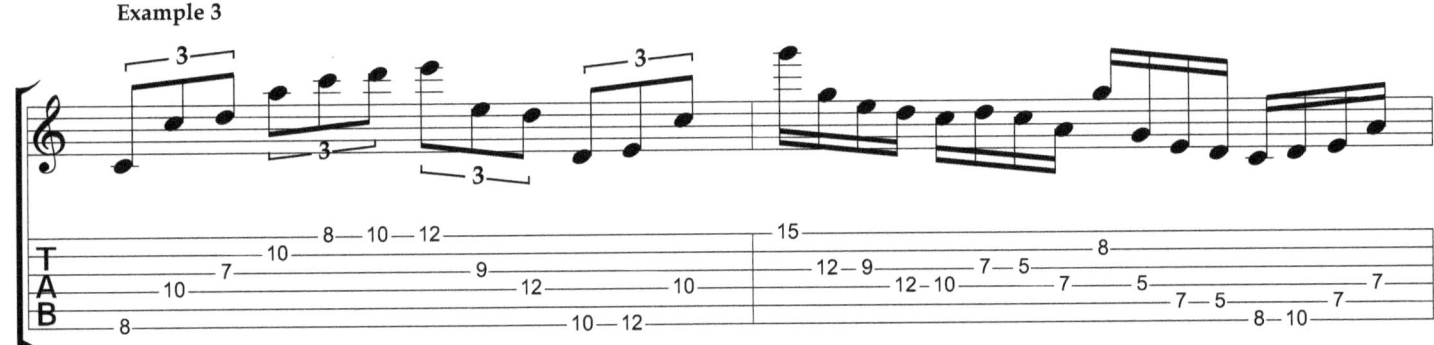

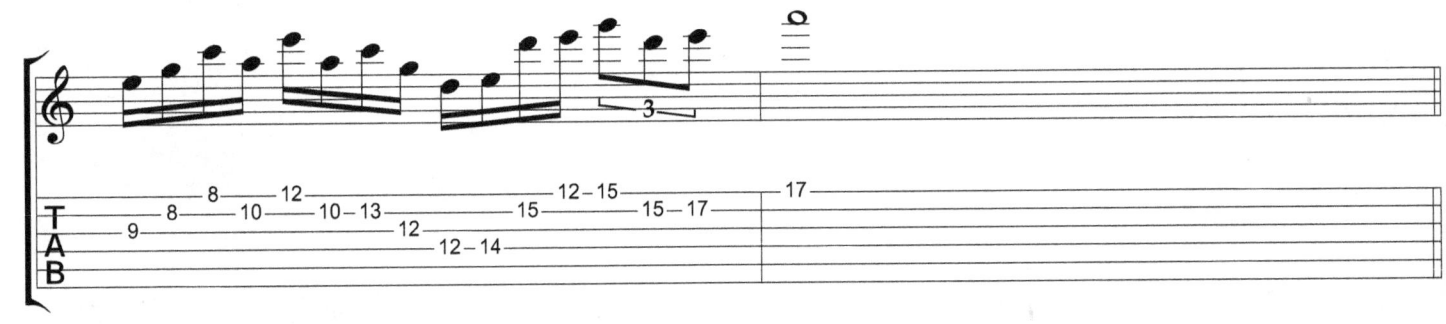

22. The Chromatic Scale

For Reference, The a minor Pentatonic Scale

23. The A Minor Pentatonic Scale with Chromatic Alterations

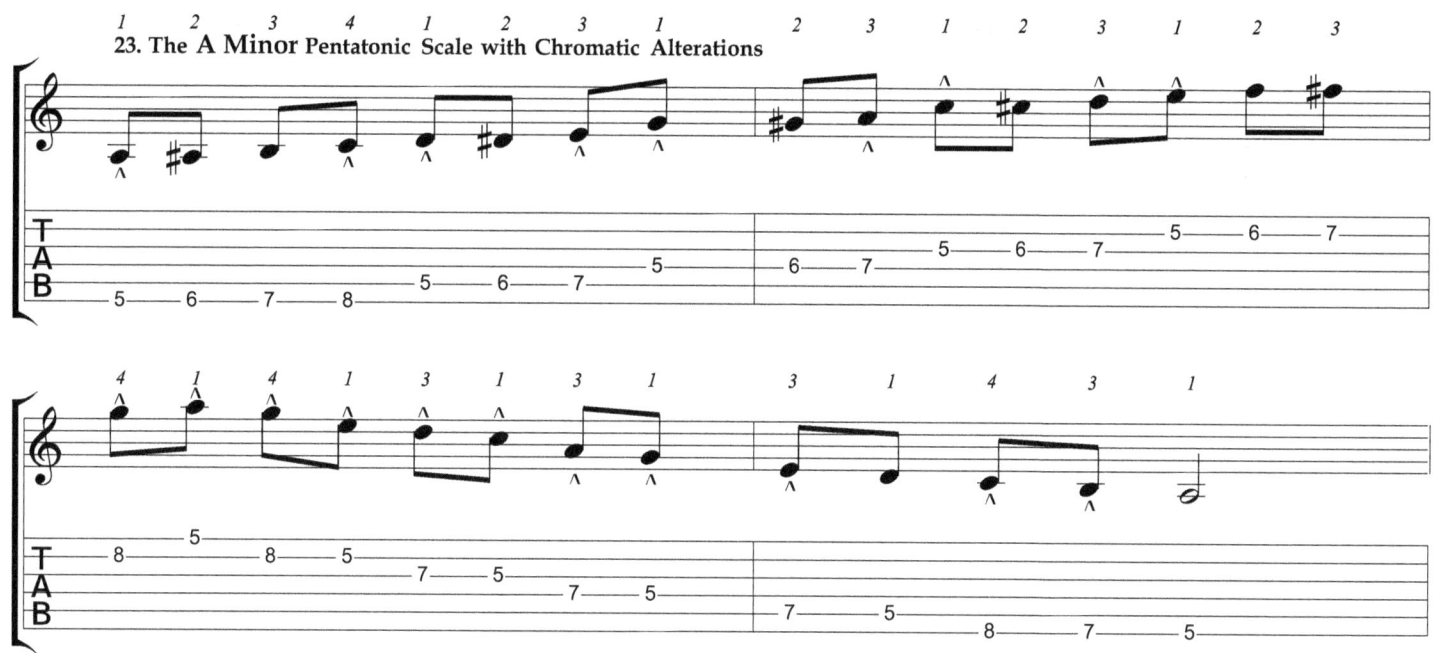

For Reference, The C Major Scale

24. The C Major Scale with Chromatic Alterations

25. The Whole Tone Scale

26. Whole Tone Arpeggios

27. Diminished Arpeggio étude Performed with Alternate Picking

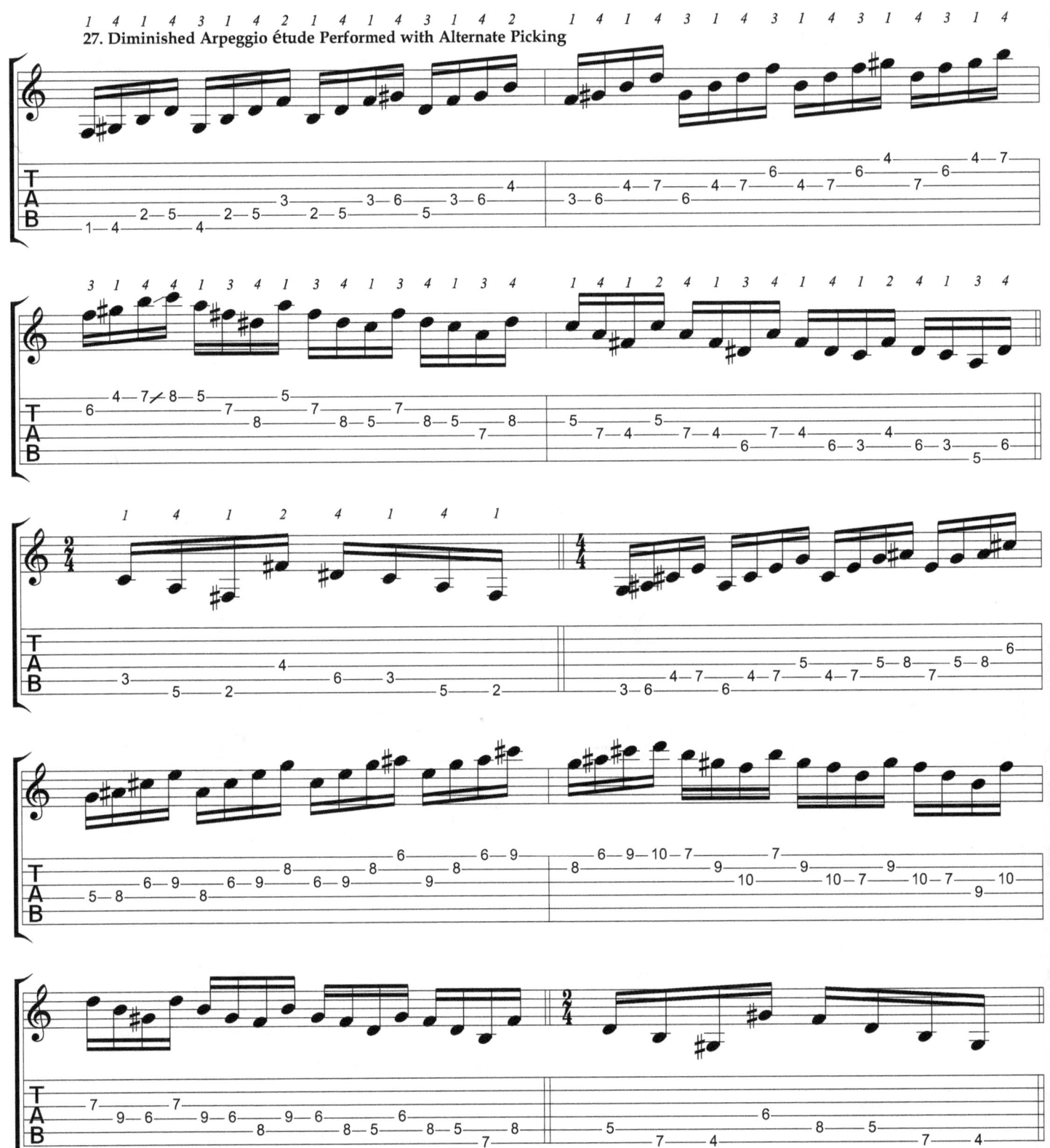

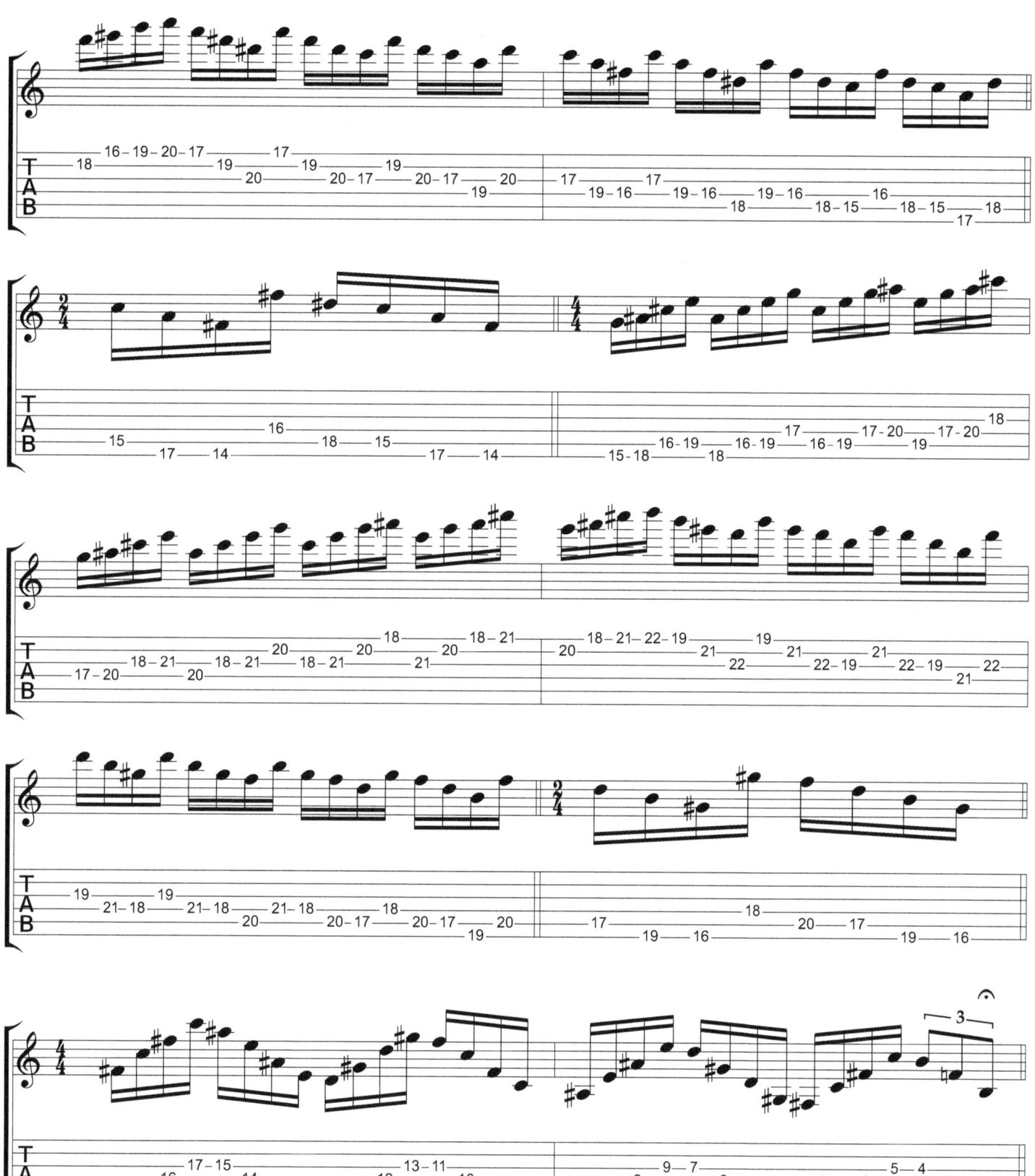

28. Melodic Development with Scales

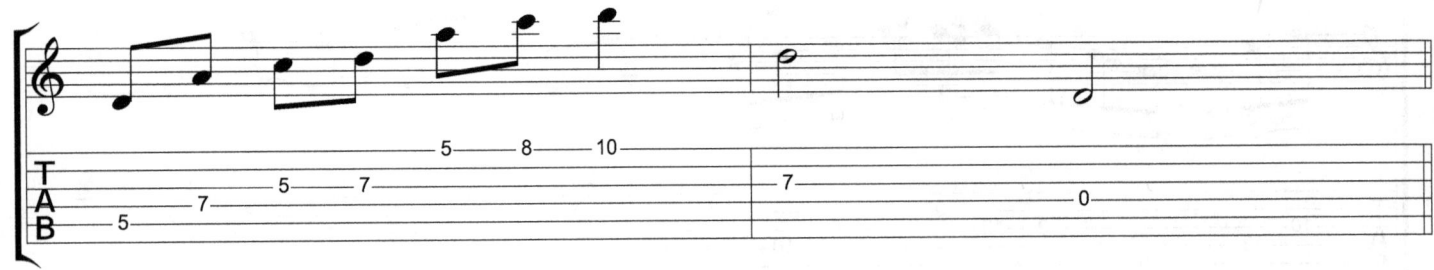

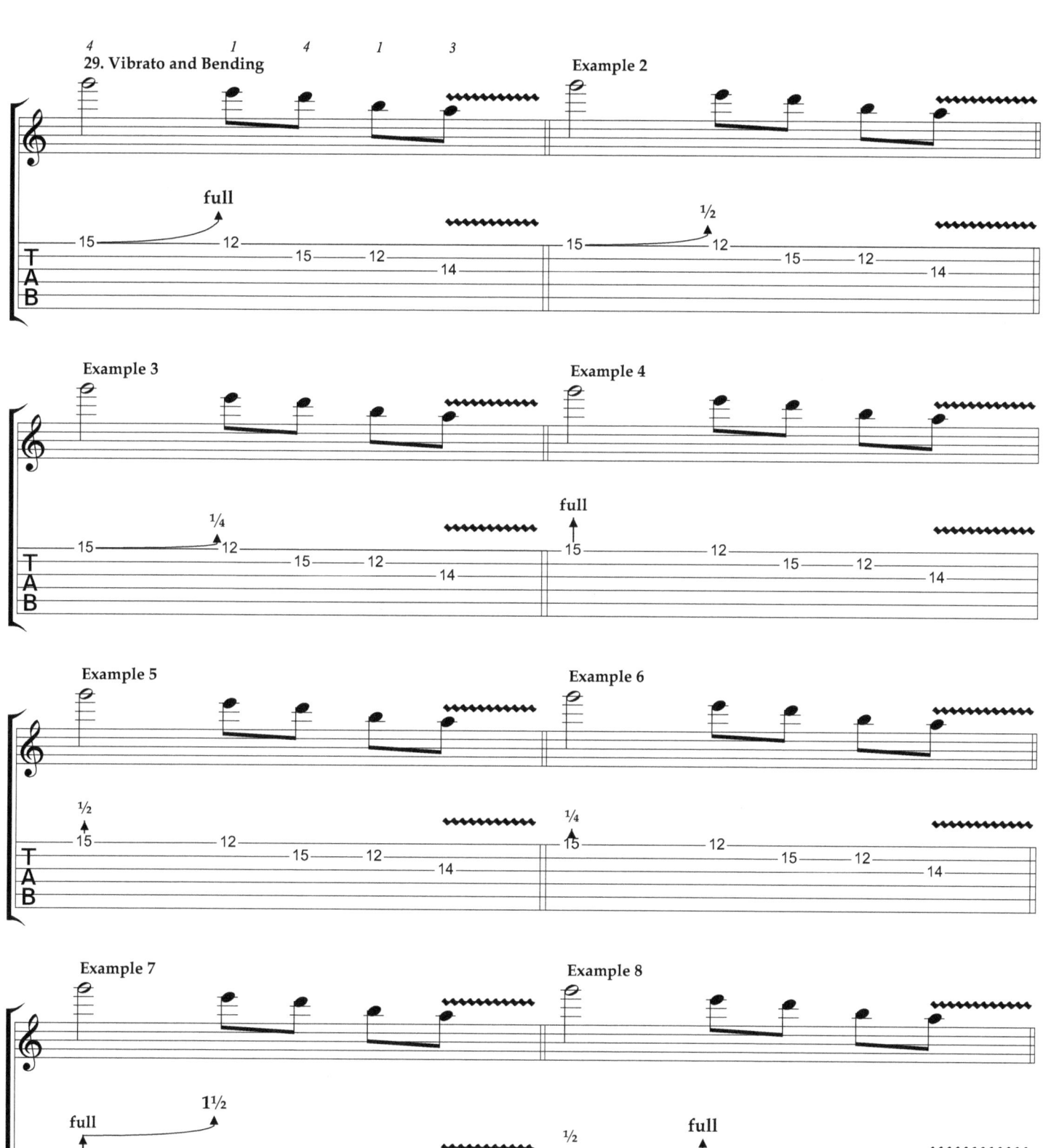

Example 9

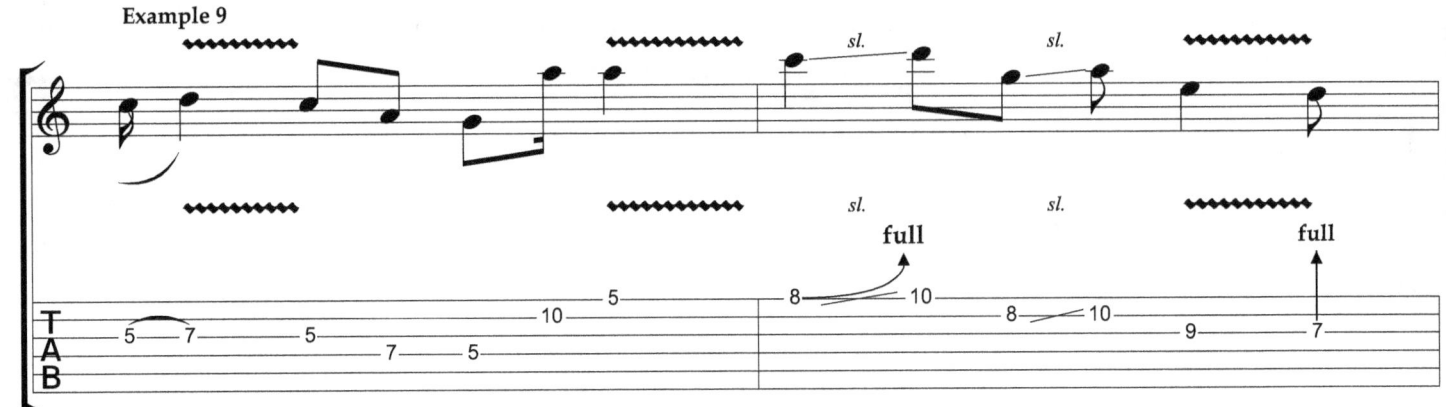
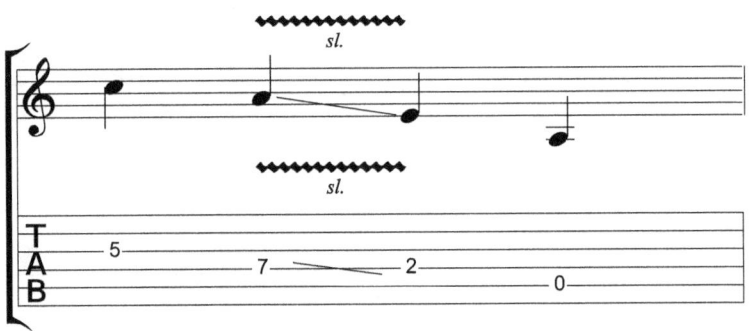

30. Vibrato and Bending in a Melodic Solo

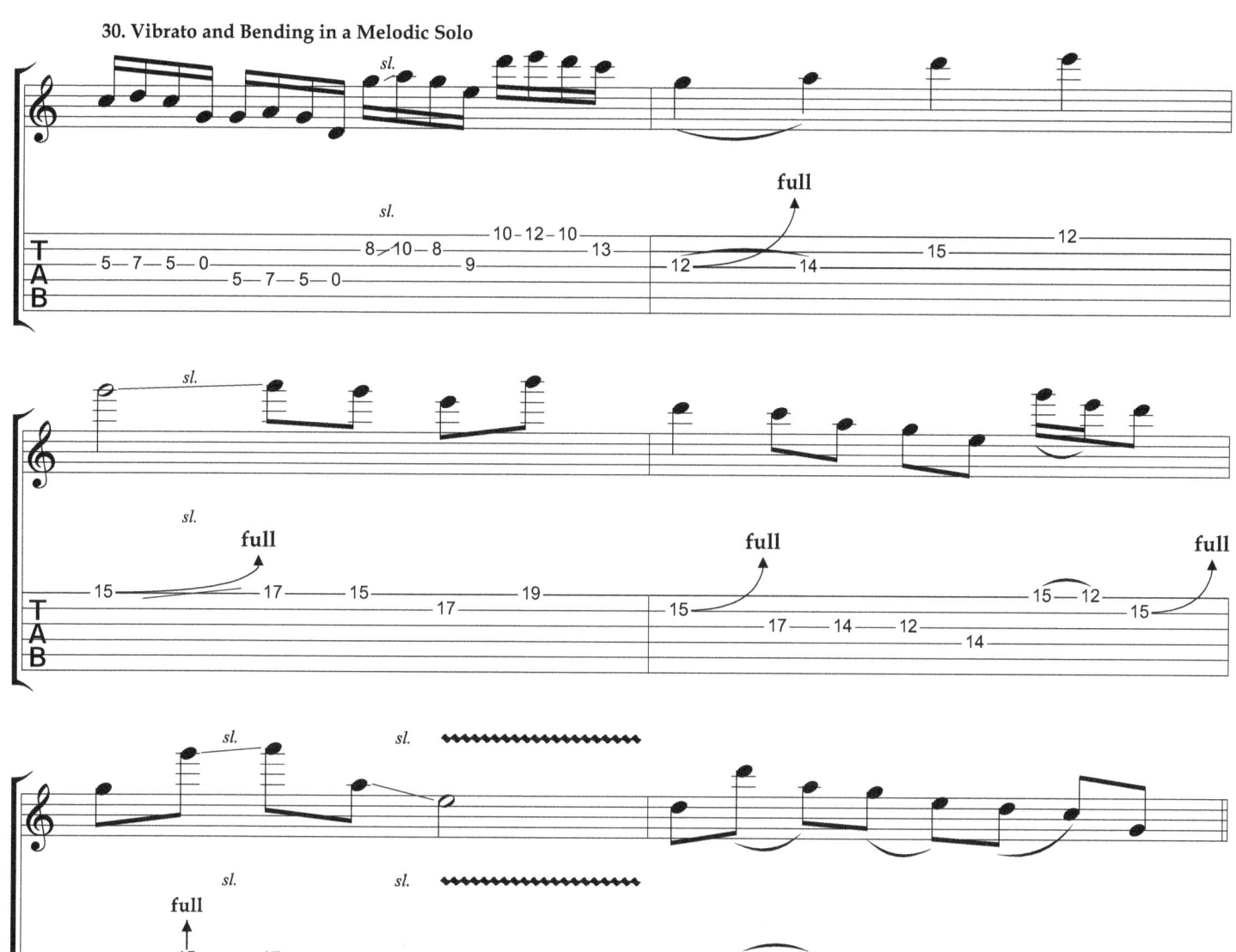

V. The Classical Guitar

Practice and Perform all of the examples with a modern right-hand classical guitar technique. The lower forearm, just before the elbow, should be resting on the top of the guitar as this creates a natural (falling down) curve and arch to the plucking wrist. The fingers should be performing the exercises at the beginning of the rosette, closest to the bridge. The contact location between the fingers and strings should be on the left side of a finger (angled), as the finger nail can easily catch without a modified angle (although can be utilized for a colorful and contrasting tonal effect).

There are two stroke methods in order to attack a single note, free-stroke and rest-stroke. With free-stroke, the string must be pressed into the guitar, and then released as the finger "hovers" just above the string. With rest-stroke, after pressing the string into the guitar, the finger falls onto the string (resting) above the previously attacked string. Fingers may be straightened for rest-strokes, and slightly curved for free-strokes.

Another subtle, but important practice is to physically find the optimal reactive string vibration from a previous attack in order to execute an ideal and economical note to follow. An optimal "bounce" in the string. This will allow you to have more rebound with the string and give you a faster and more economical way of playing. This is very effective with tremolo and rest-stroke scales.

All a-m-i and p-a-m-i scales are treated as a traditional classical guitar tremolo with a high level of string-crossing. It is preferred to utilize free-strokes as it creates a more athletic hand when transitioning from scales to arpeggios and tremolos.

Your fingers must remain as close to the strings as possible both before and after playing free-strokes, rest-strokes and tremolos.

Nails are very important to the performance of the classical and flamenco guitar. A combination of flesh and nail will produce quality tone and give adequate volume. Nail shape and length can take on many variations depending on the player. I would suggest a slight file of the left side of the nail in order to create a smooth "ramp" that will not catch on the string.

The strums of the classical and flamenco guitar, known as the Rasgueado, will require a great deal of wrist-action and finger-independence when triggering each strum. "Flicking" the wrist and "firing" each finger will give you a loud and percussive flamenco strum. Each finger must leave with complete physical independence and rhythmic equality. A good practice is to make a fist, and then fire independently in order (c), (a), (m), (i), keeping each previous finger extended. The continuous rasgueado has the (i) finger pull the fist back together with an up-stroke (after c, a, m, i, have followed through each with individual down strokes). The thumb can rest on any lower string not needed or even the body of the guitar, above the 6th string. There are many variations to rasgueado patterns depending on the rhythmic situation.

The Classical Guitar

31. Arpeggios 103-104
32. Villa-Lobos étude 1 Arpeggio Pattern 105
33. Tremolo 106
34. Flamenco Tremolo 106
35. The Never-ending Tremolo/Trill 106
36. Joe Hartnett Tremolo 106-108
37. Cross-String Arpeggio/Tremolo by Joe Hartnett 109-110
38. i-m Alternation with Rest-Stroke and Free-Stroke 111
39. a-m-i Scales 112-113
40. p-a-m-i Scales 114
41. p-a-m-i Scales with String Skipping 115
42. Strums and Rasgueado 116
43. The Barre 116
44. Arpeggio étude 117-119
45. Tremolo étude 120-123

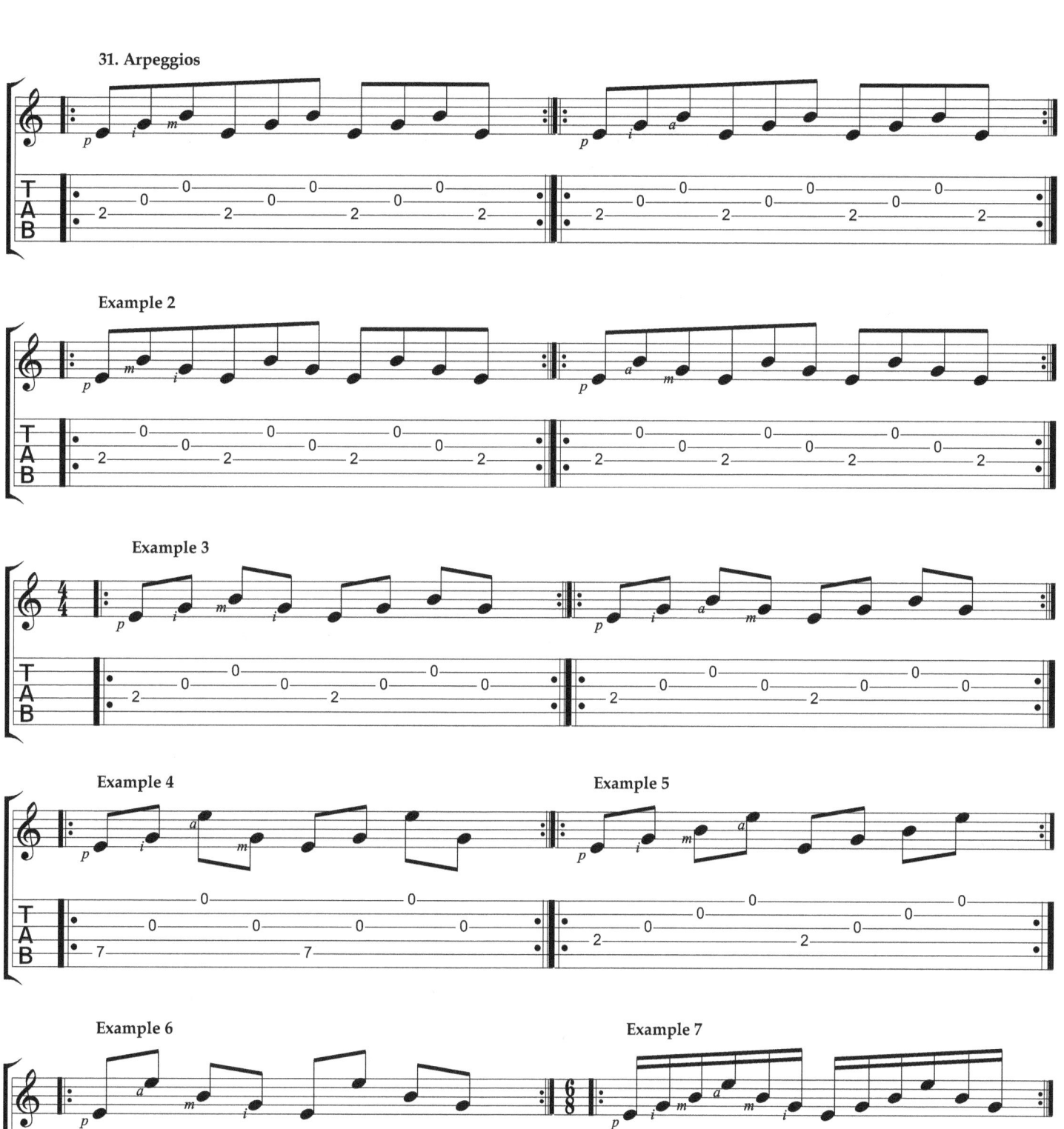

32. Villa-Lobos étude 1 Arpeggio Pattern

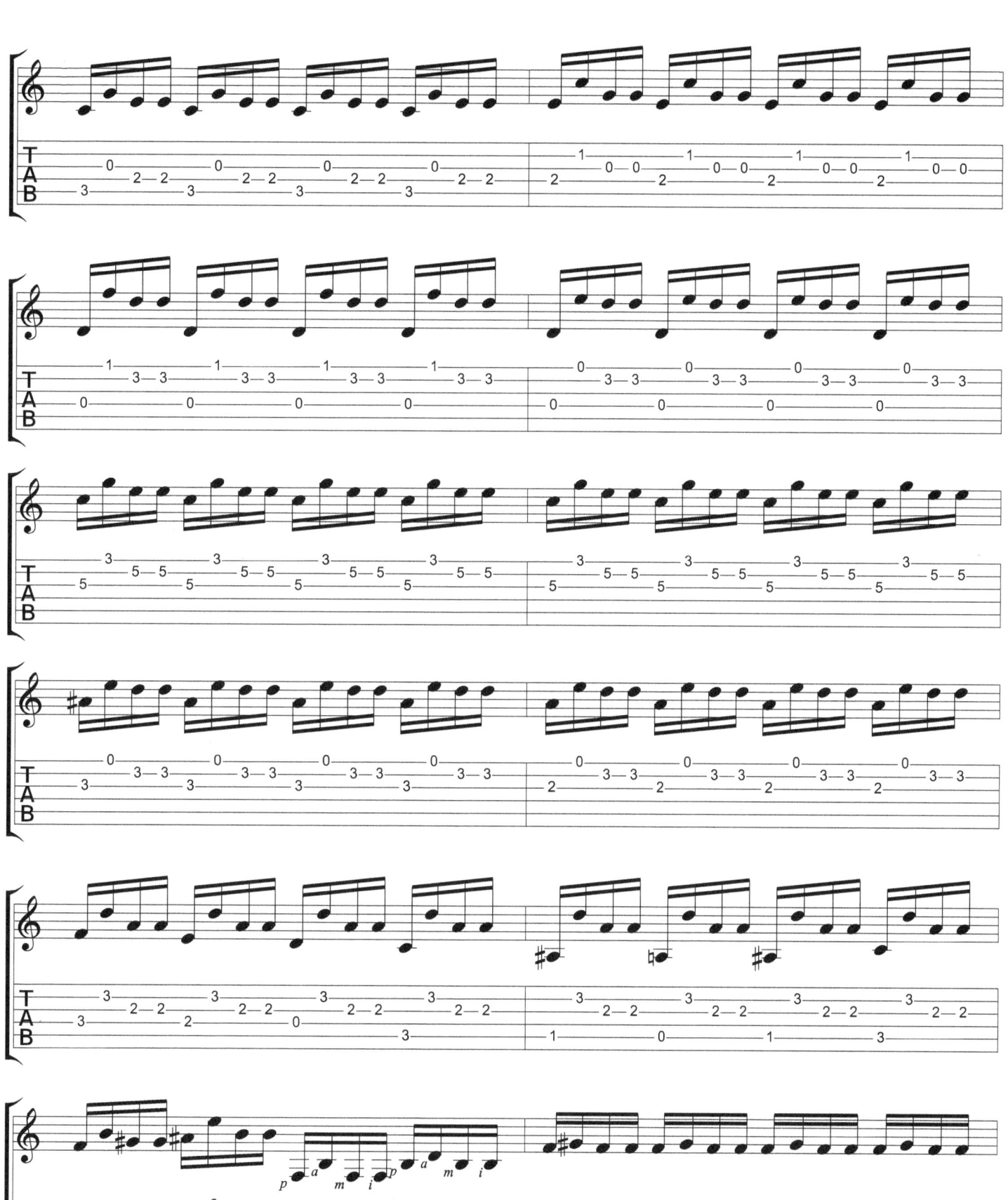

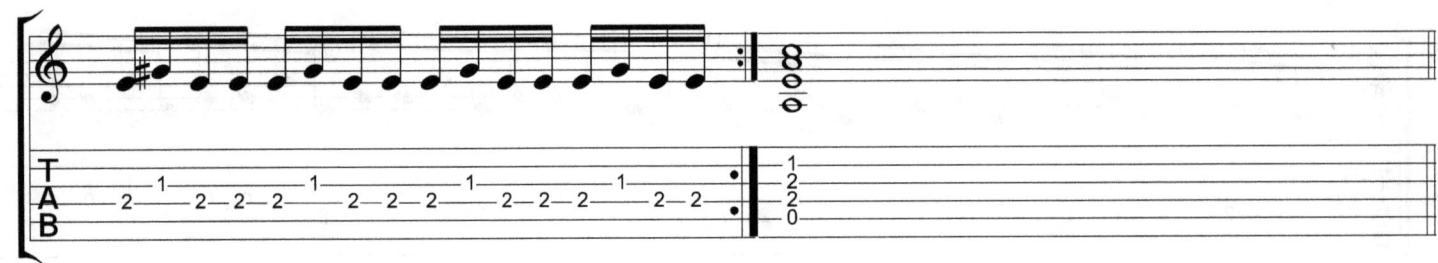

37. Cross-String Arpeggio/Tremolo by Joe Hartnett

Slide The Barre Pattern

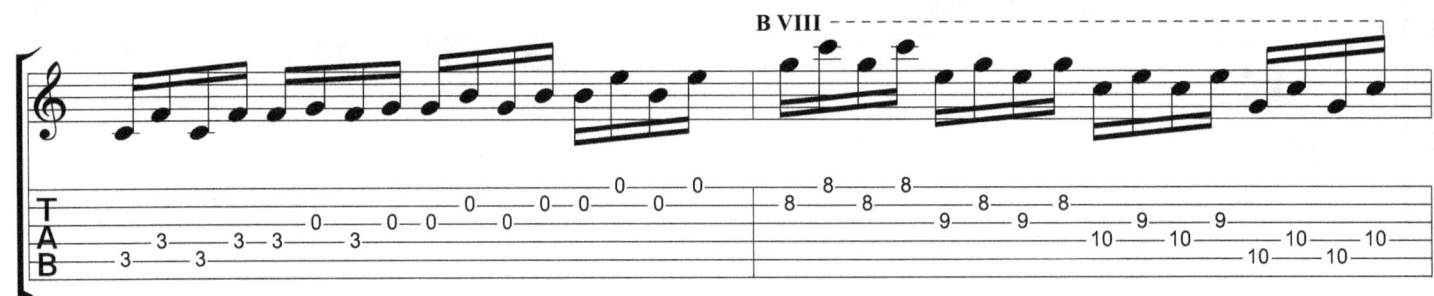

38. i-m Alternation with Rest-Stroke and Free-Stroke

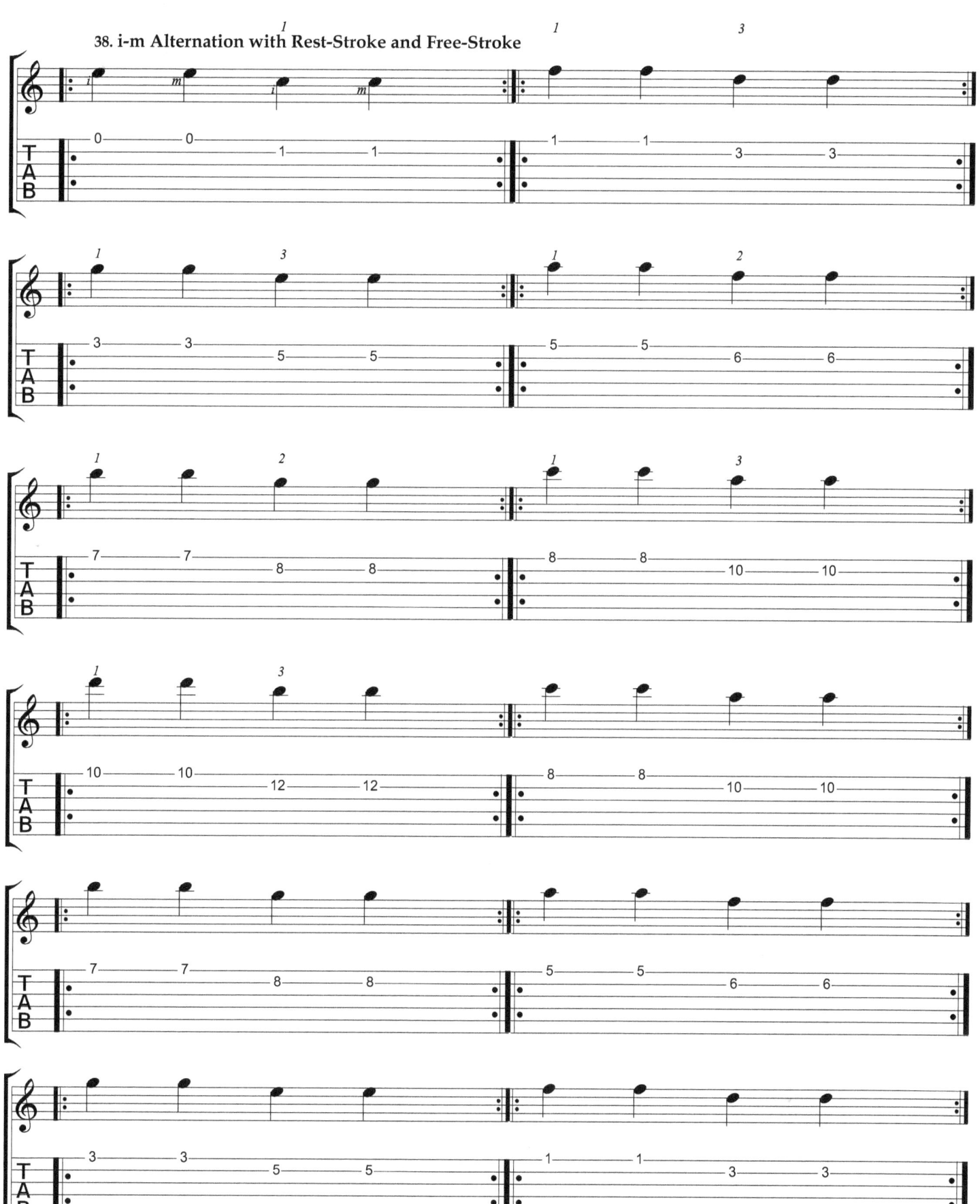

39. a-m-i Scales (Free-Stroke)

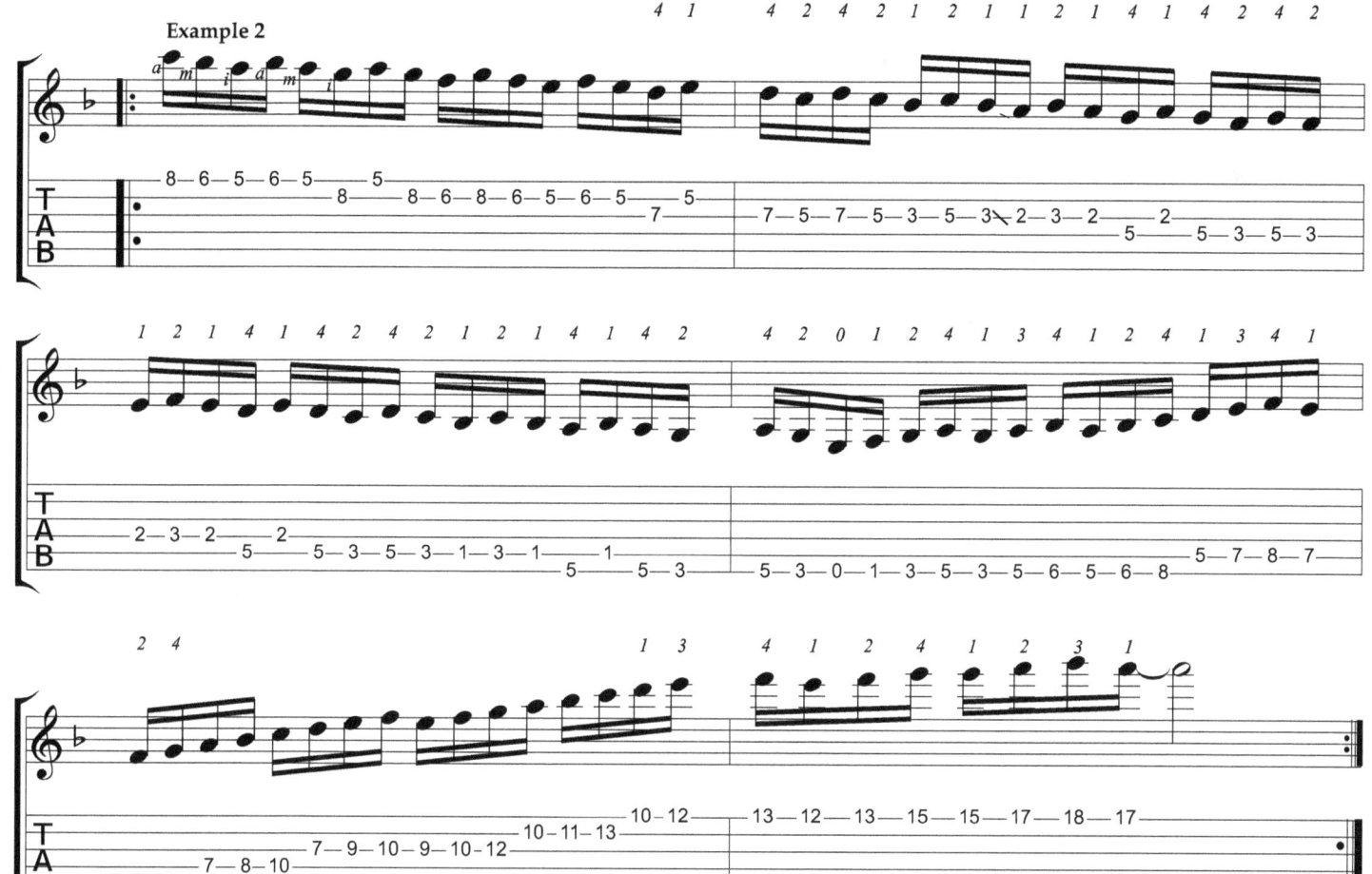

40. p-a-m-i Scales

41. p-a-m-i Scales with String Skipping

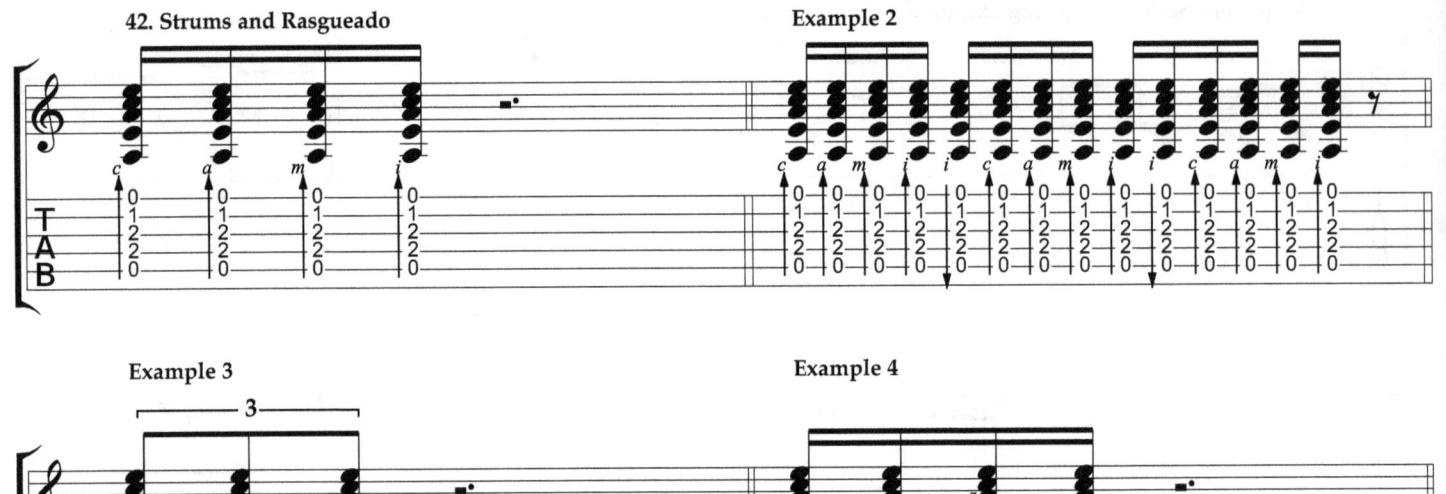

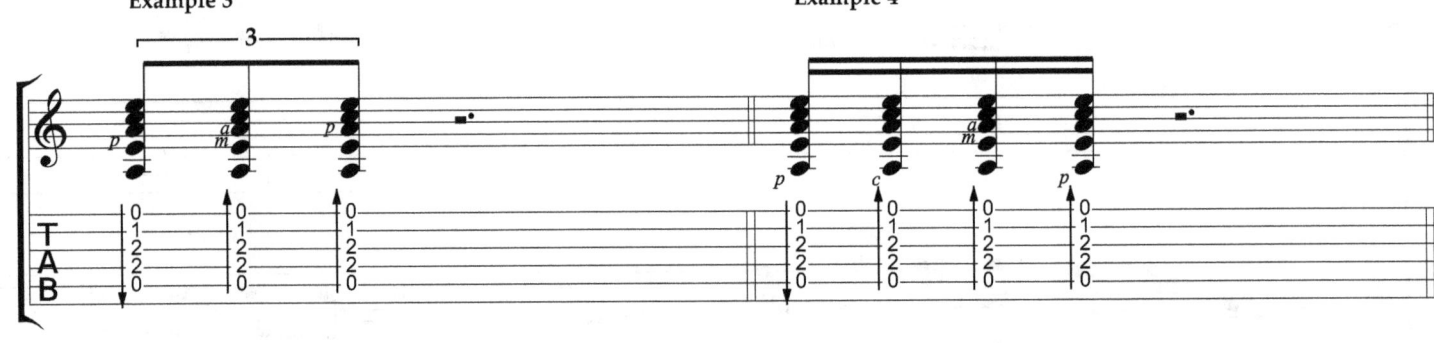

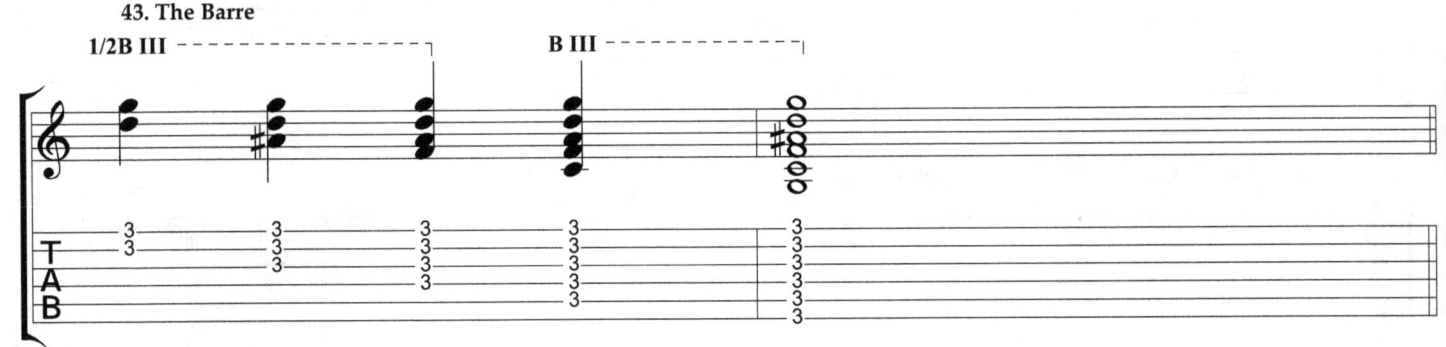

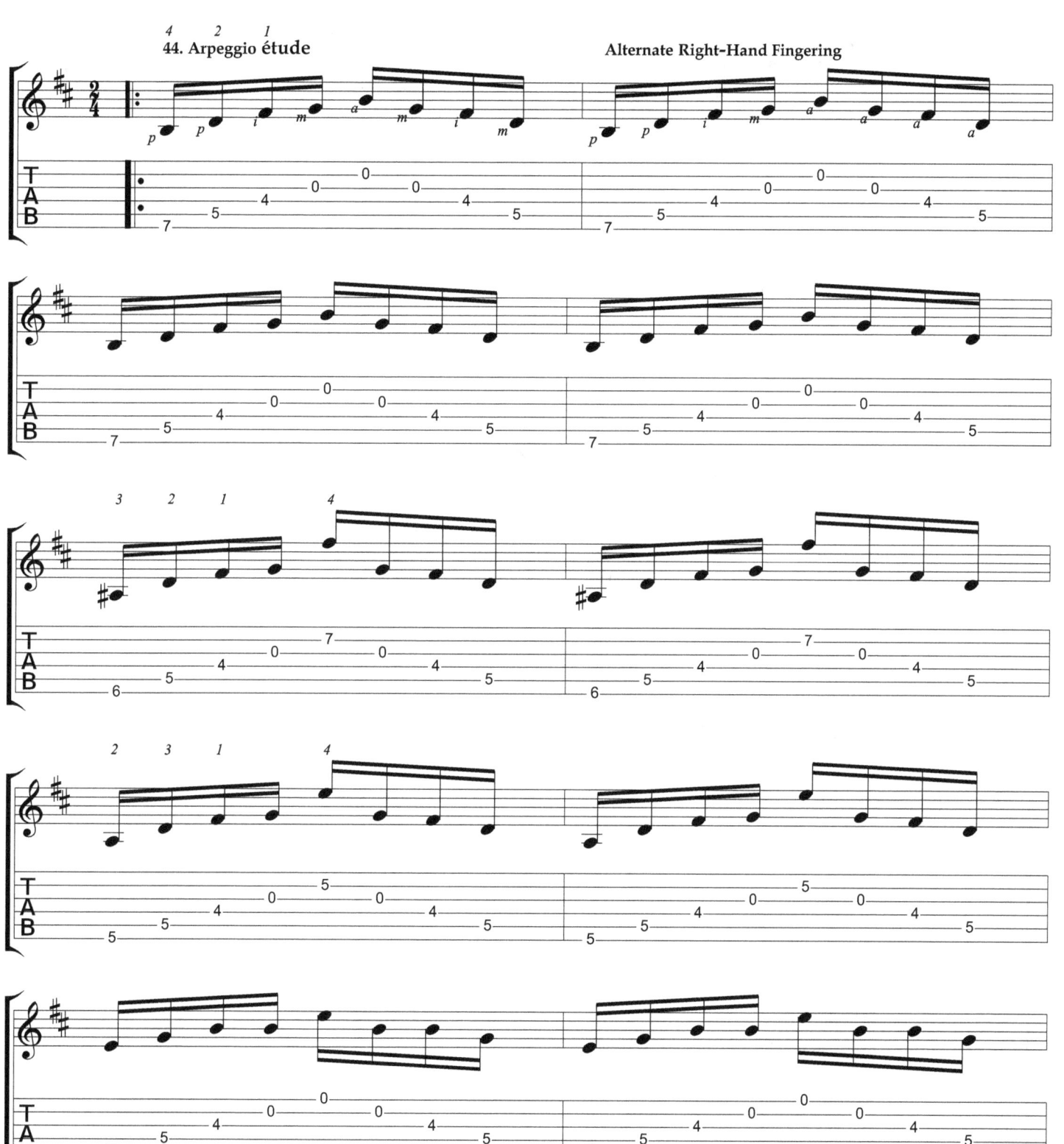

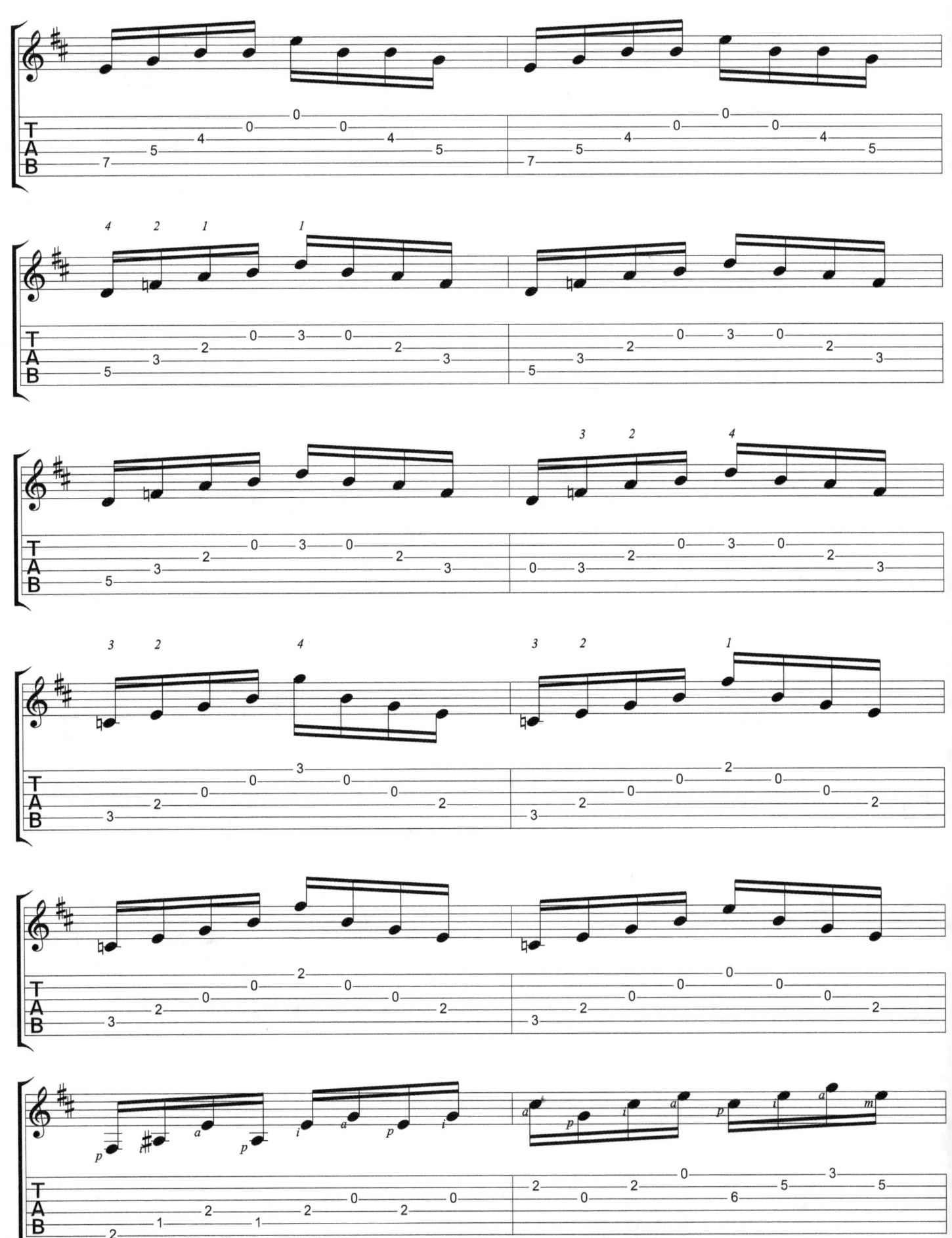

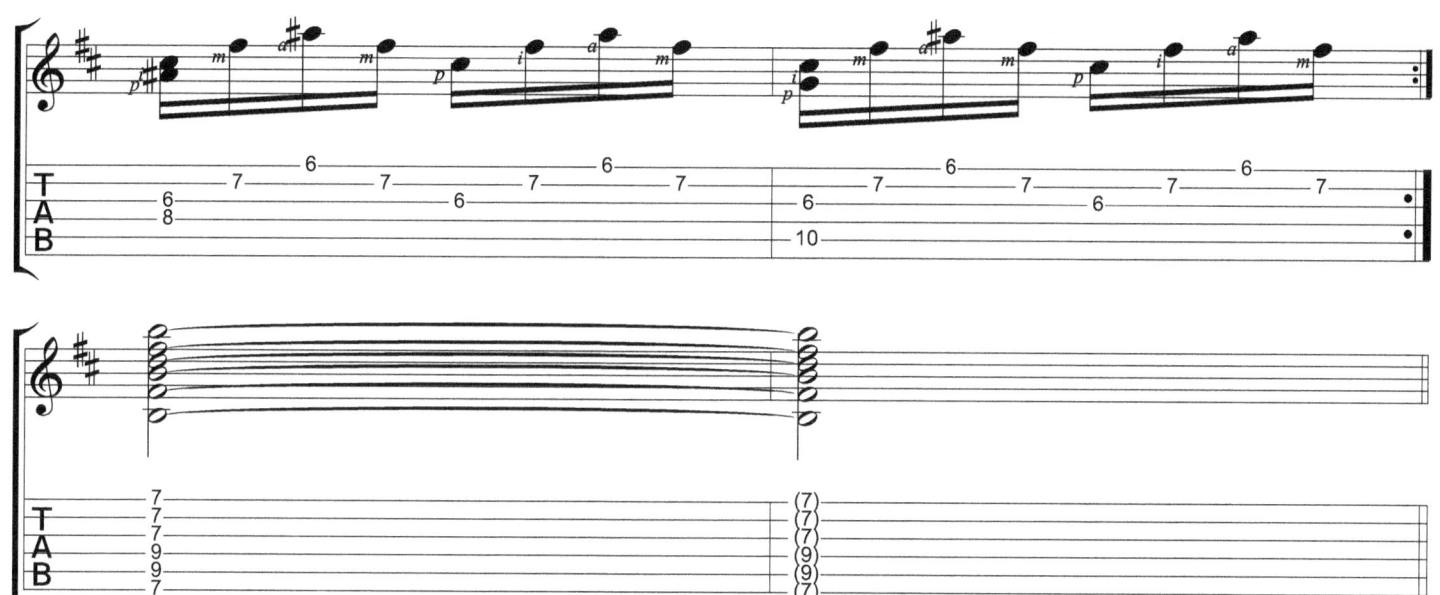

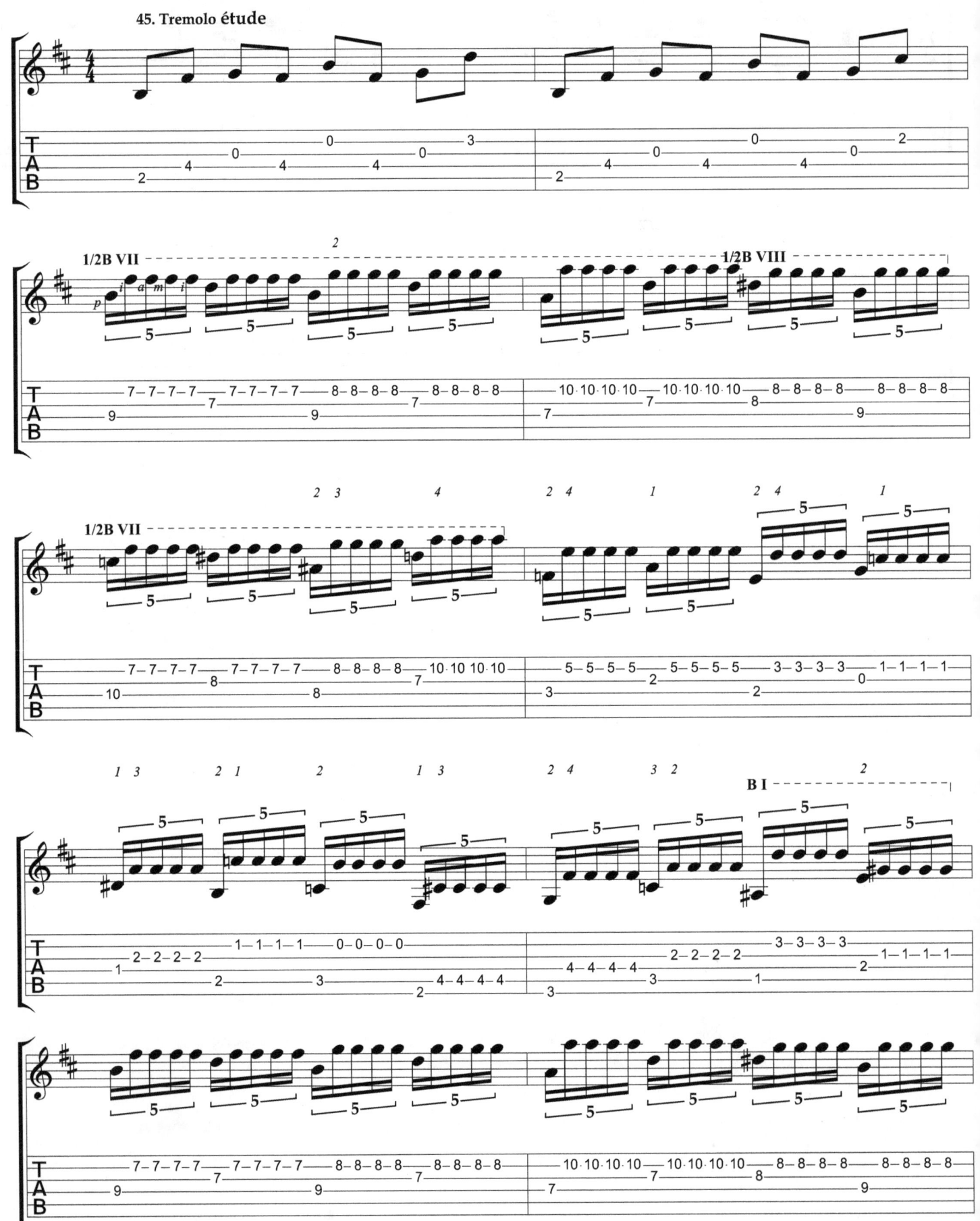

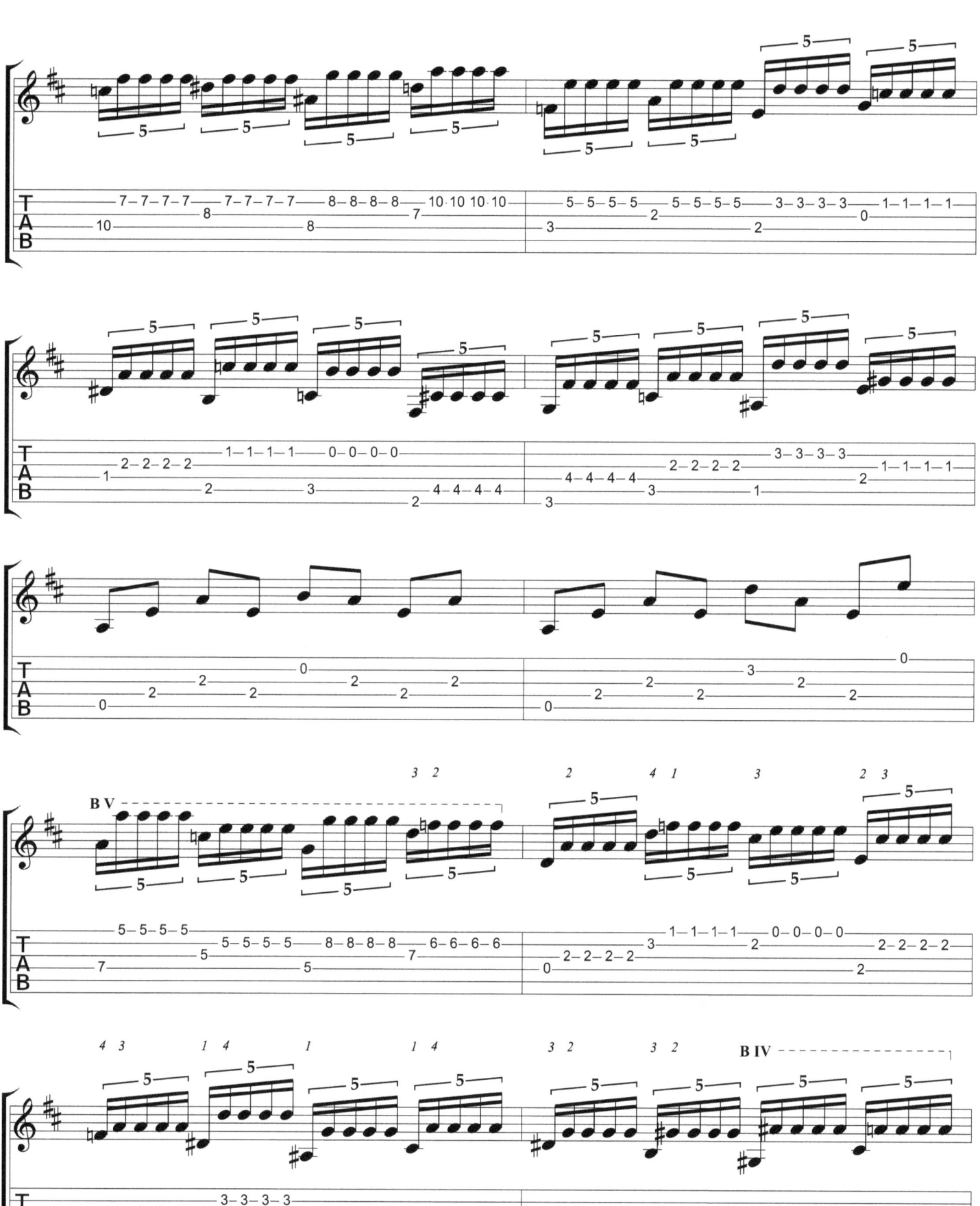

VI. Transcriptions, Arrangements, and Compositions

Transcriptions, Arrangements, and Compositions

46. Fortress for Electric Guitar 126-141
47. Snowstorm for Electric Guitar 142-147
48. Darkness for Electric Guitar 148-151
49. Summit for Electric Guitar 152-161
50. Destroyer for Electric Guitar 162-167
51. Shadows for Classical Guitar 168-176
52. Malagueñas for Classical Guitar 177-190
53. BWV 1002 Sarabande for Classical Guitar 191-194
54. BWV 1003 Allegro for Classical Guitar 195-205
55. BWV 1004 Sarabande for Classical Guitar 206-208
56. BWV 1006 Prelude for Classical Guitar 209-223
57. BWV 988 Aria for Classical Guitar 224-227
58. The Incendiary Guitar Lick for Classical Guitar 228-229
59. The Formidable Guitar Lick for Classical Guitar 230-234
60. Reflection for Classical Guitar 236-241

Fortress
for Electric Guitar
Joe Hartnett

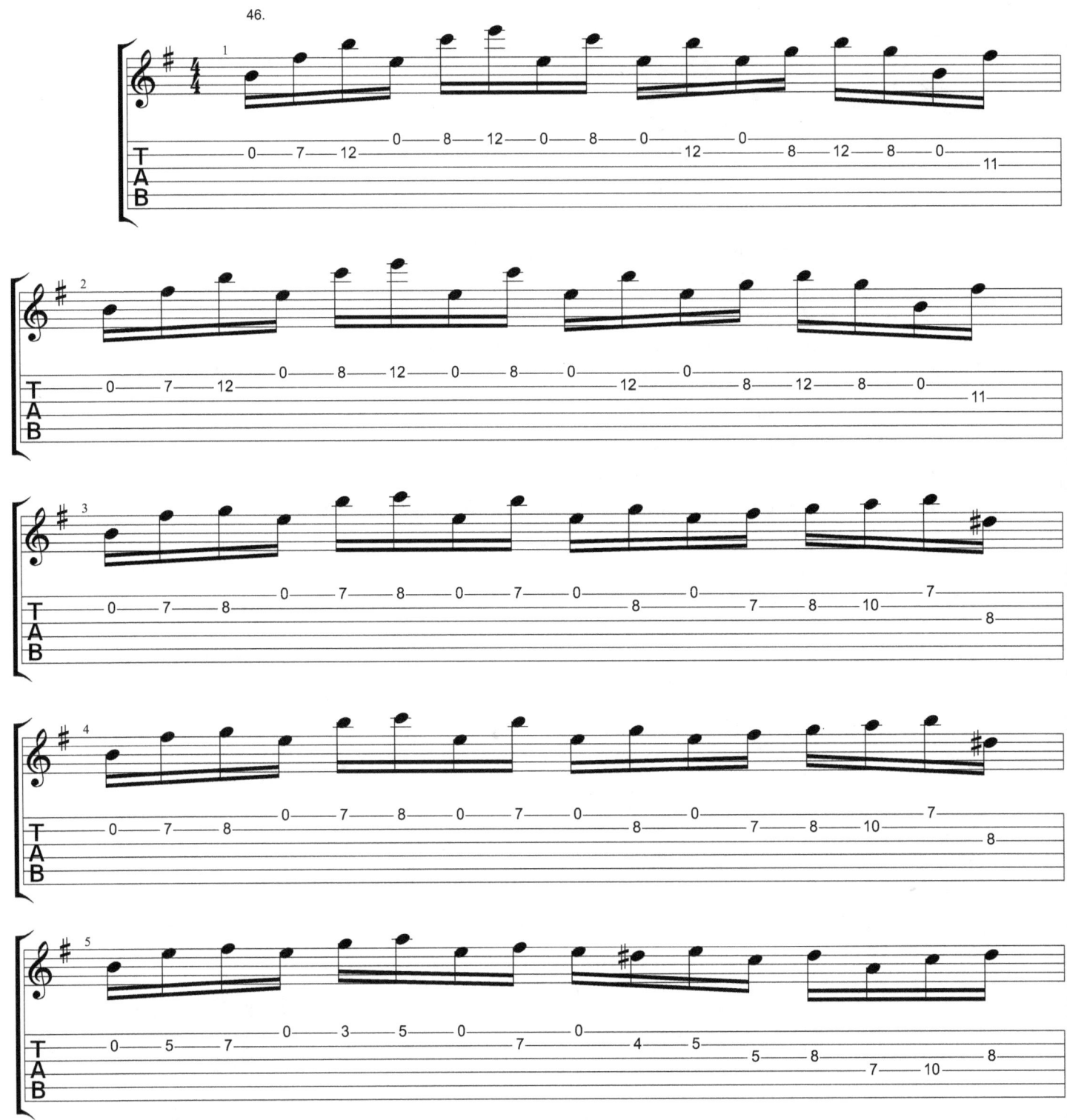

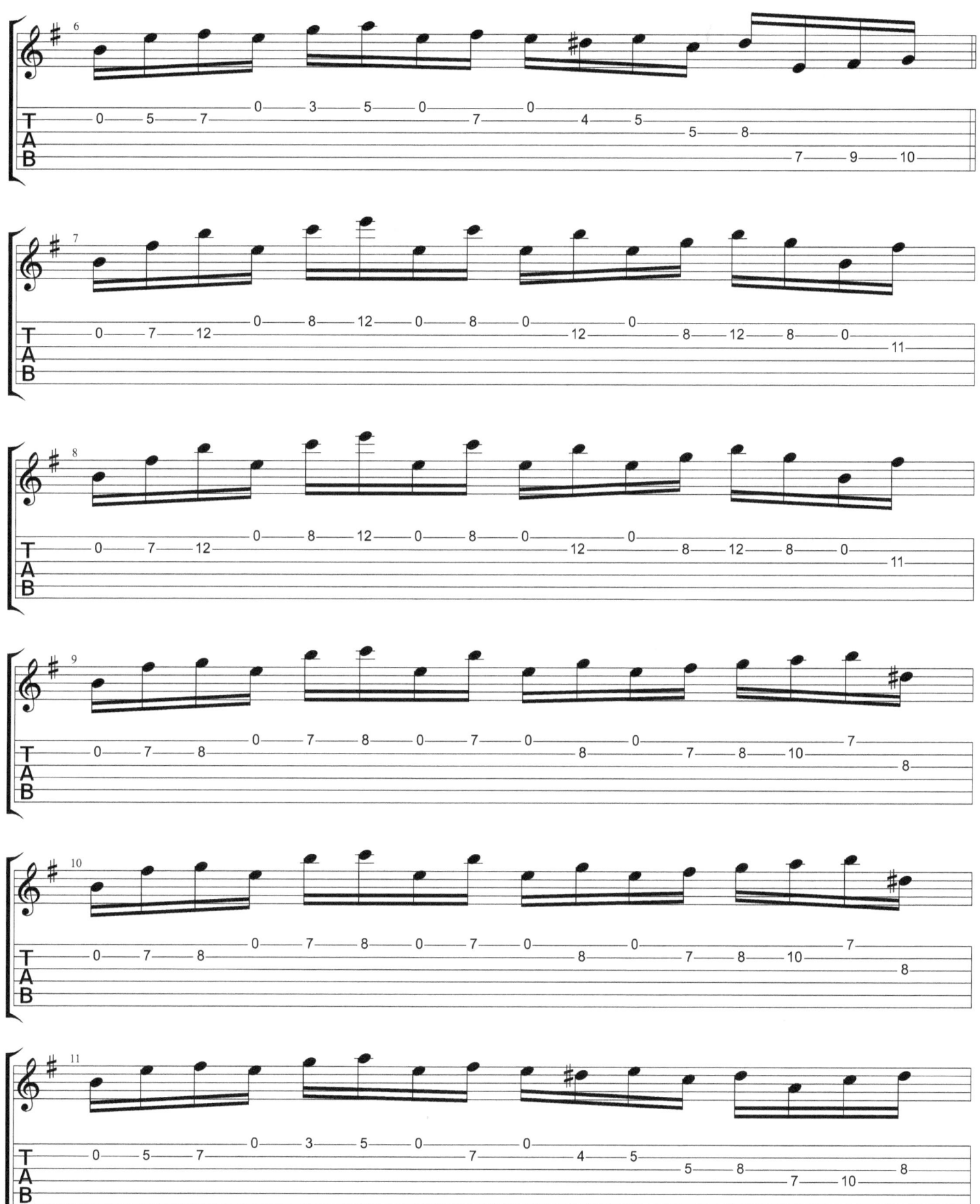

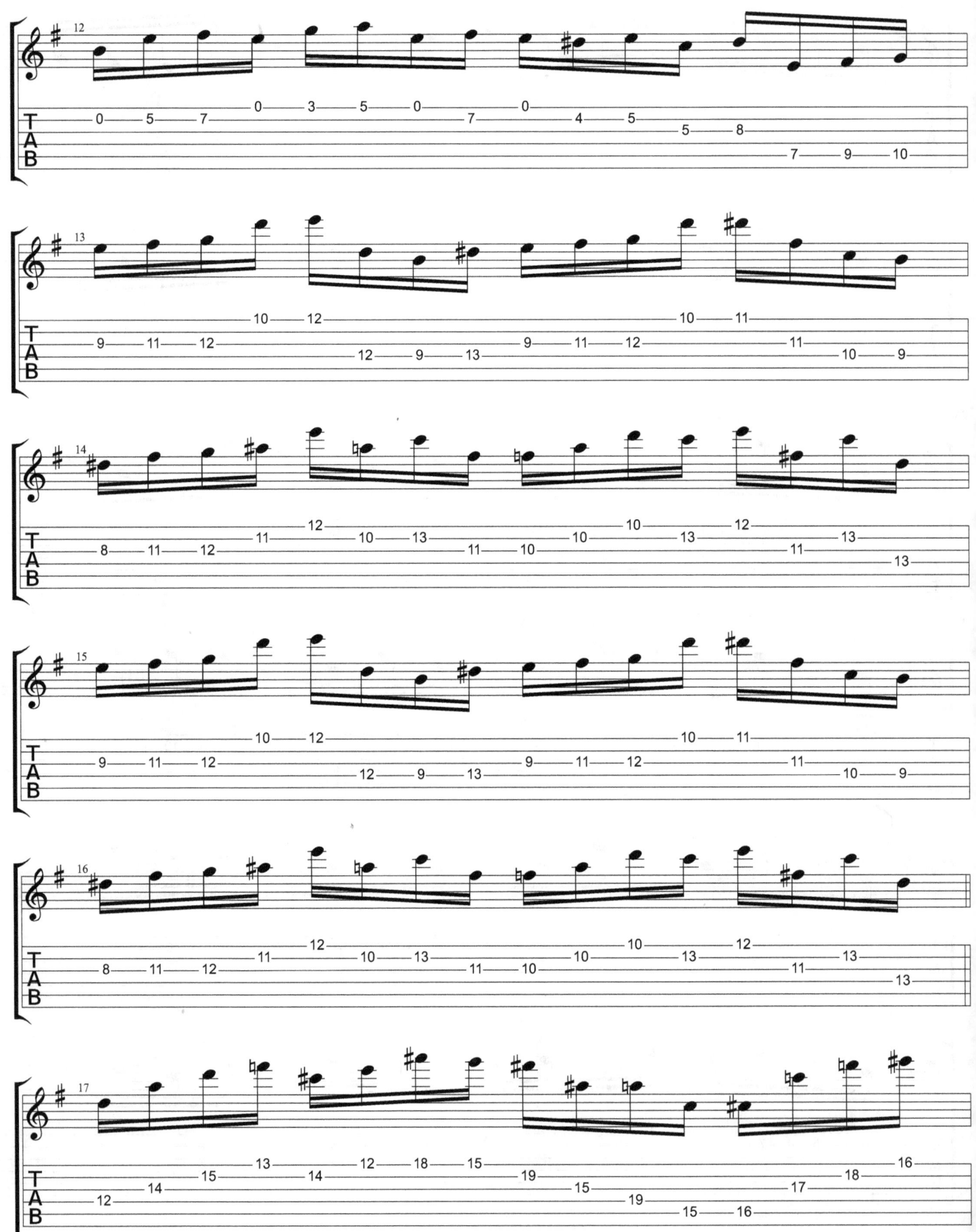

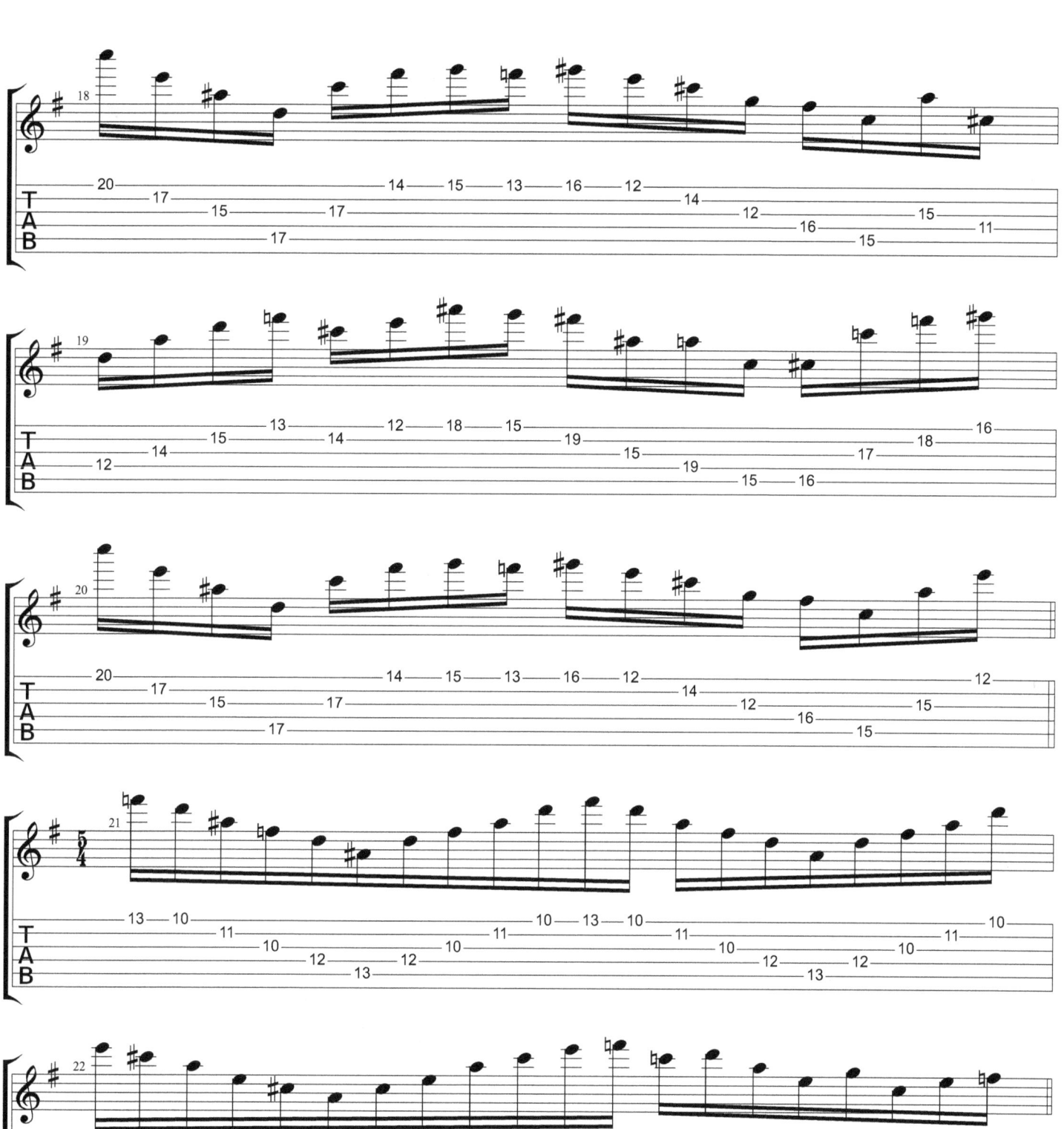

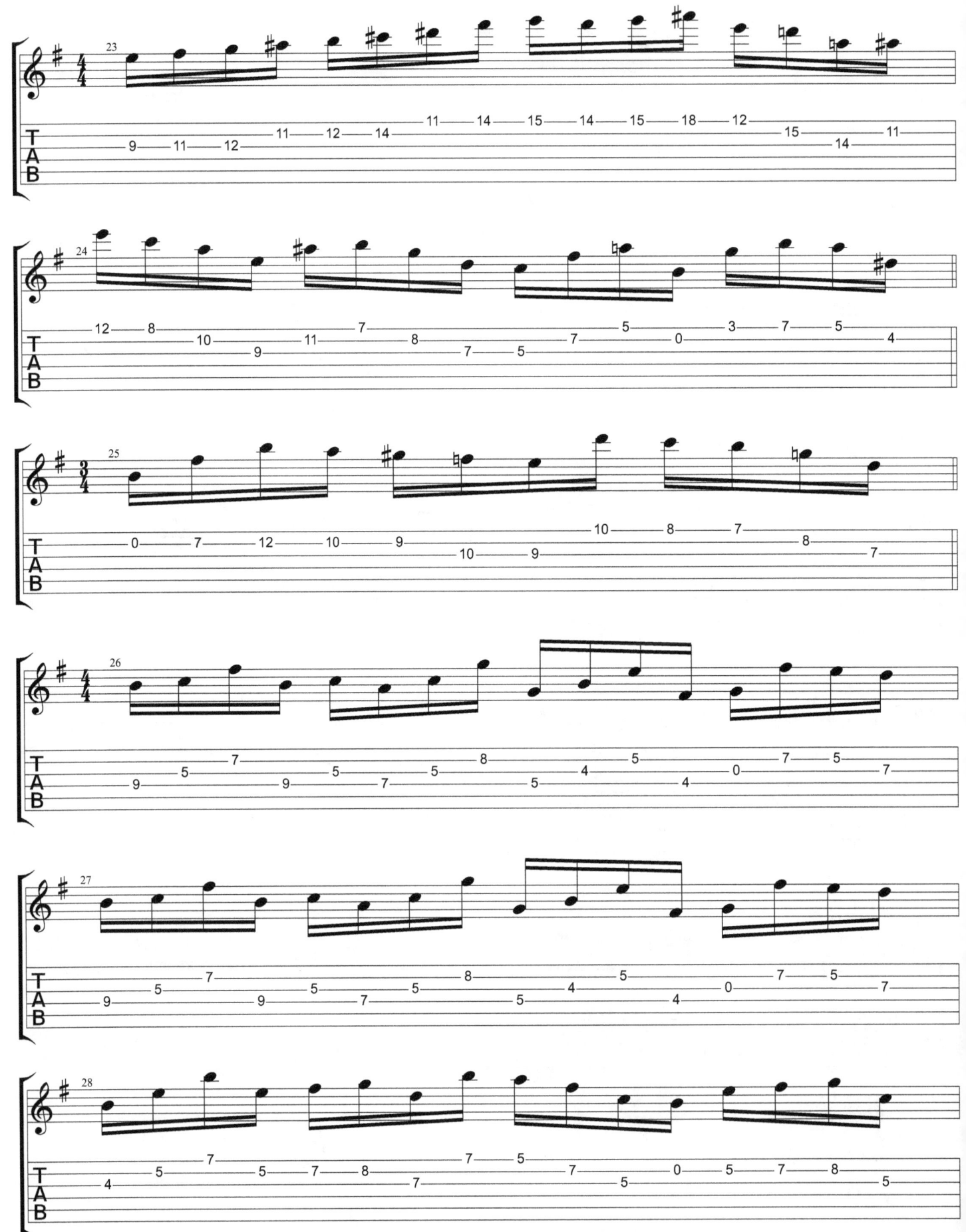

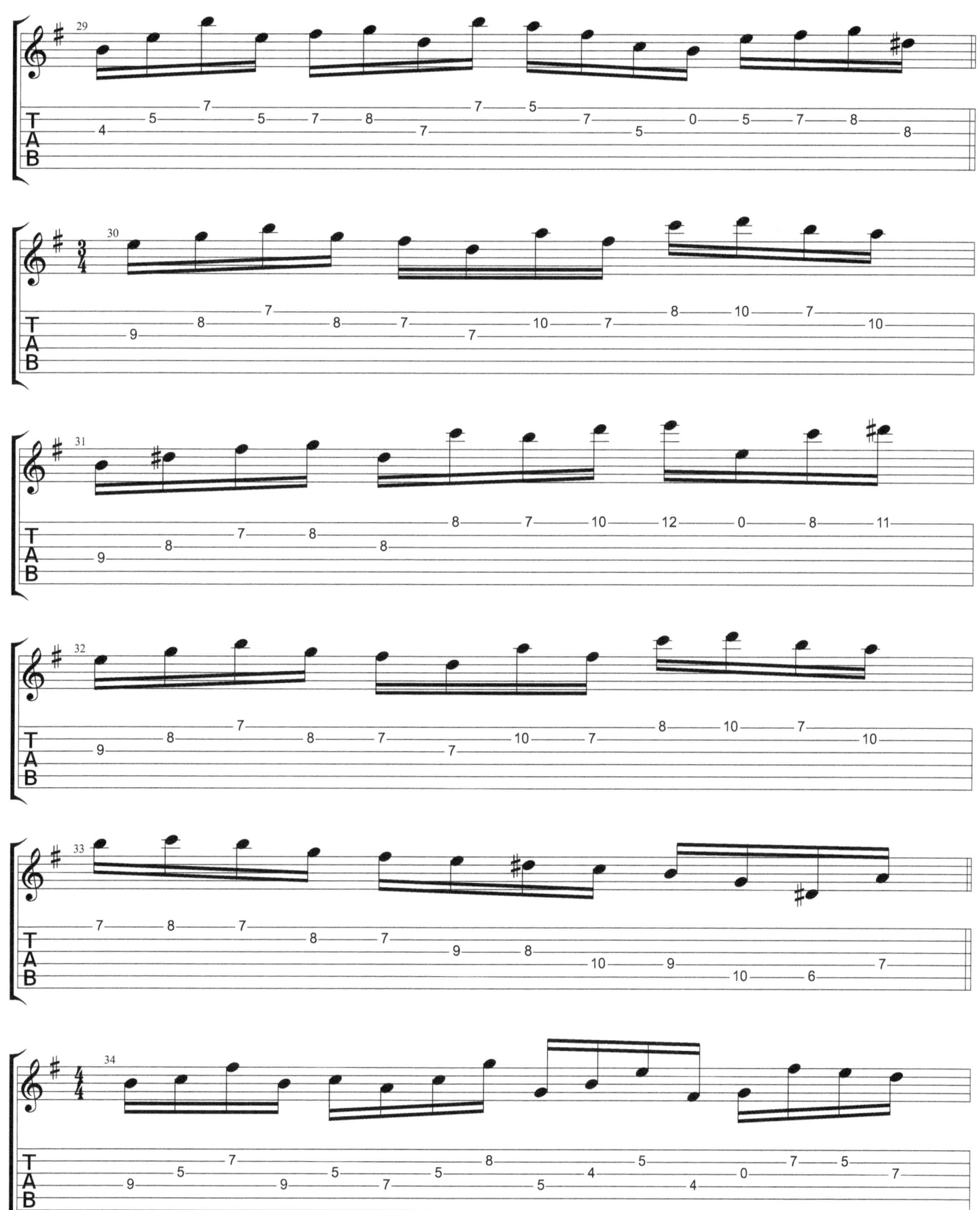

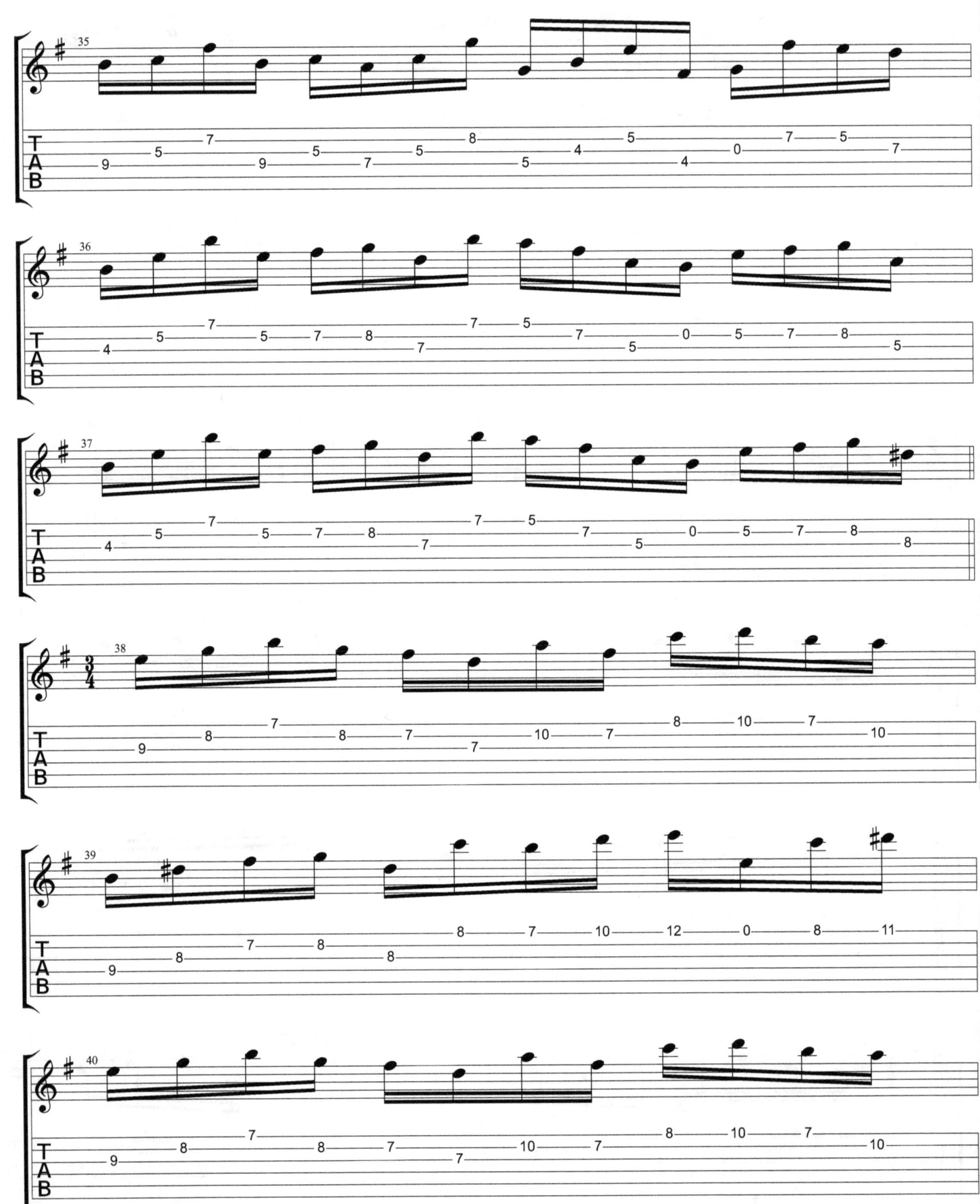

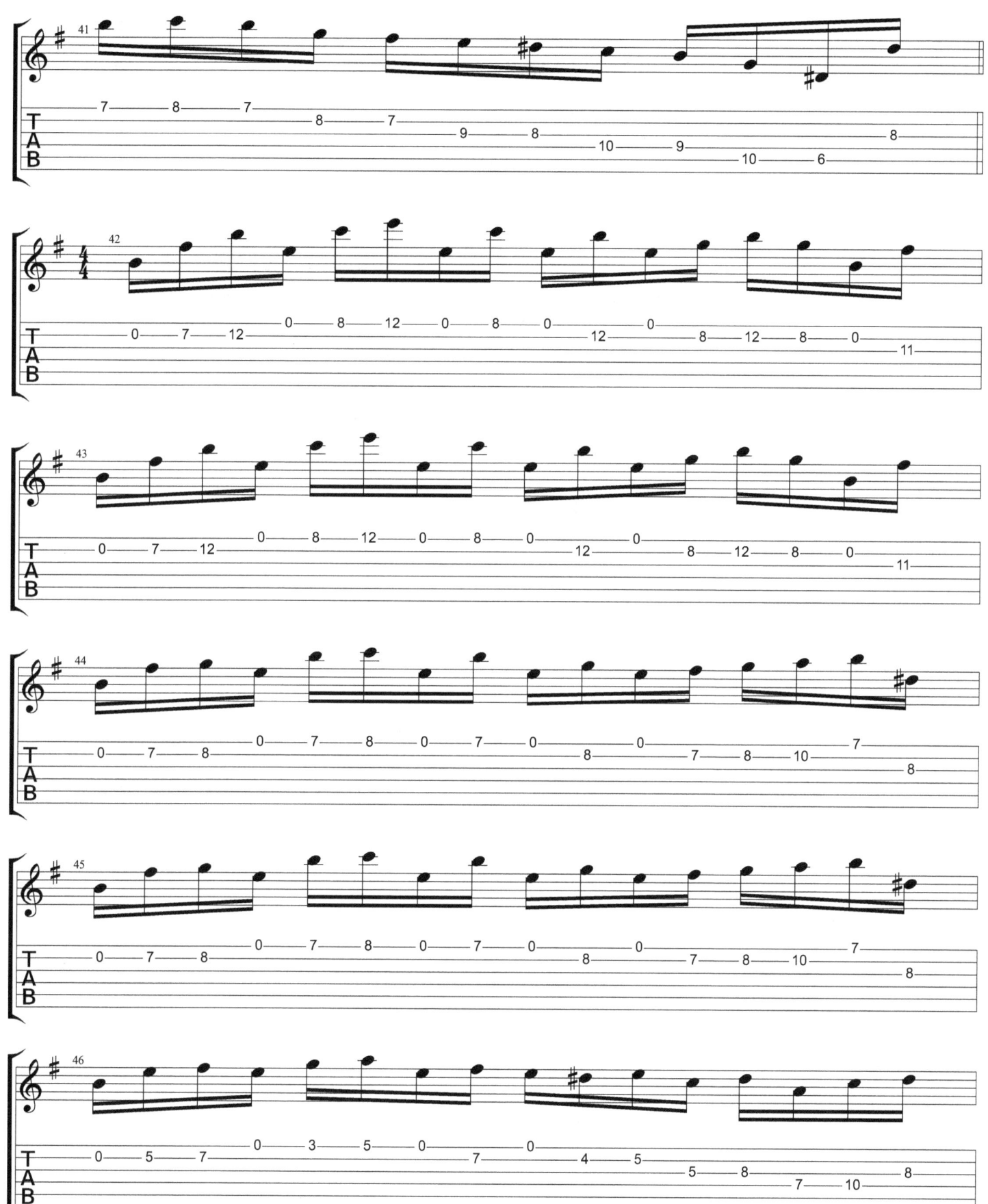

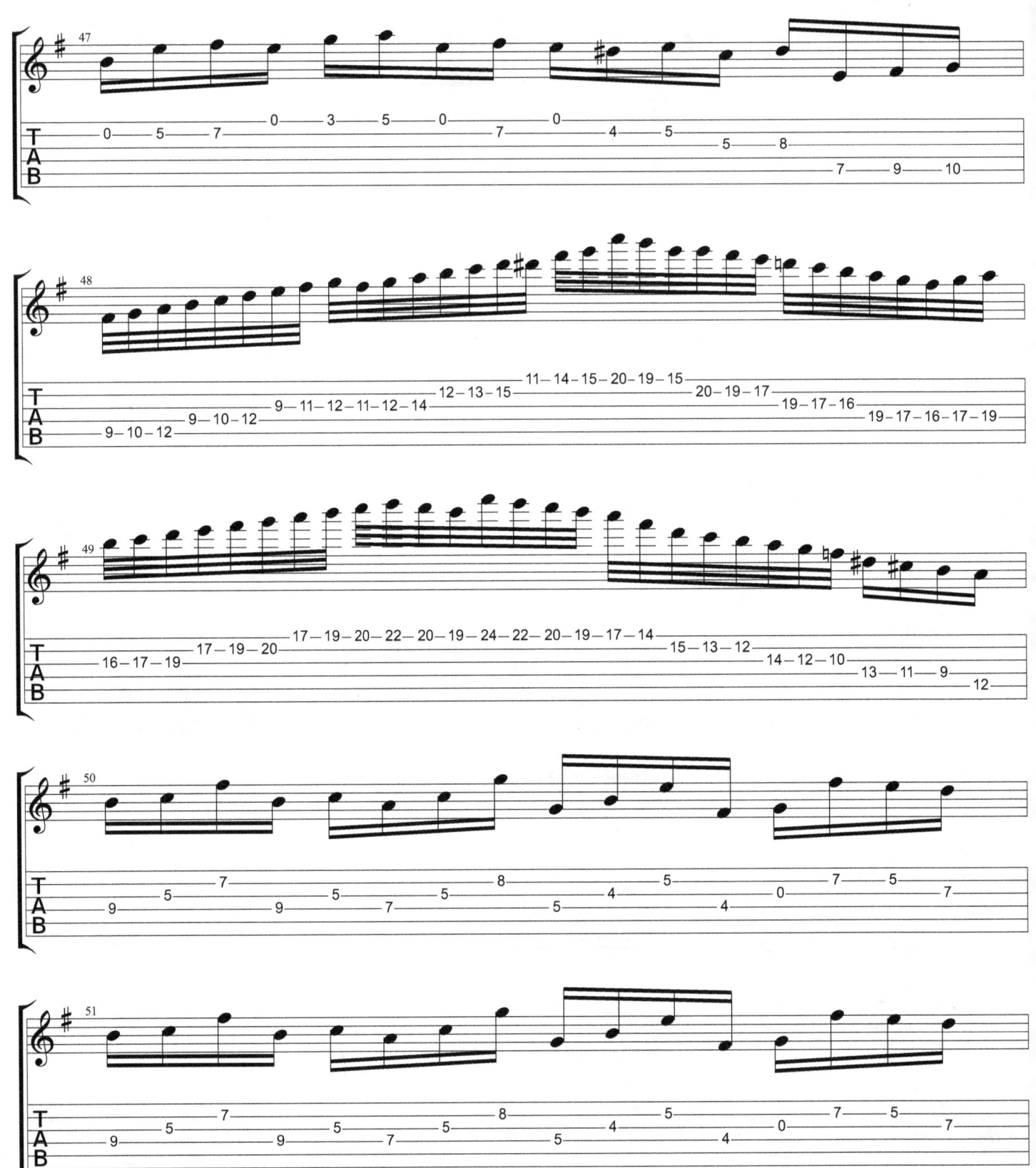

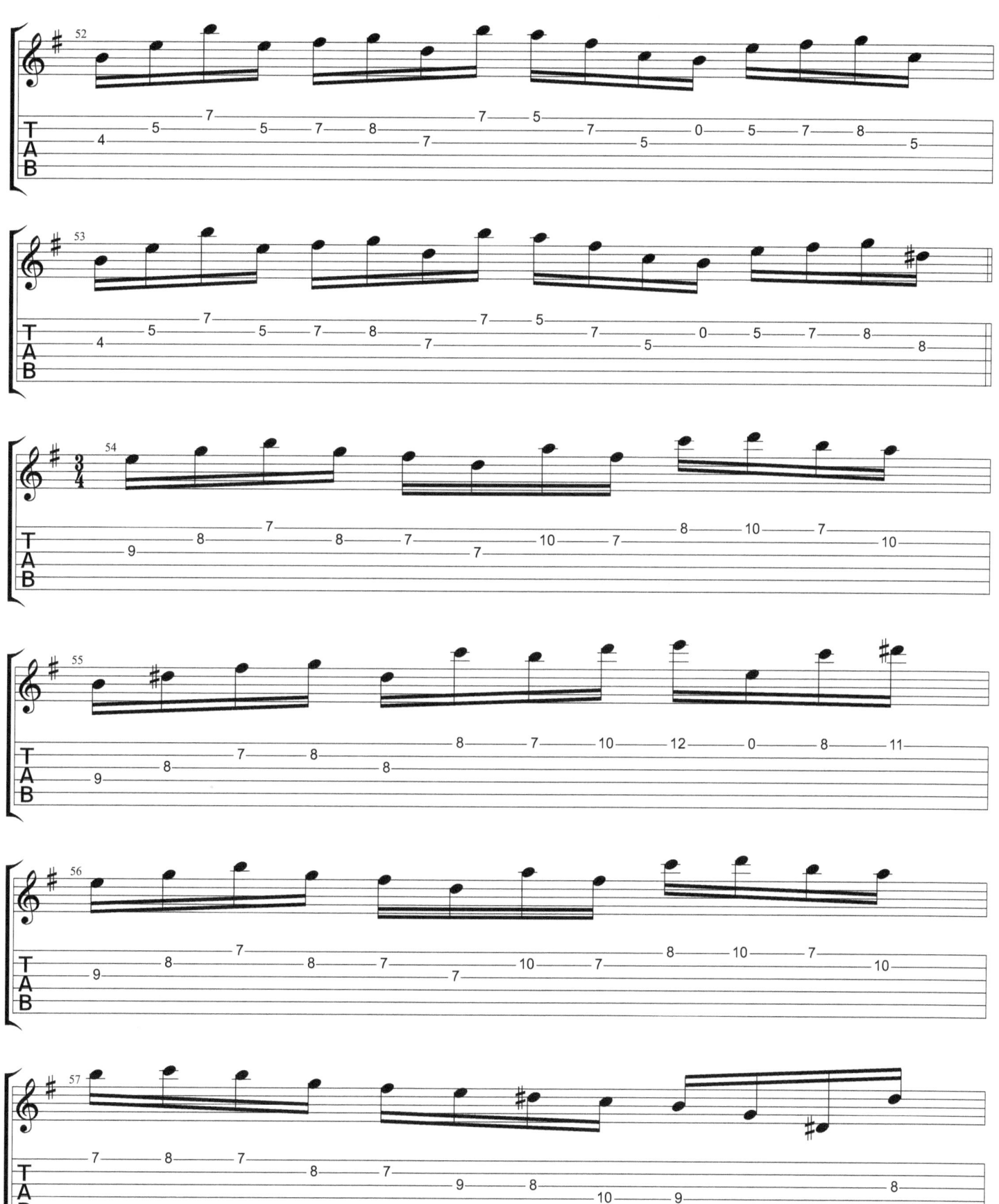

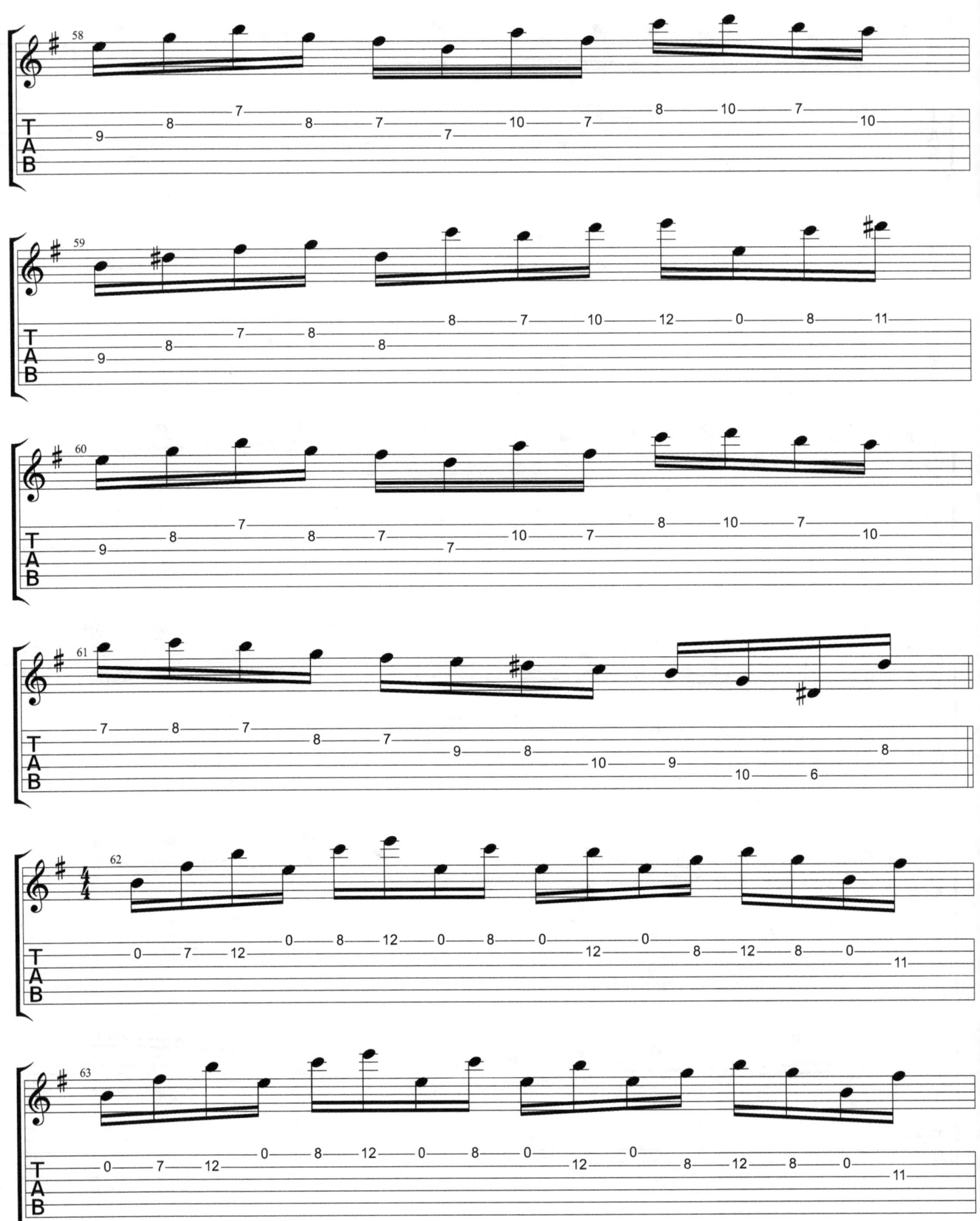

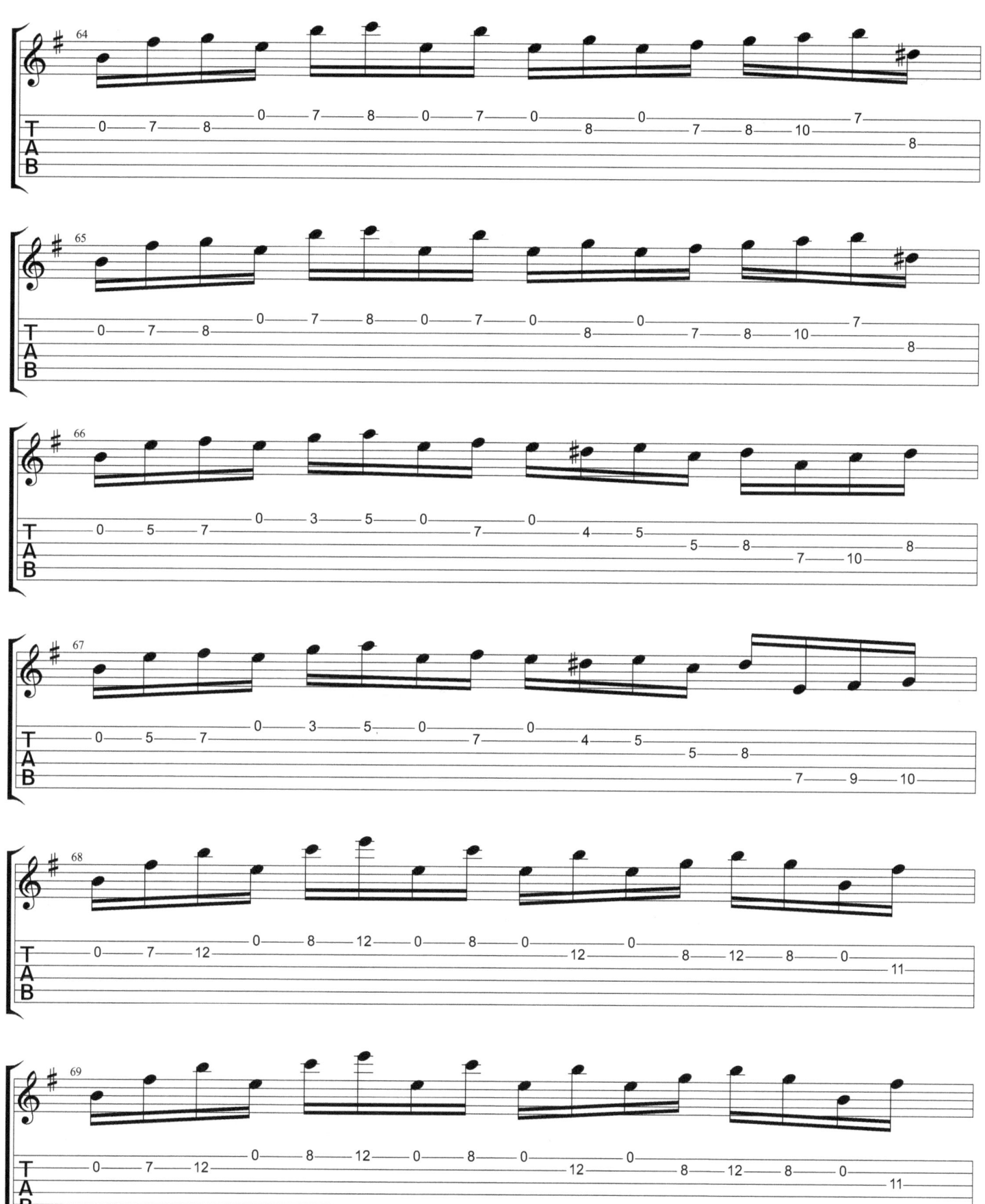

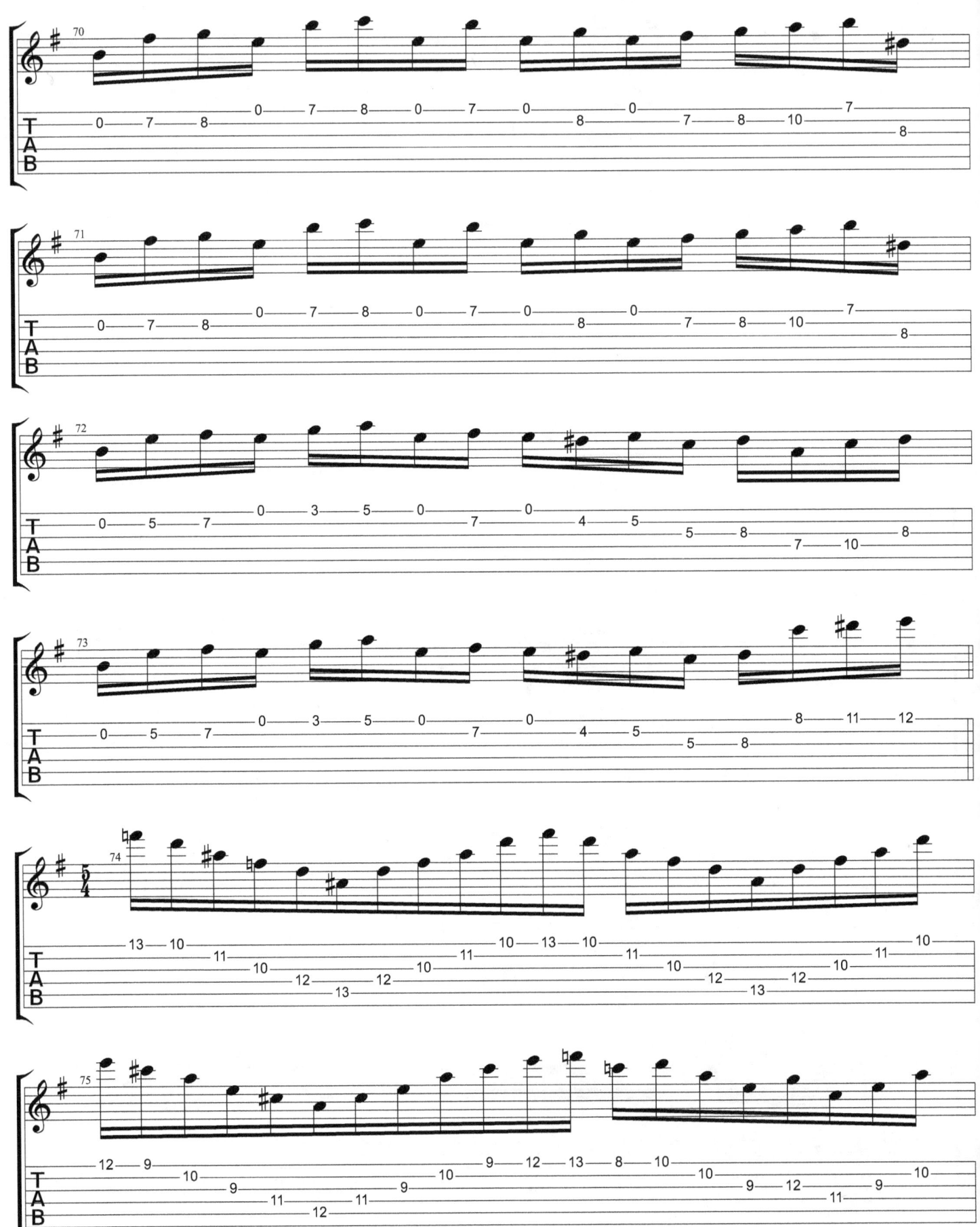

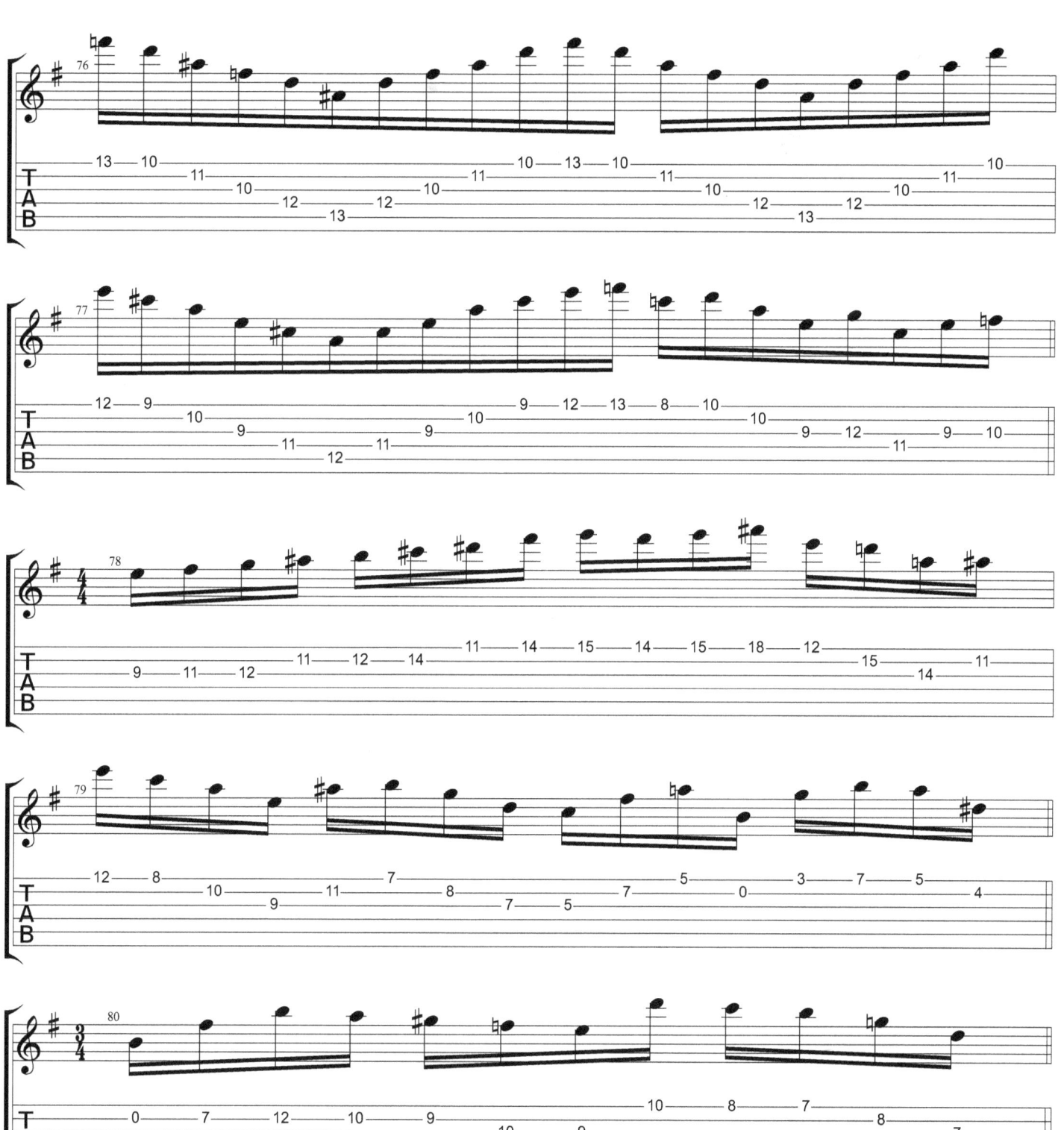

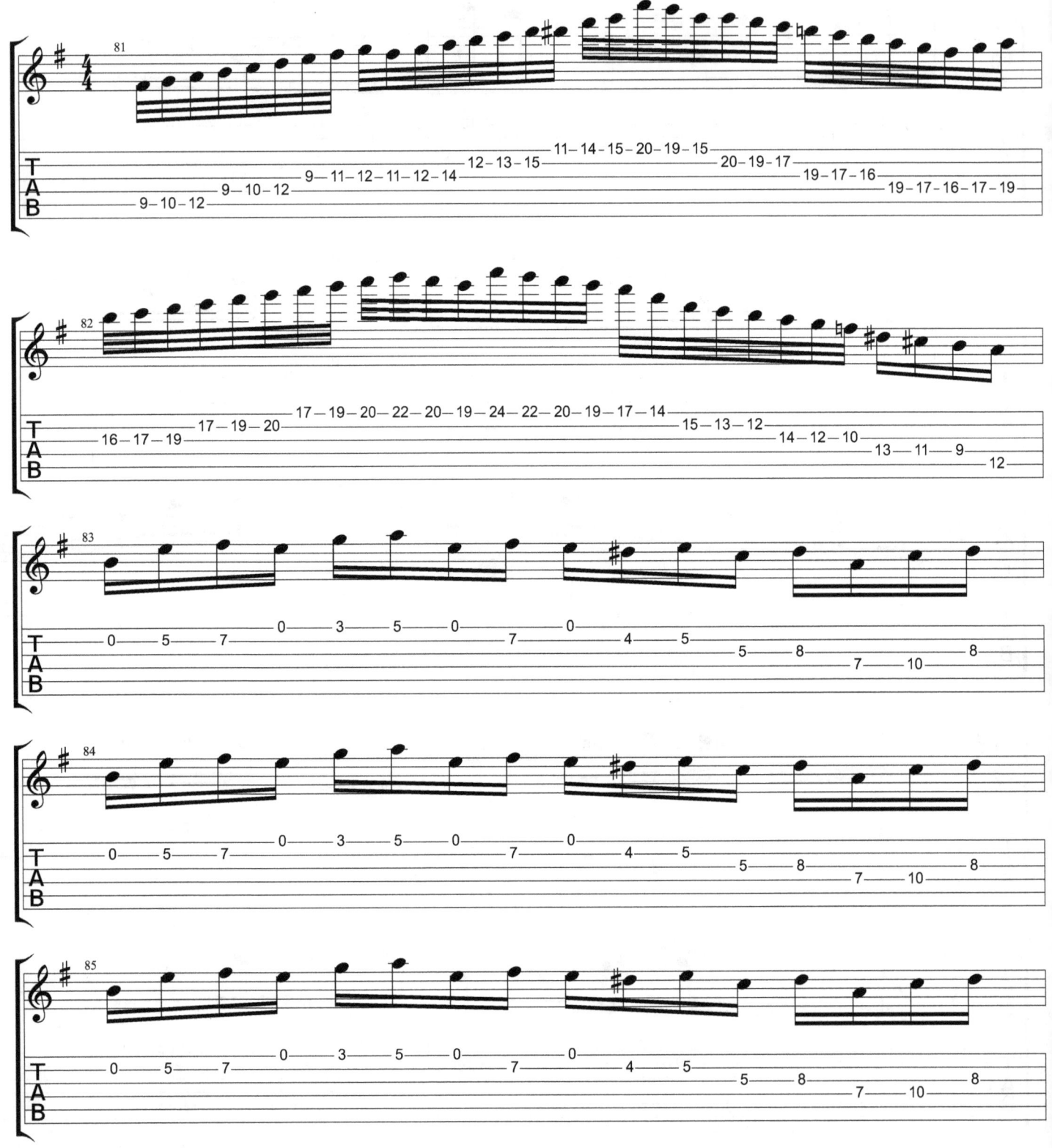

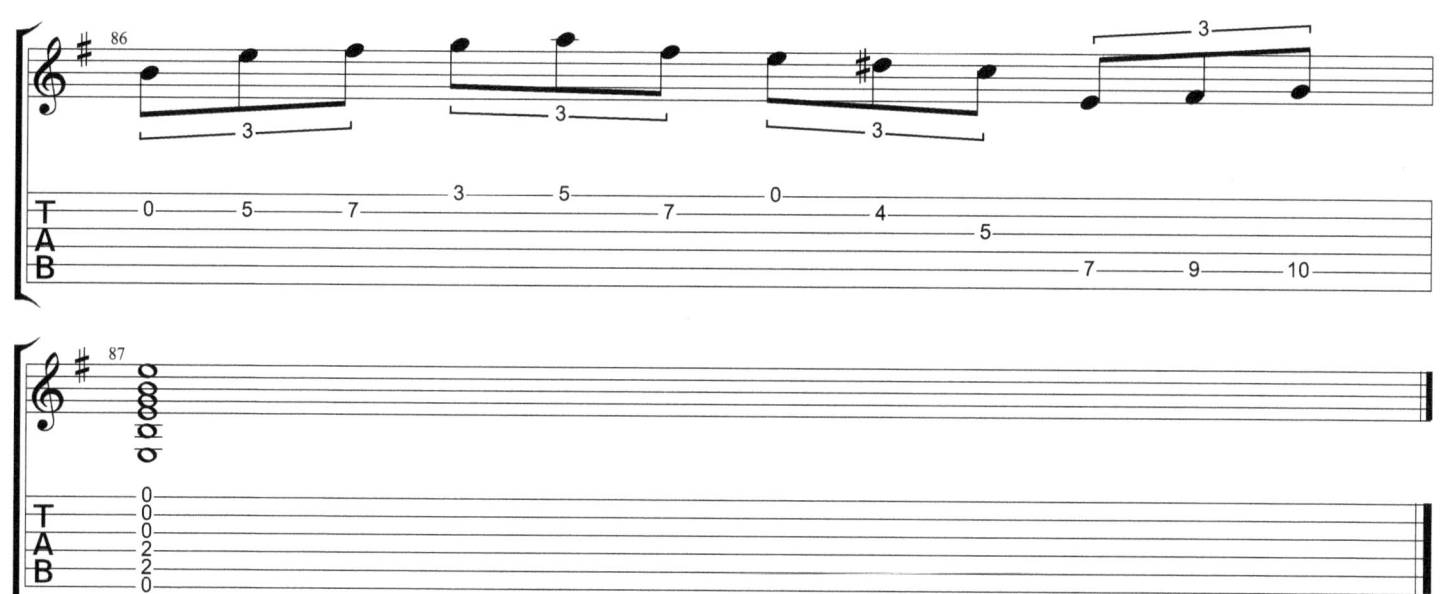

141

Snowstorm
for Electric Guitar
Joe Hartnett

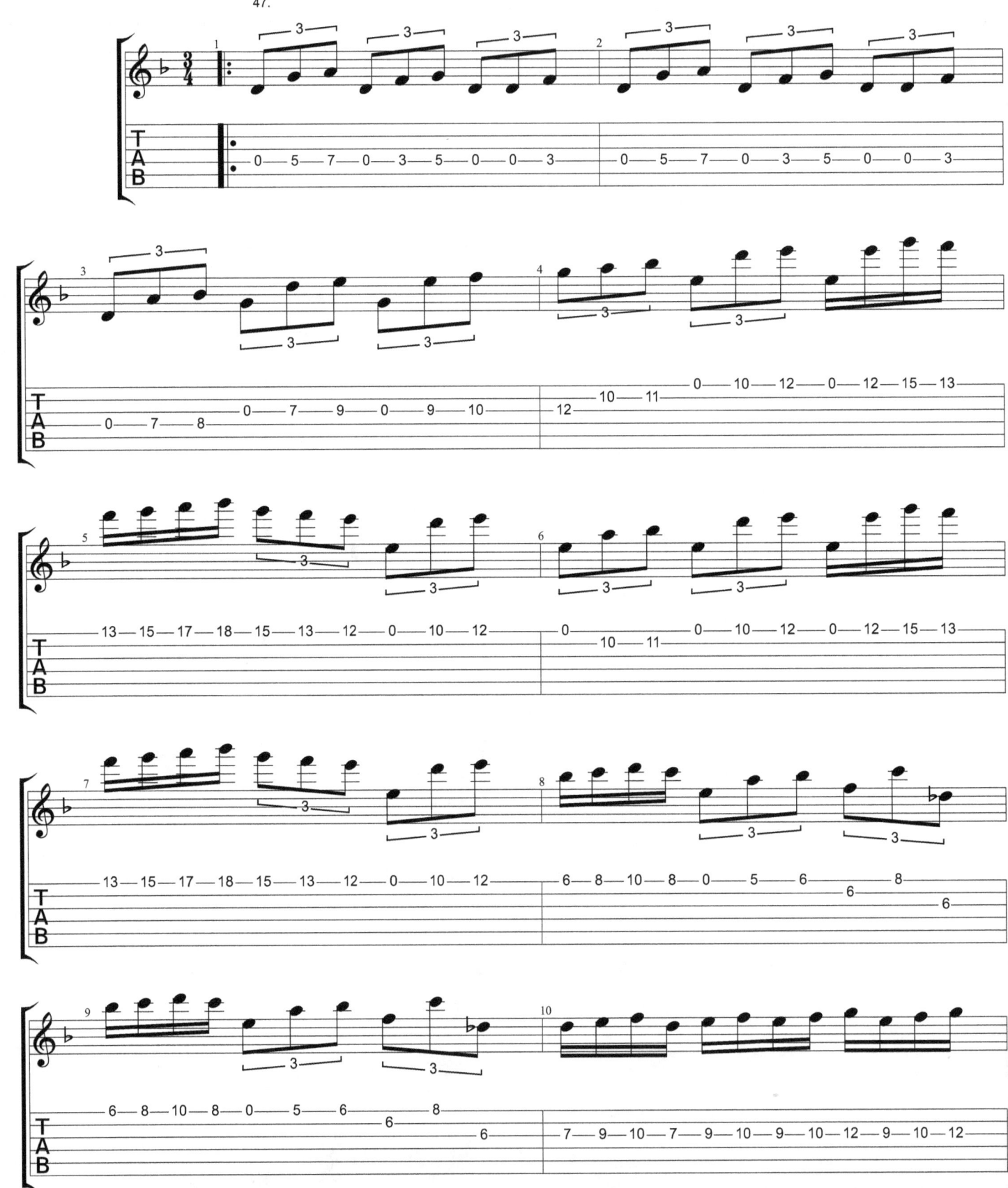

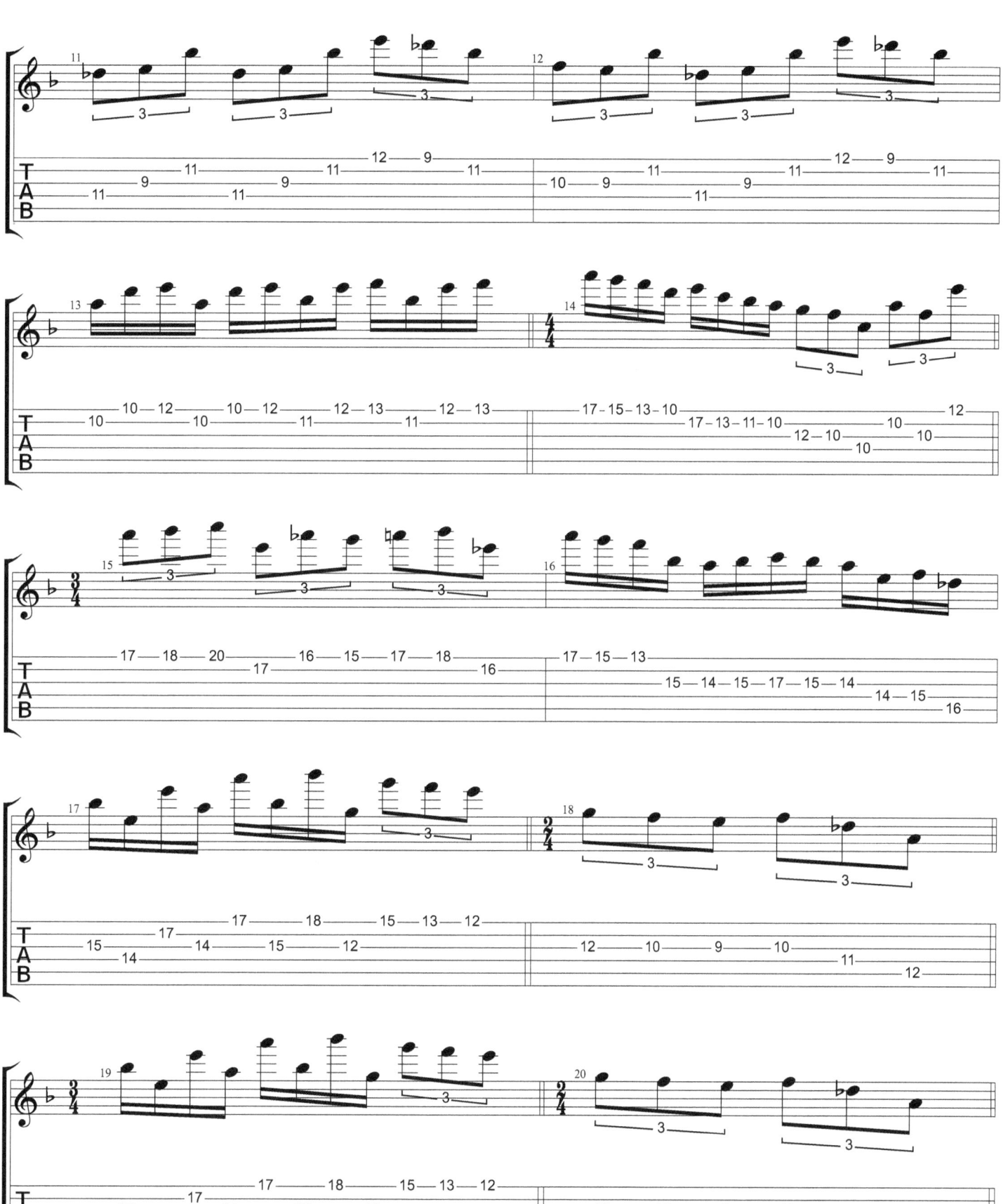

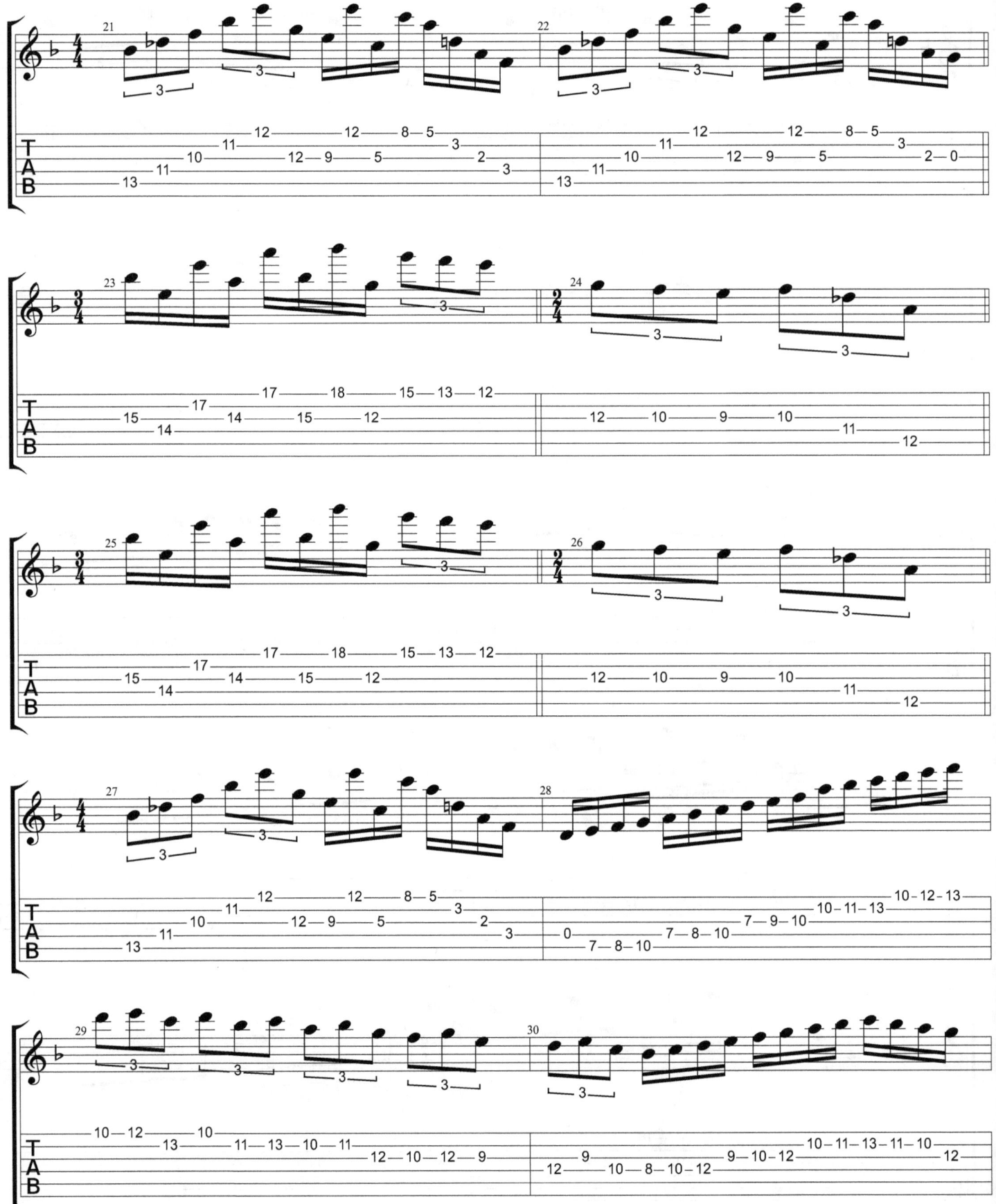

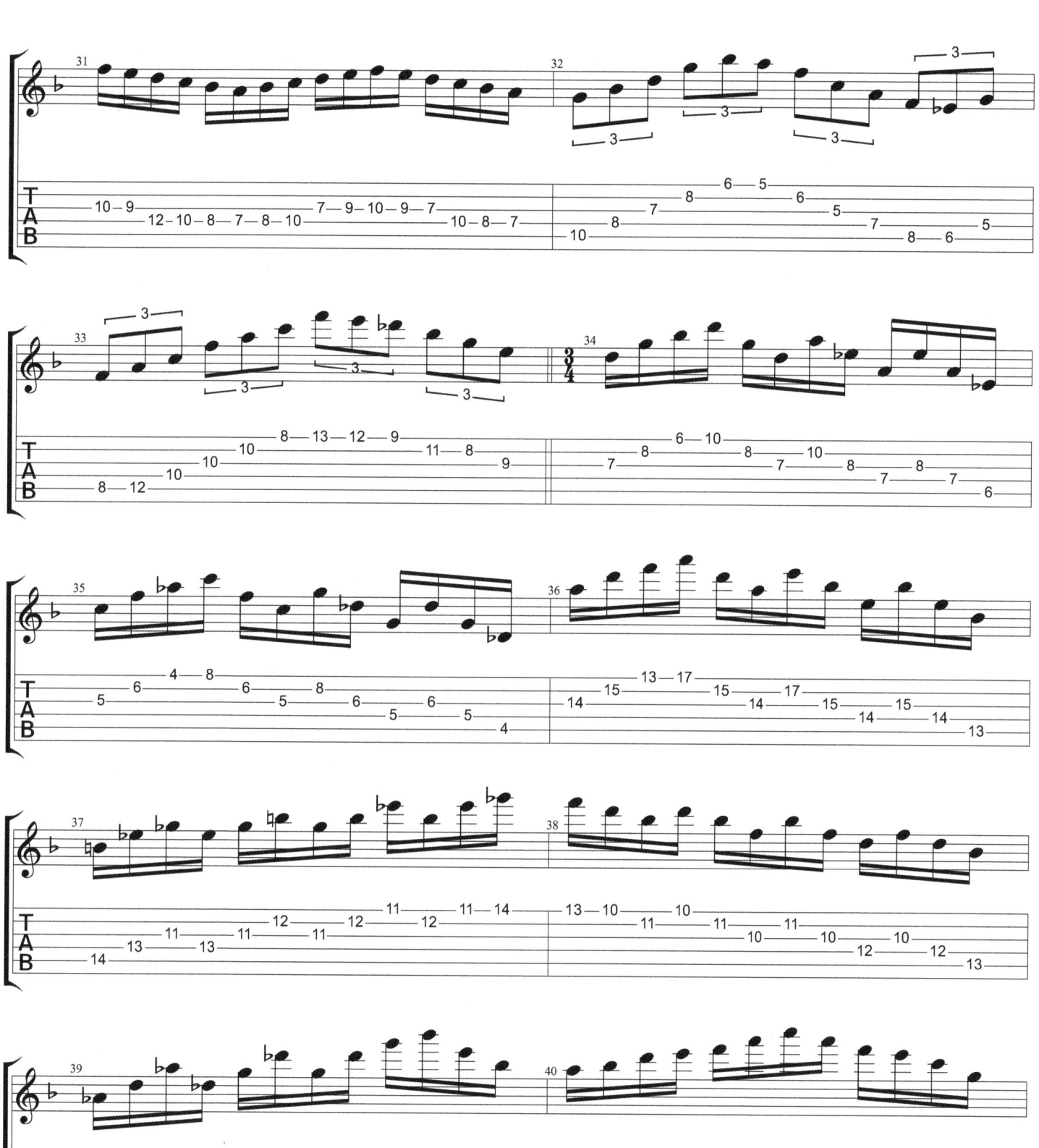

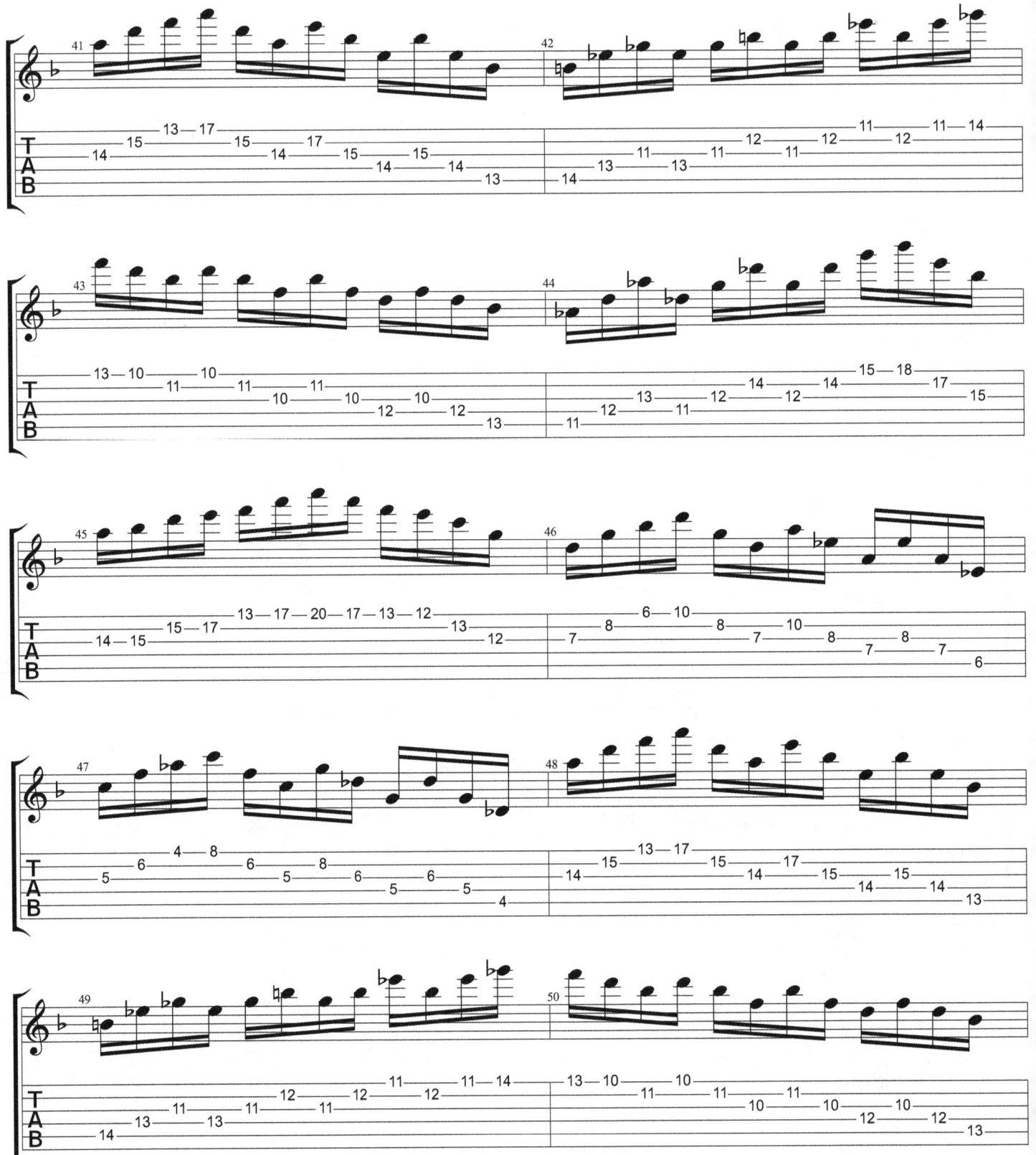

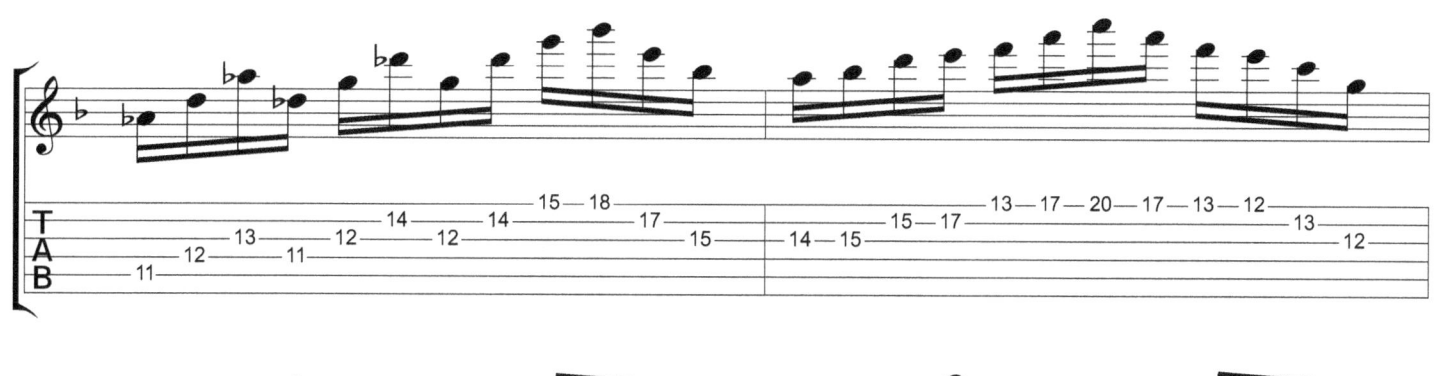

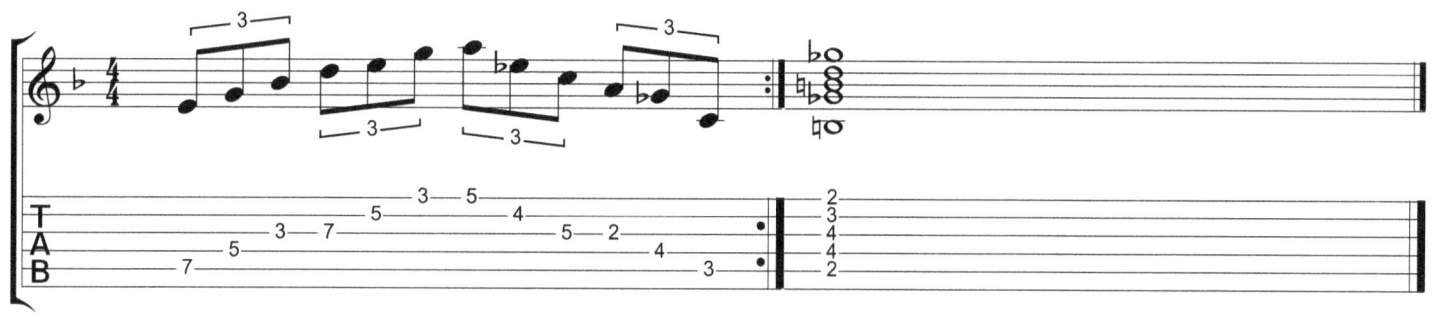

Darkness
for Electric Guitar
Joe Hartnett

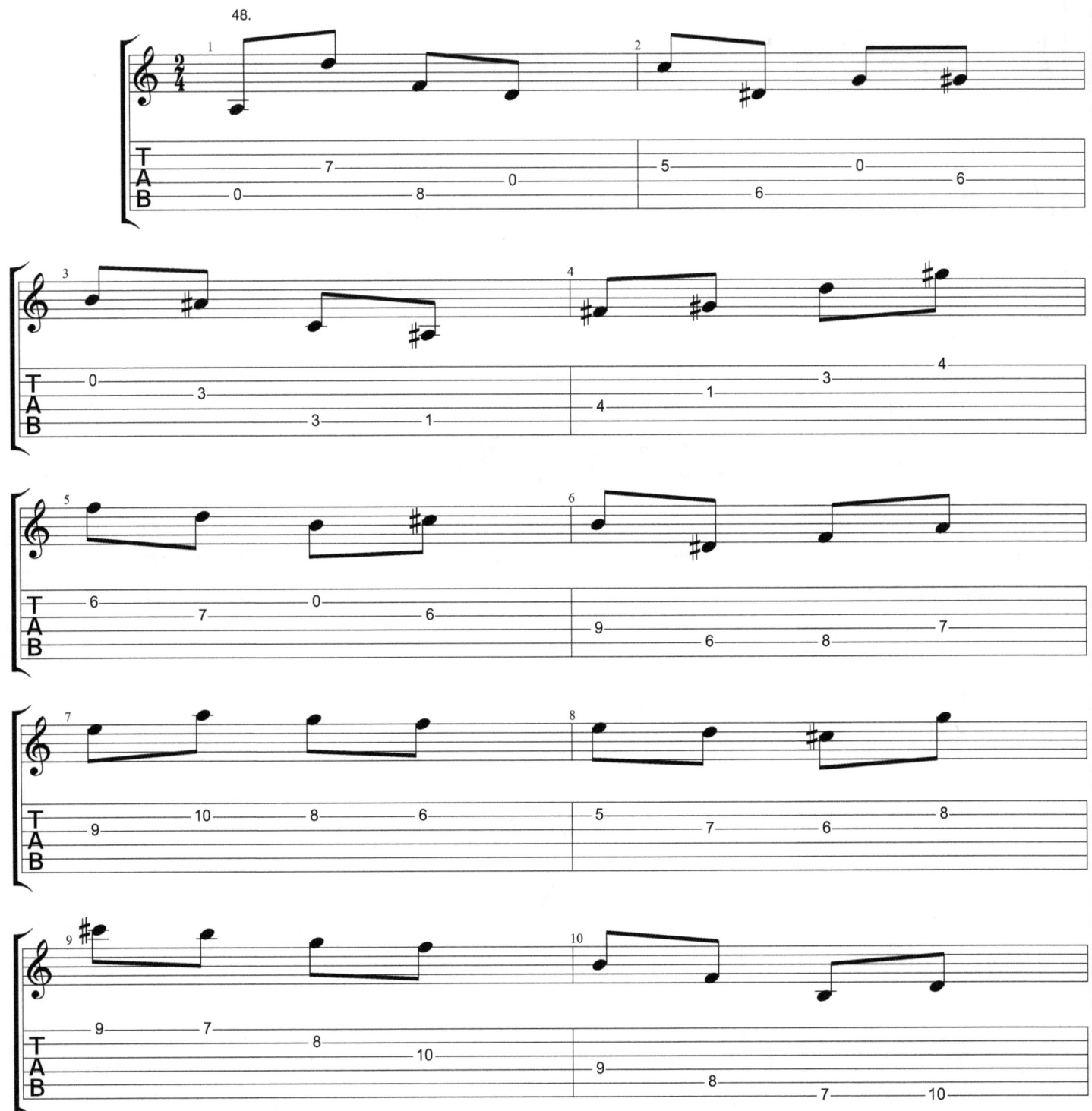

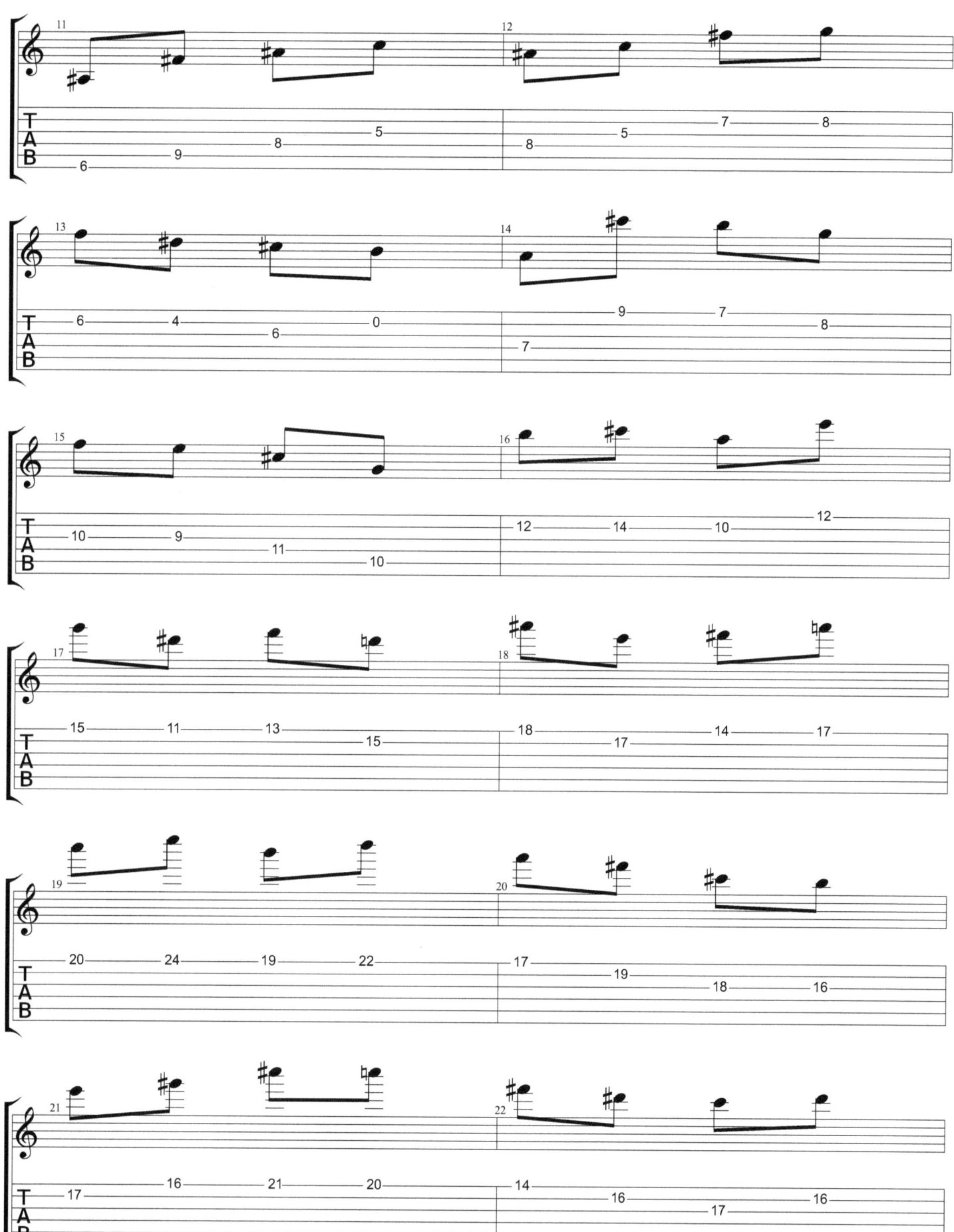

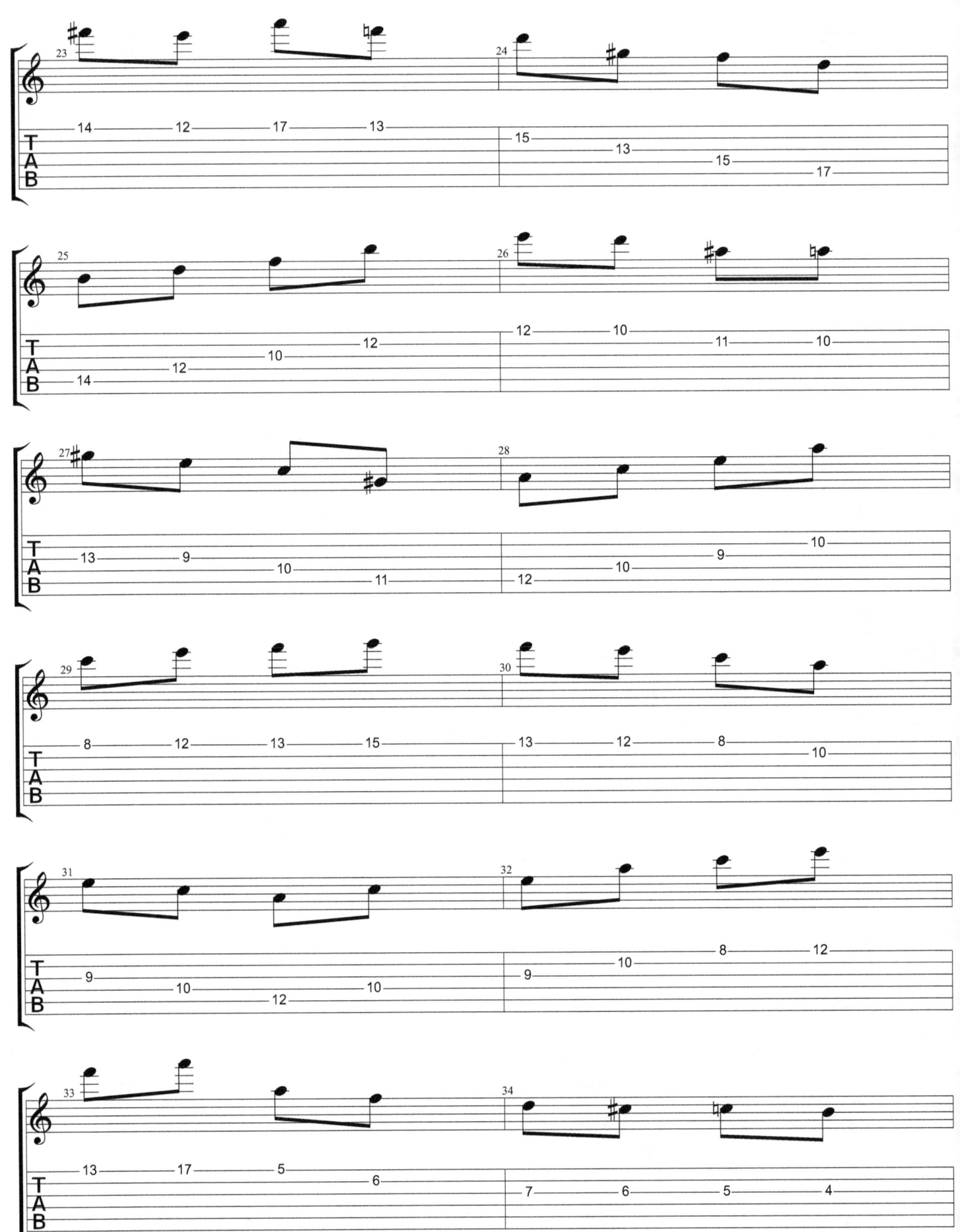

Summit
for Electric Guitar
Joe Hartnett

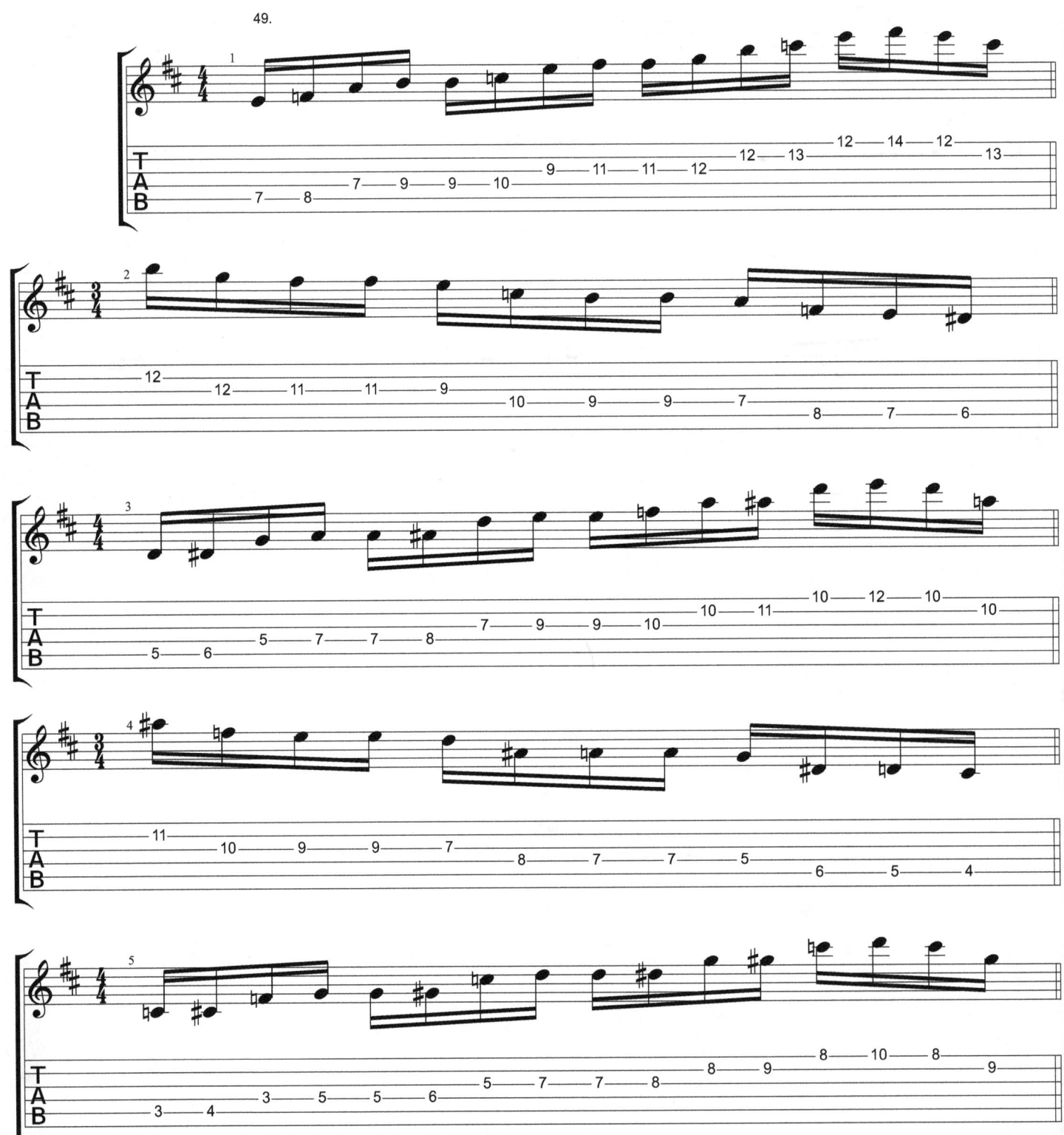

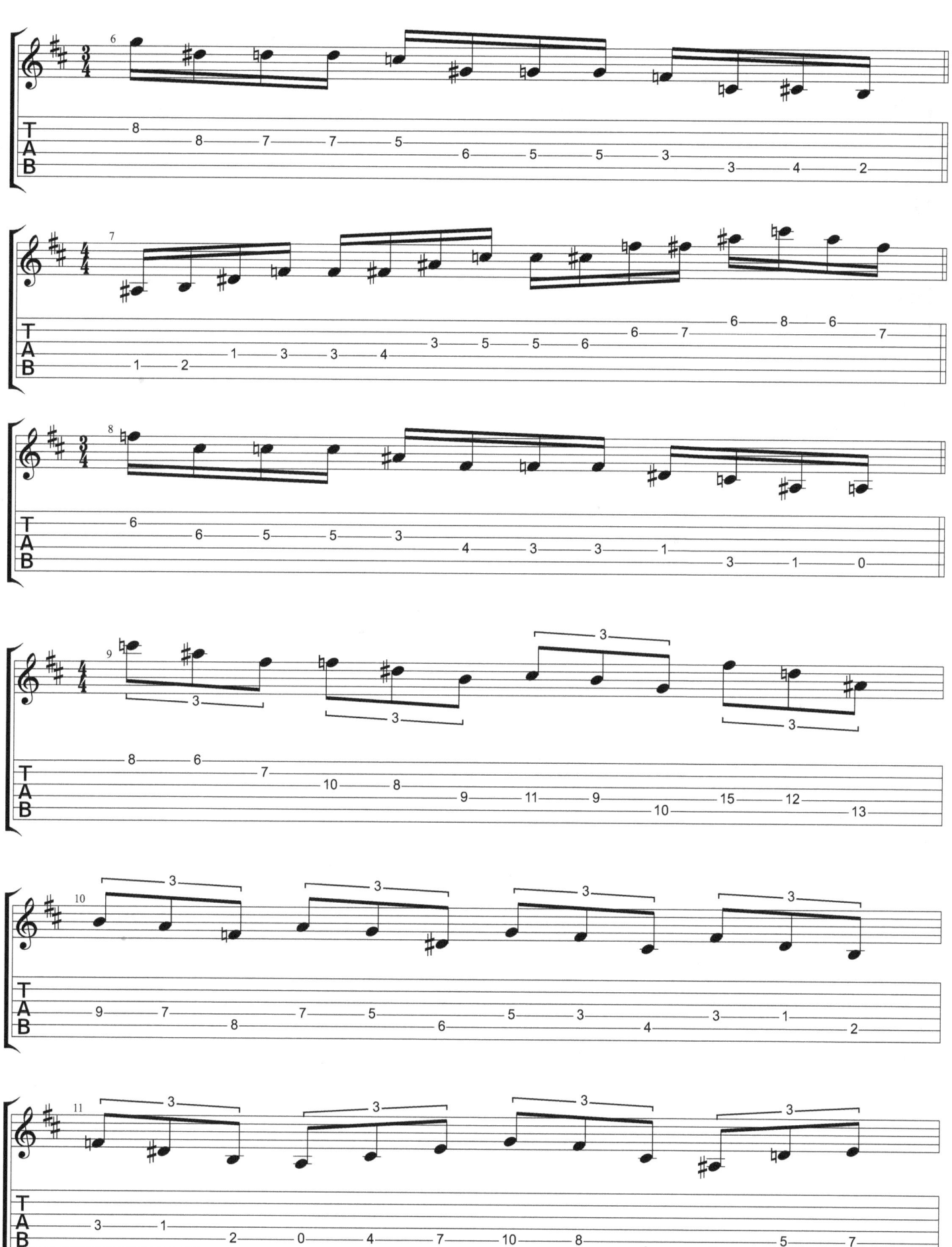

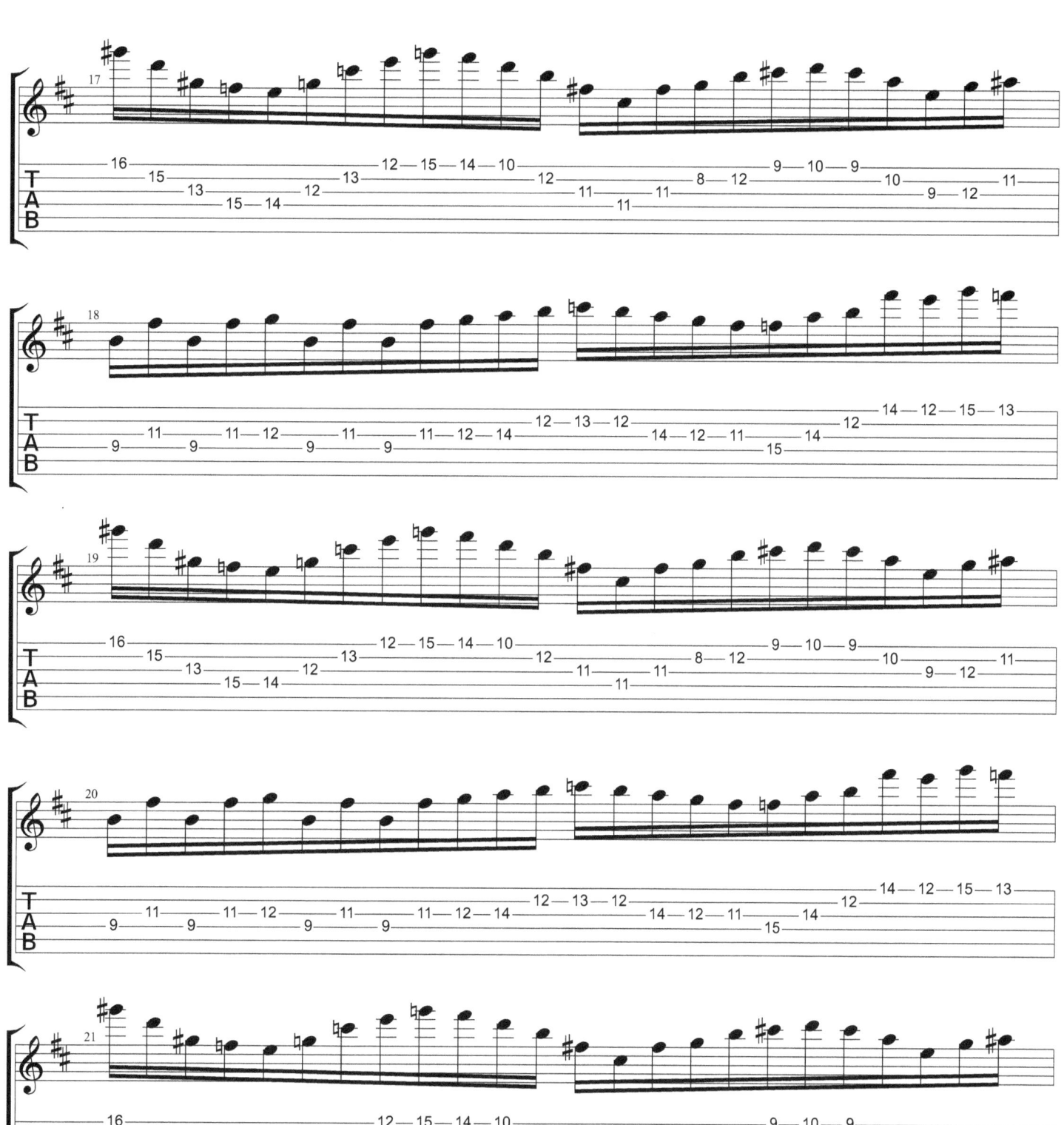

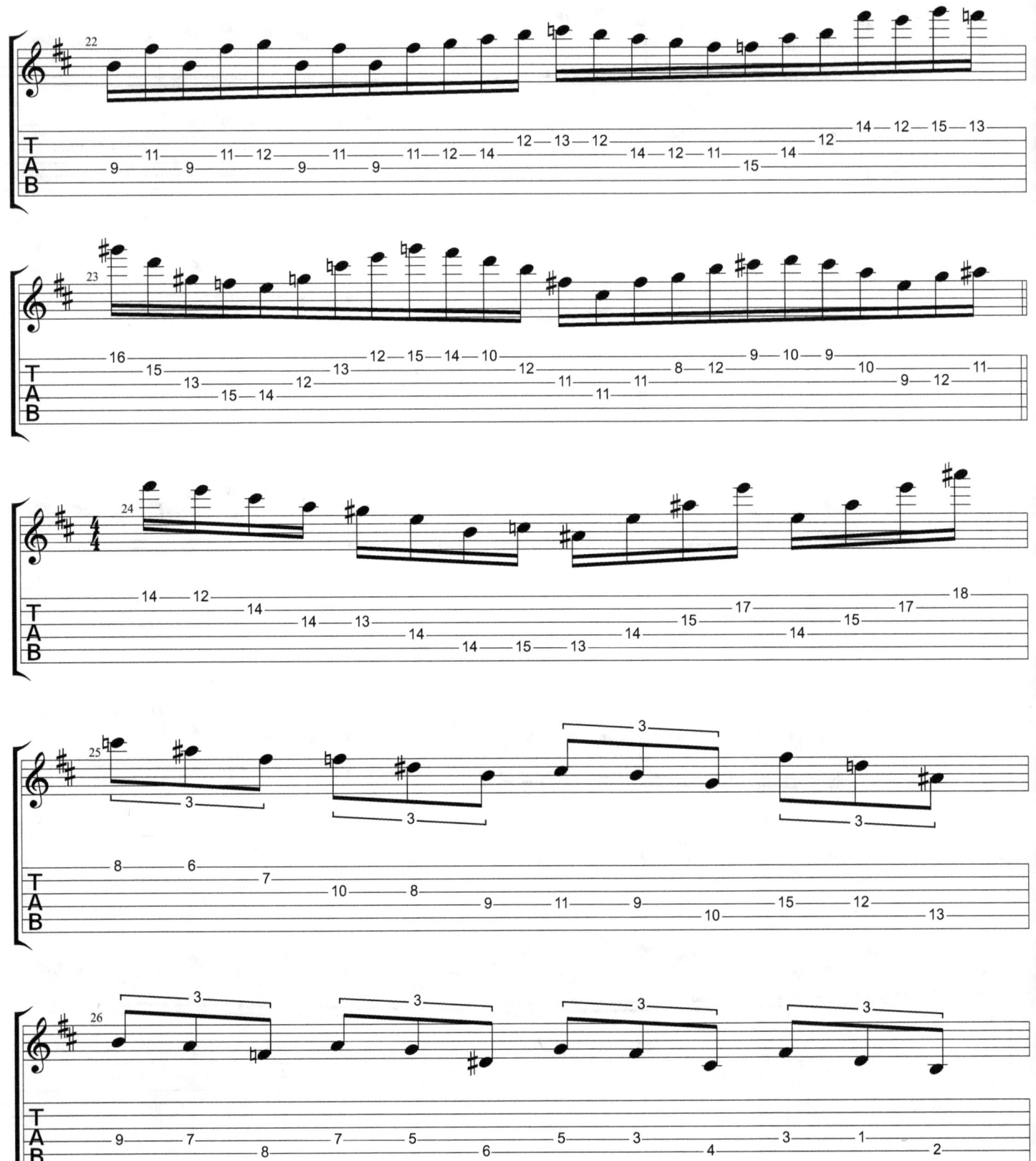

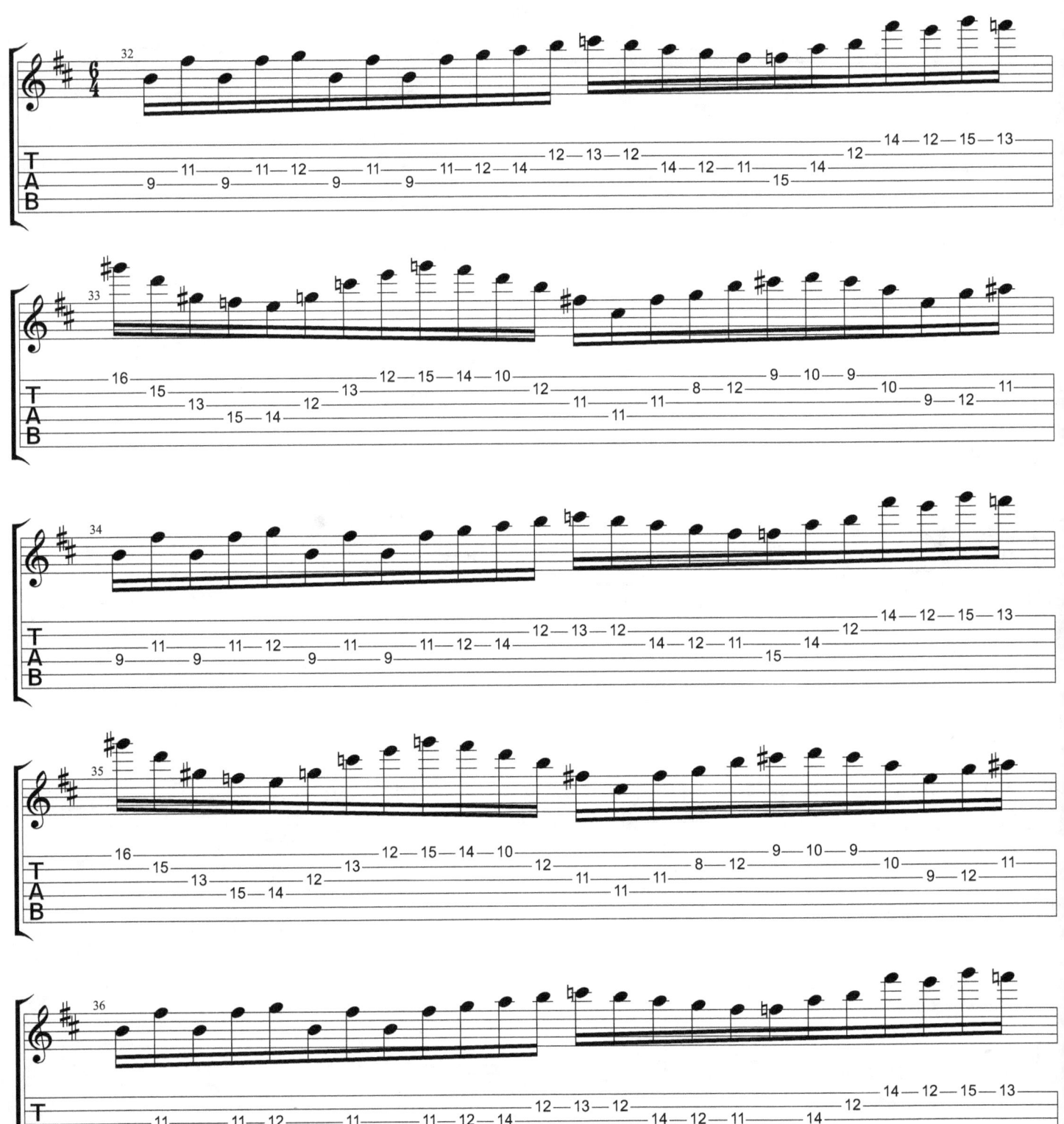

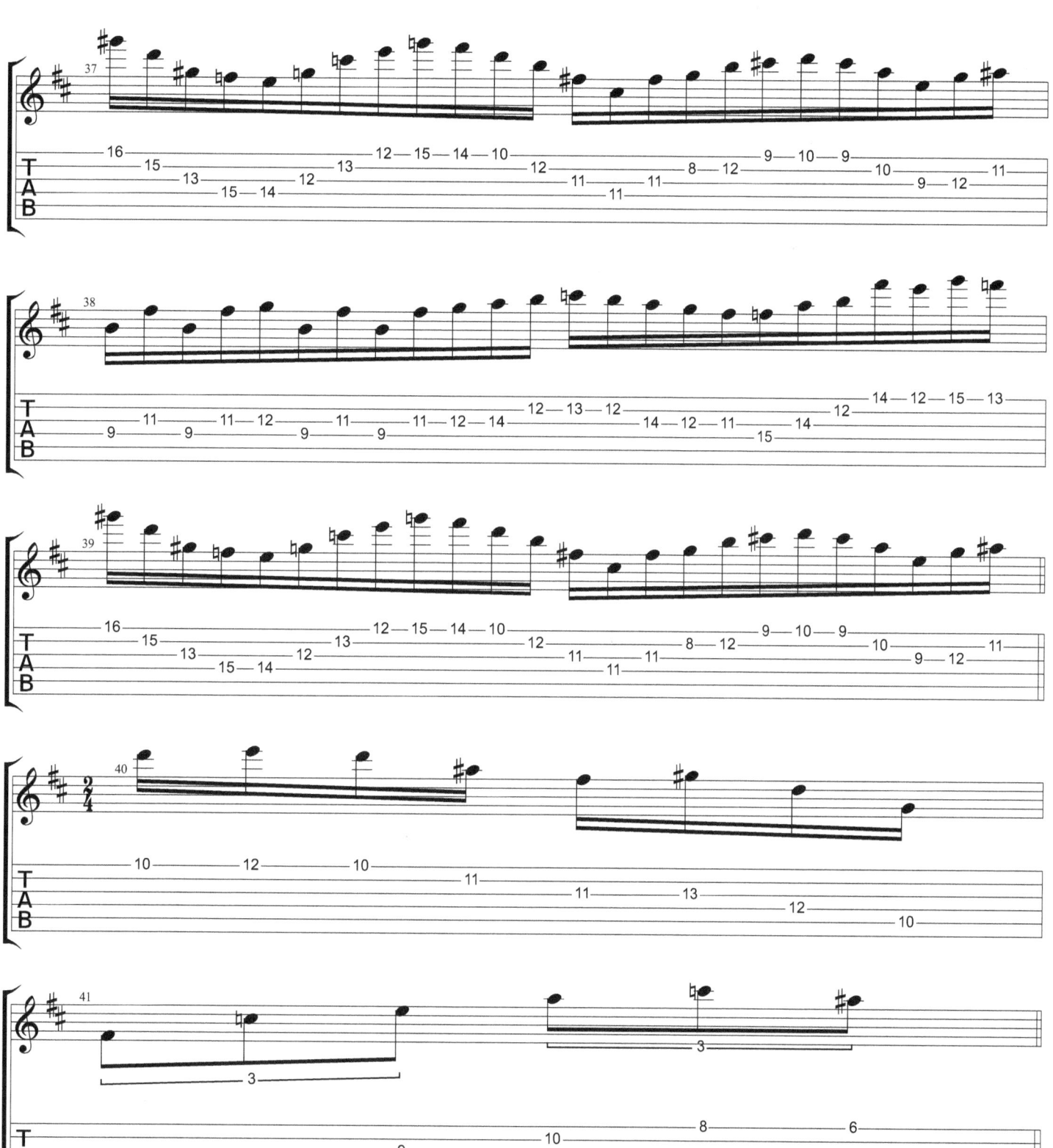

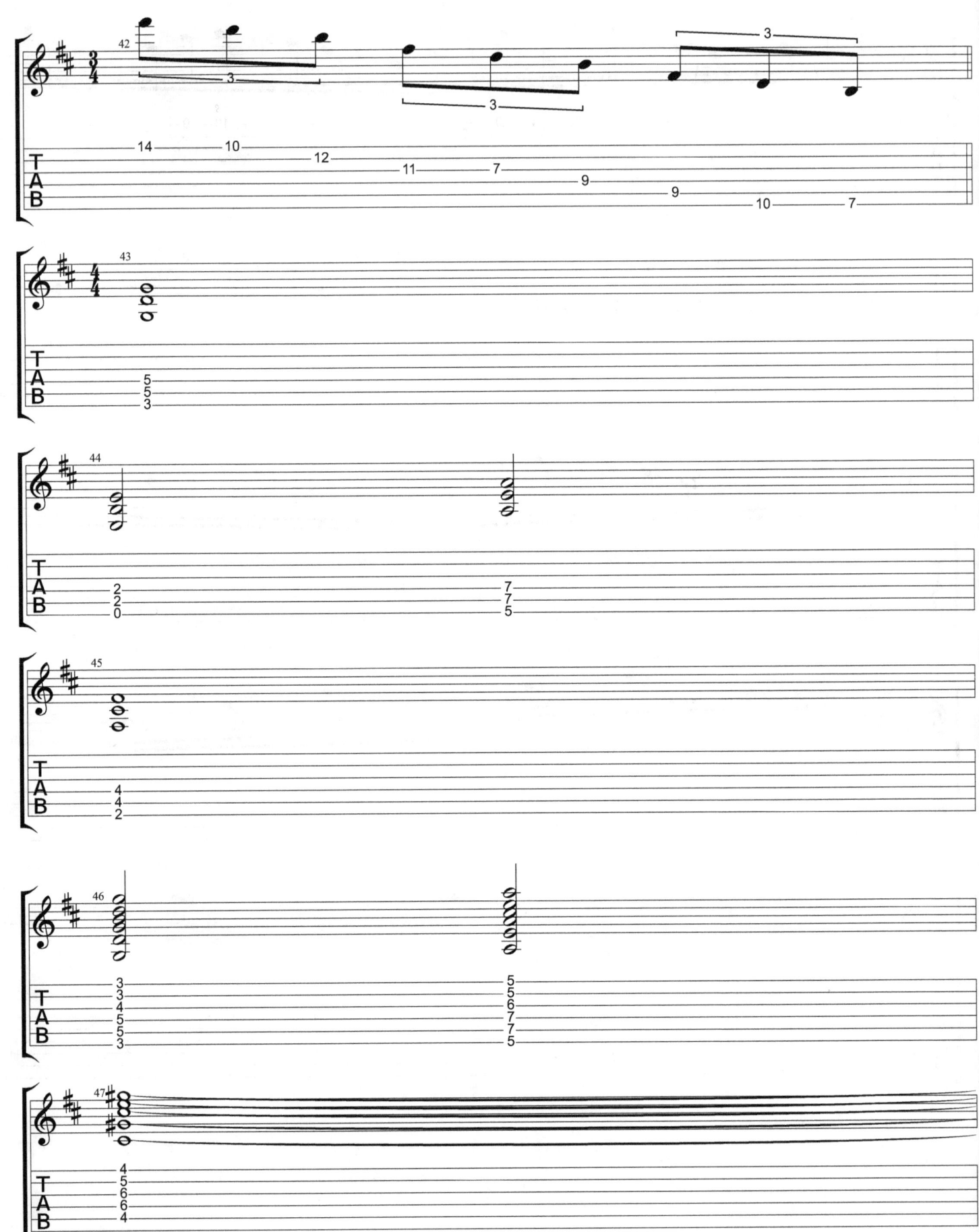

Destroyer
for Electric Guitar
Joe Hartnett

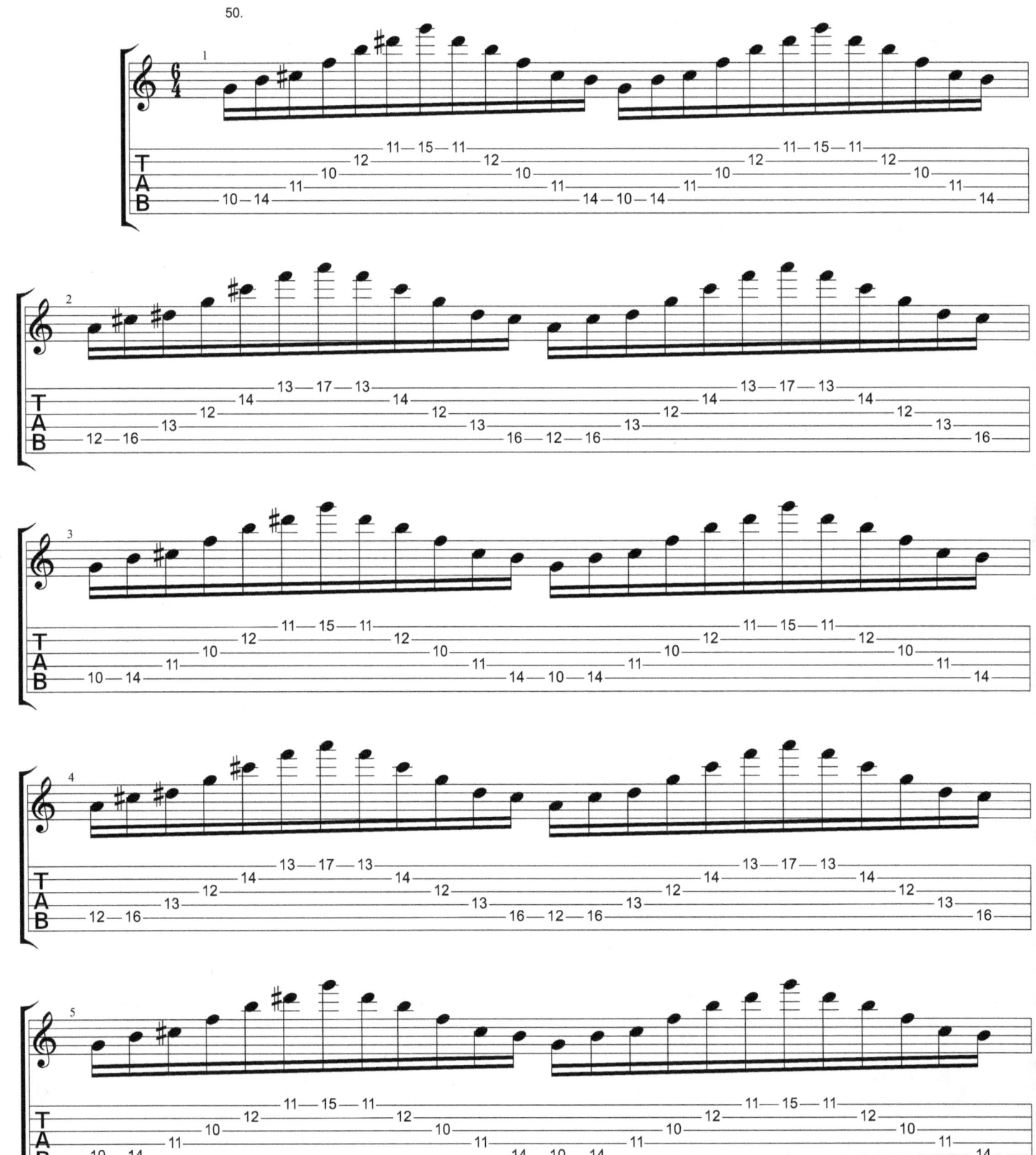

162

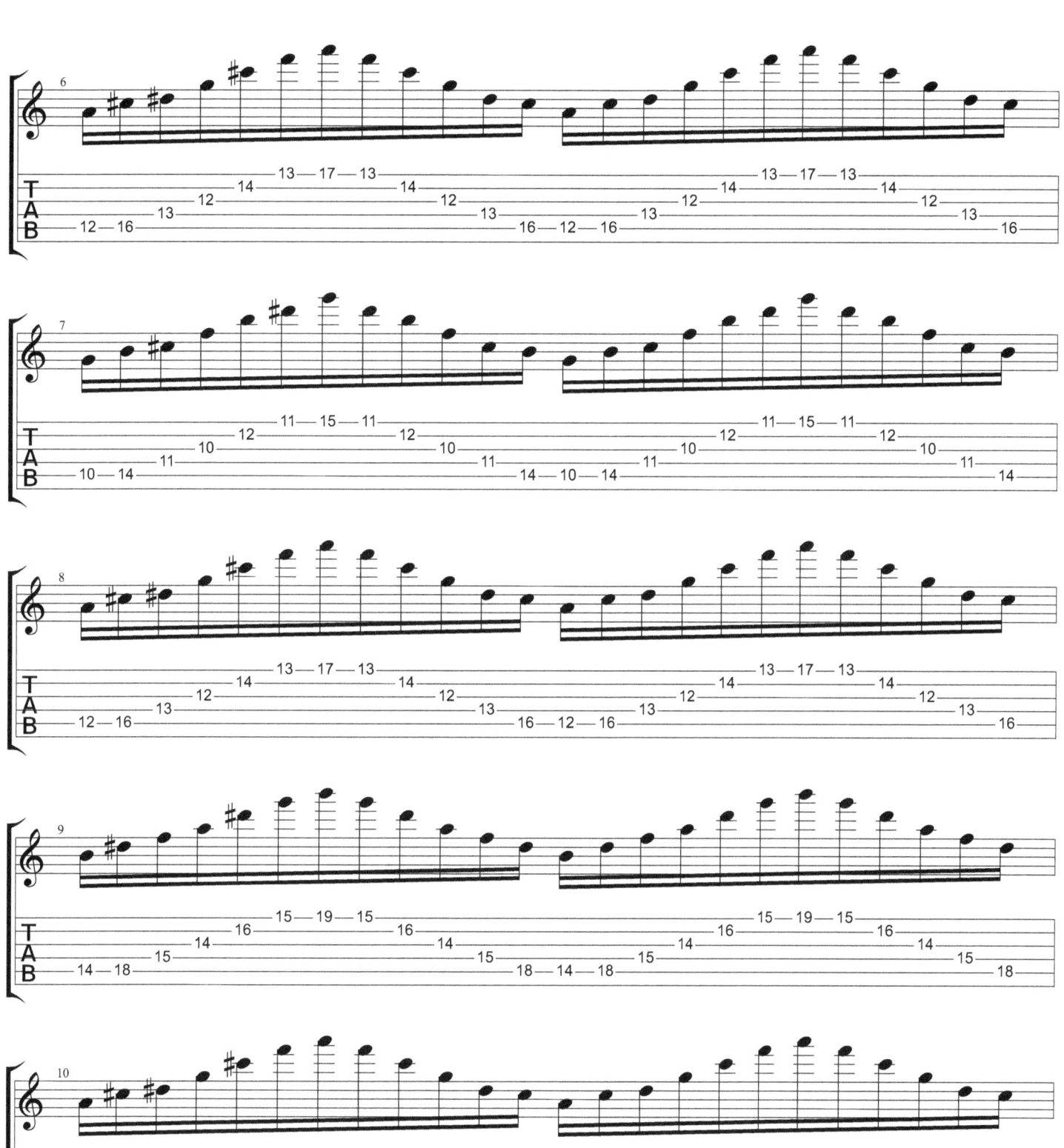

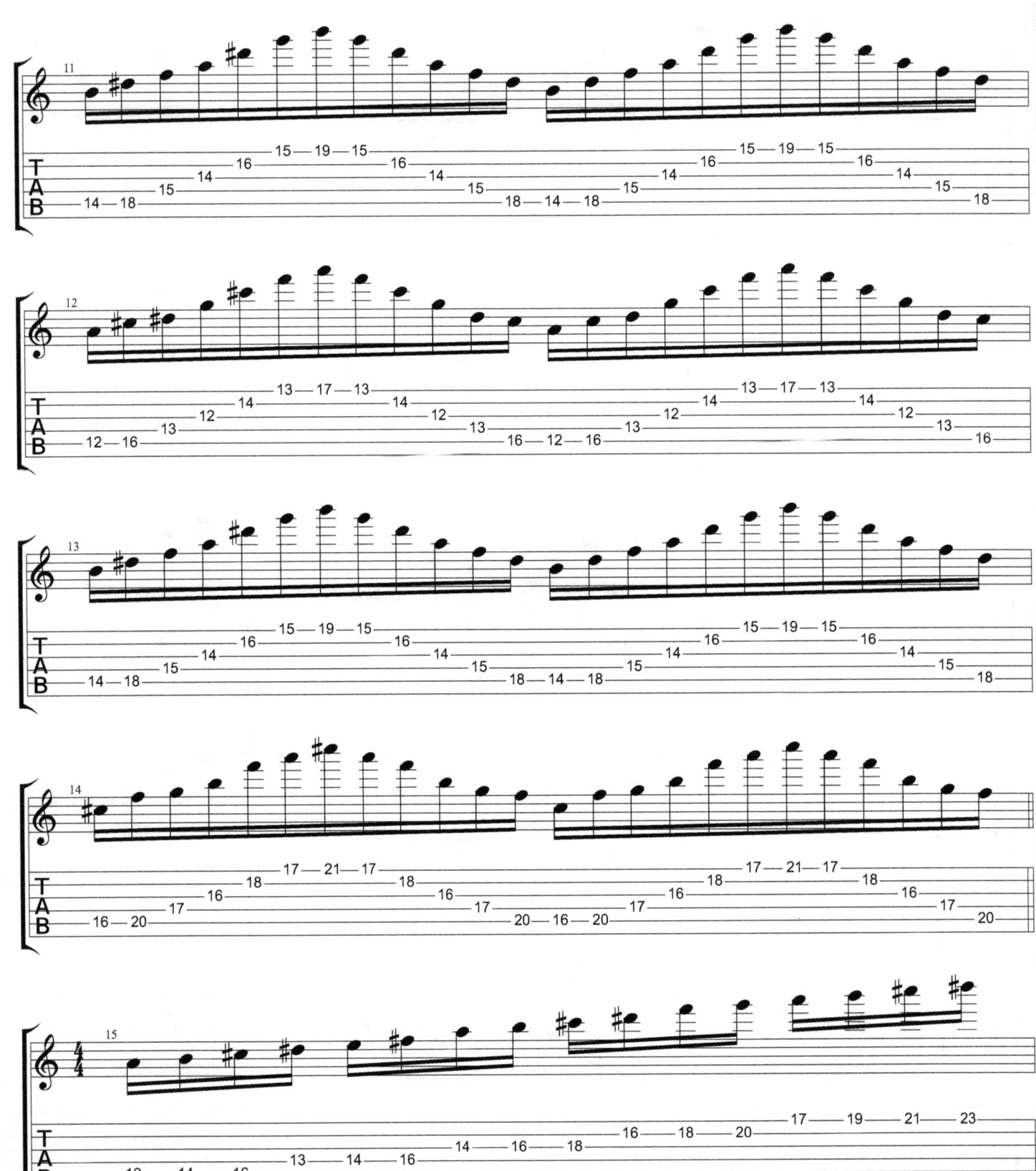

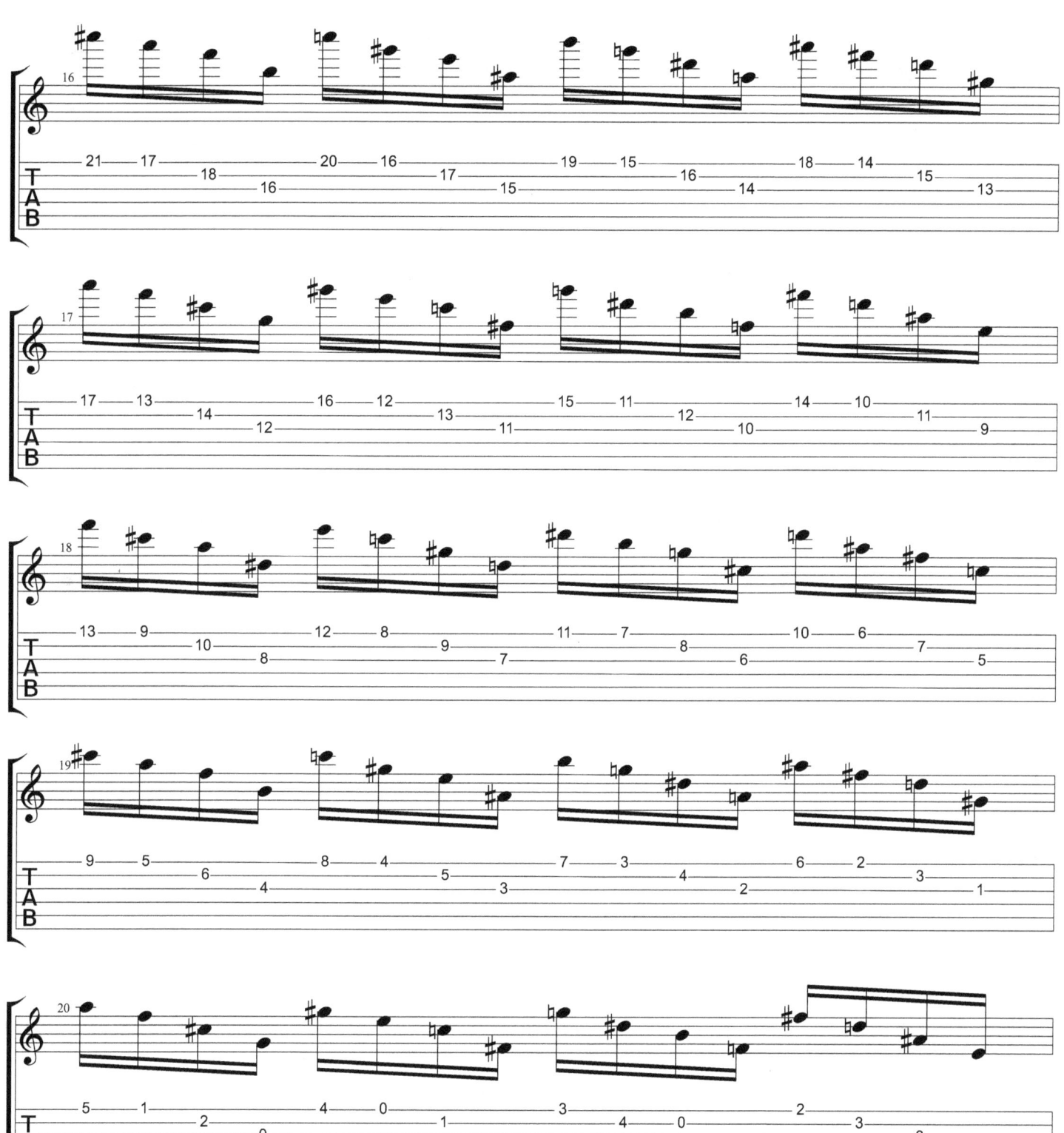

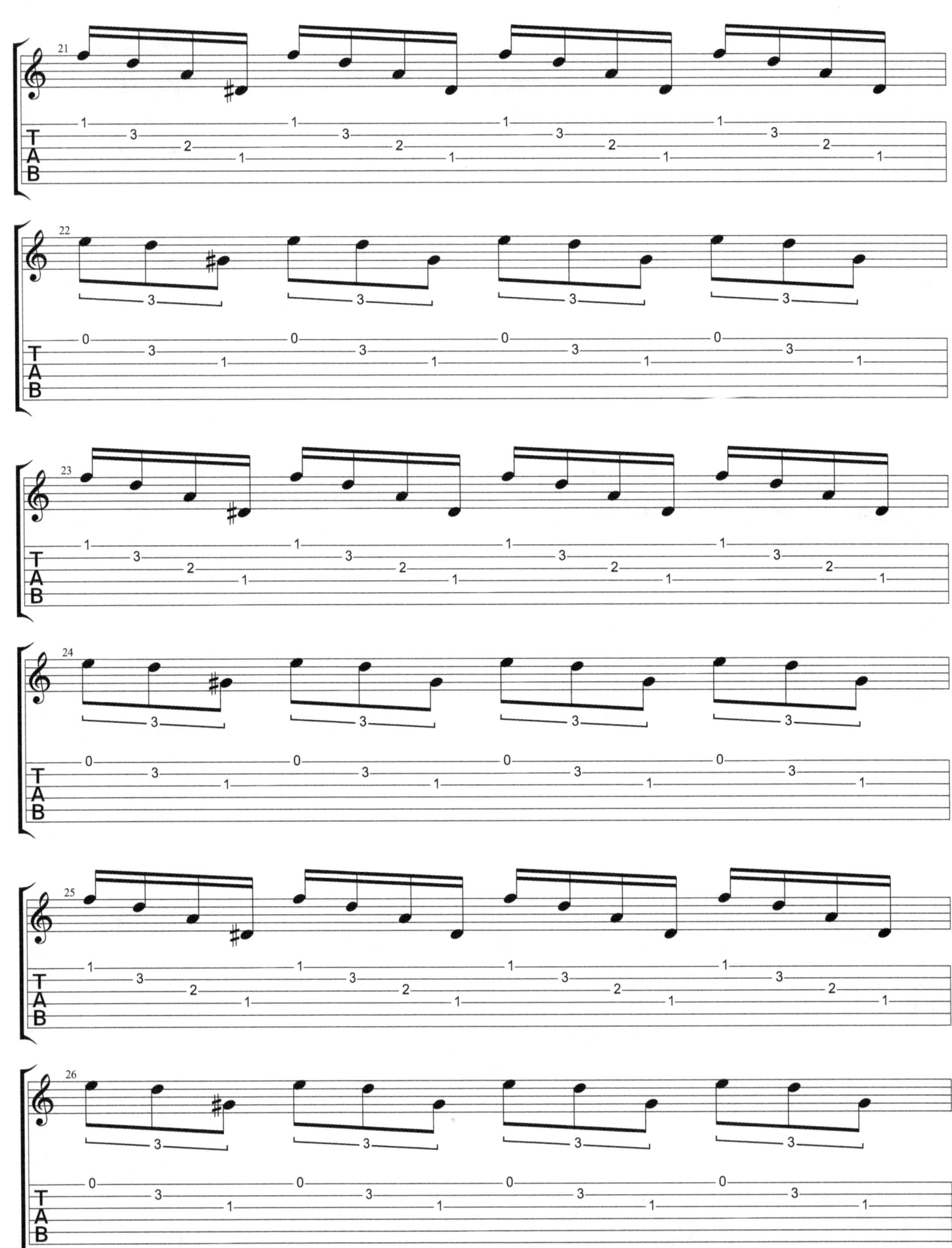

166

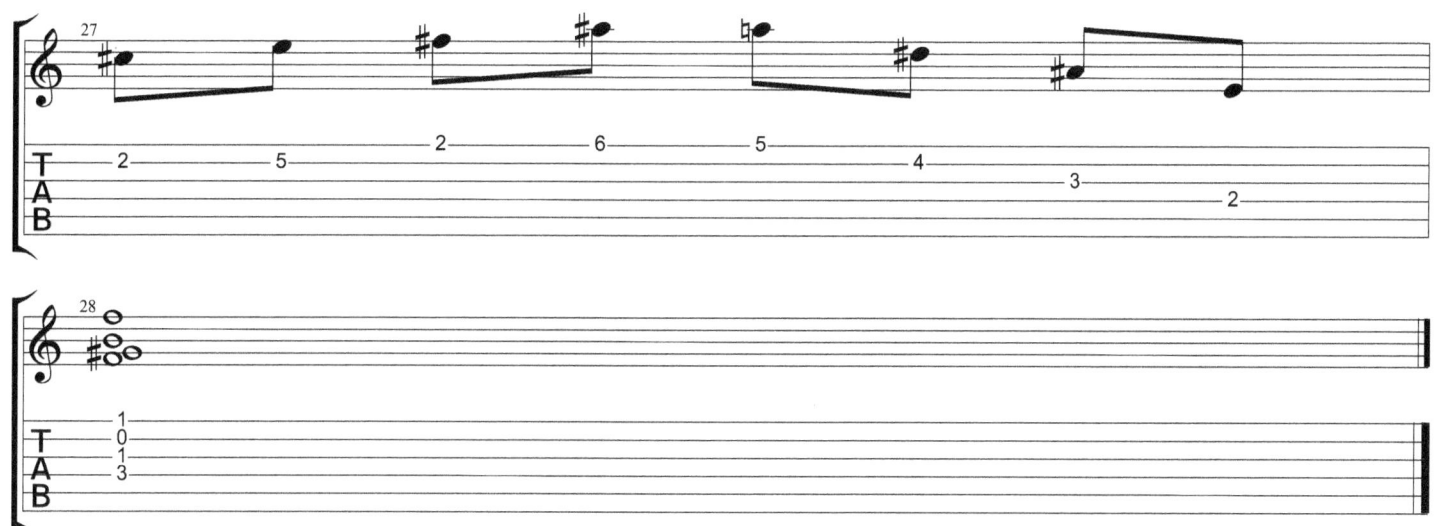

Shadows
for Classical Guitar
Joe Hartnett

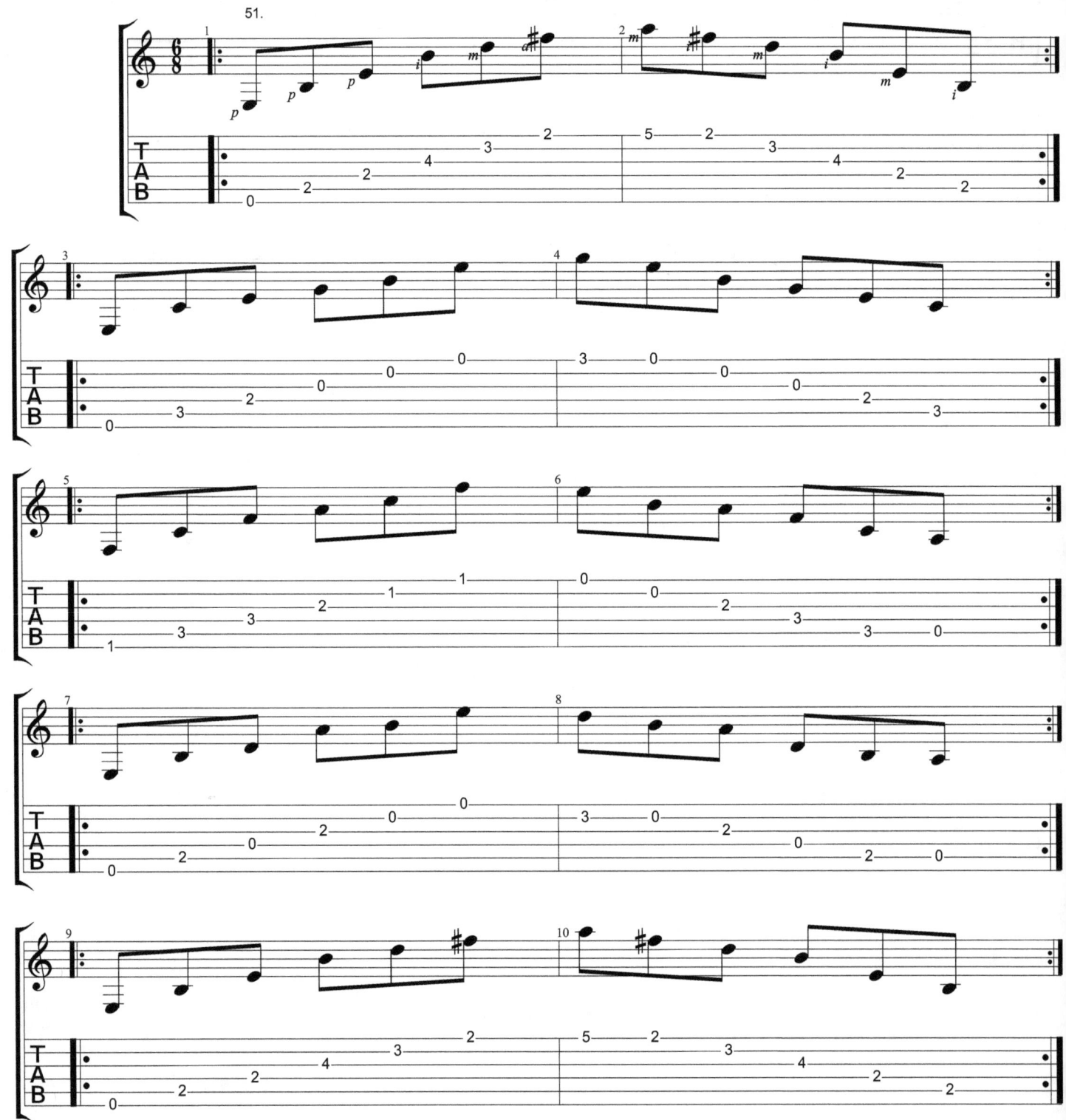

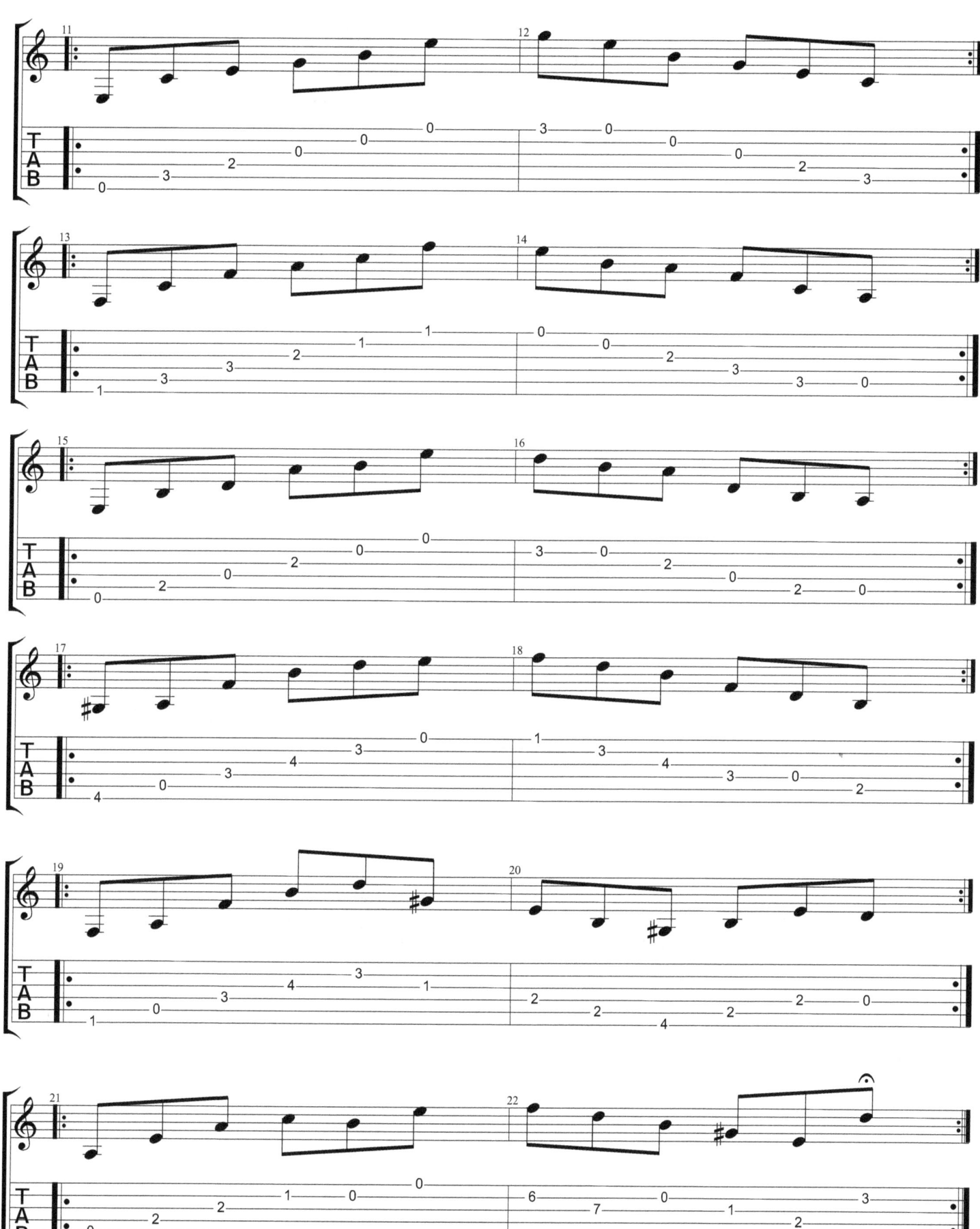

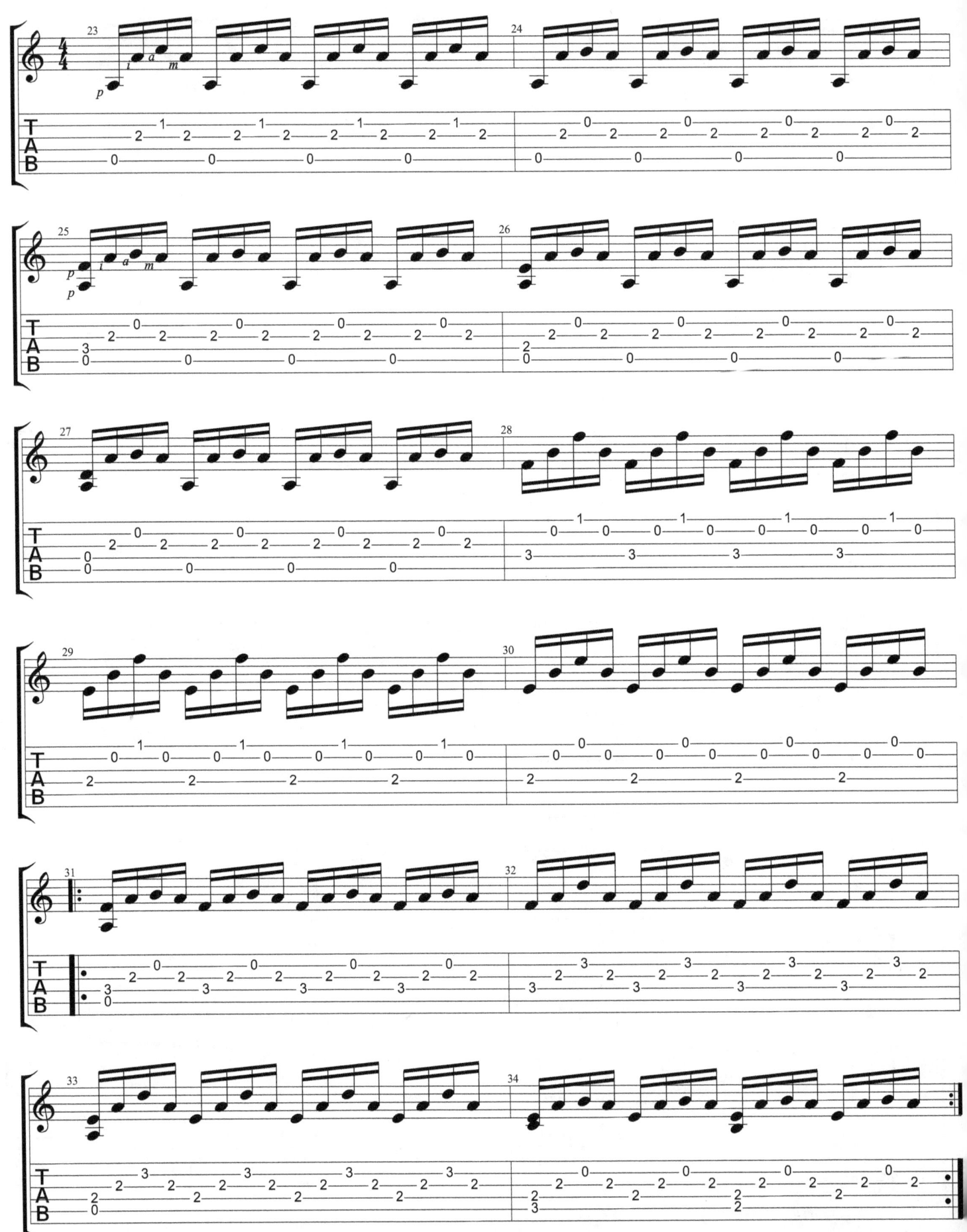

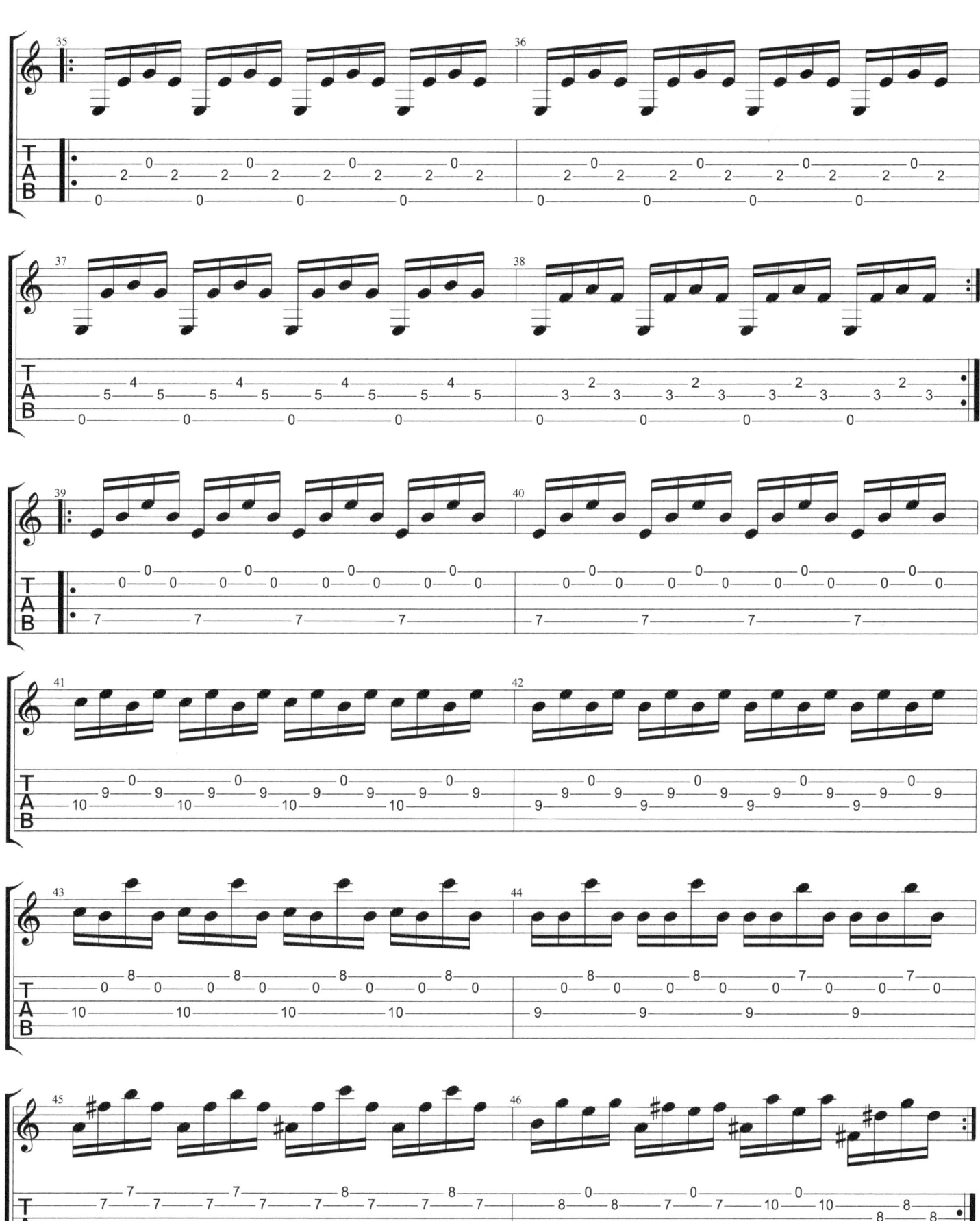

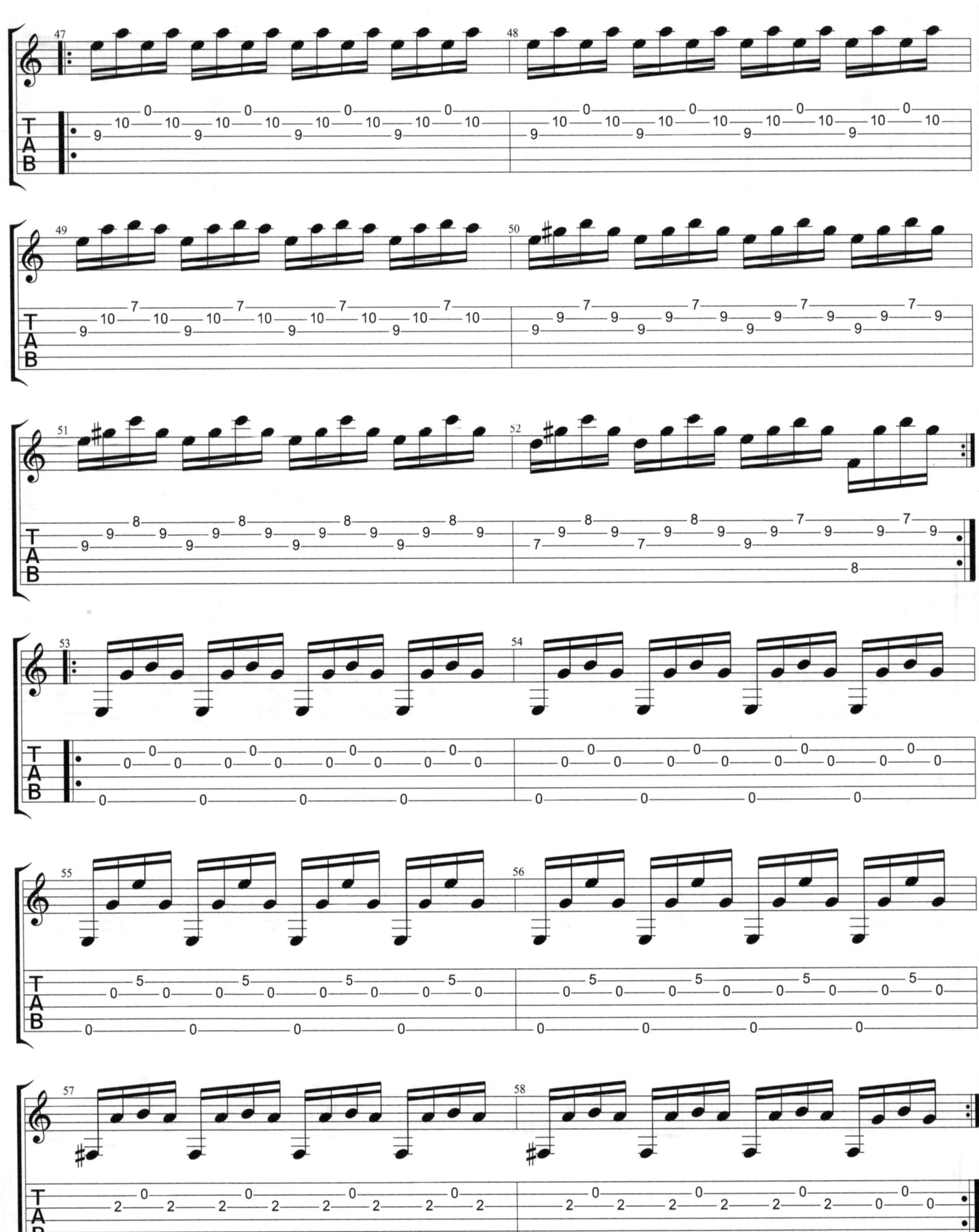

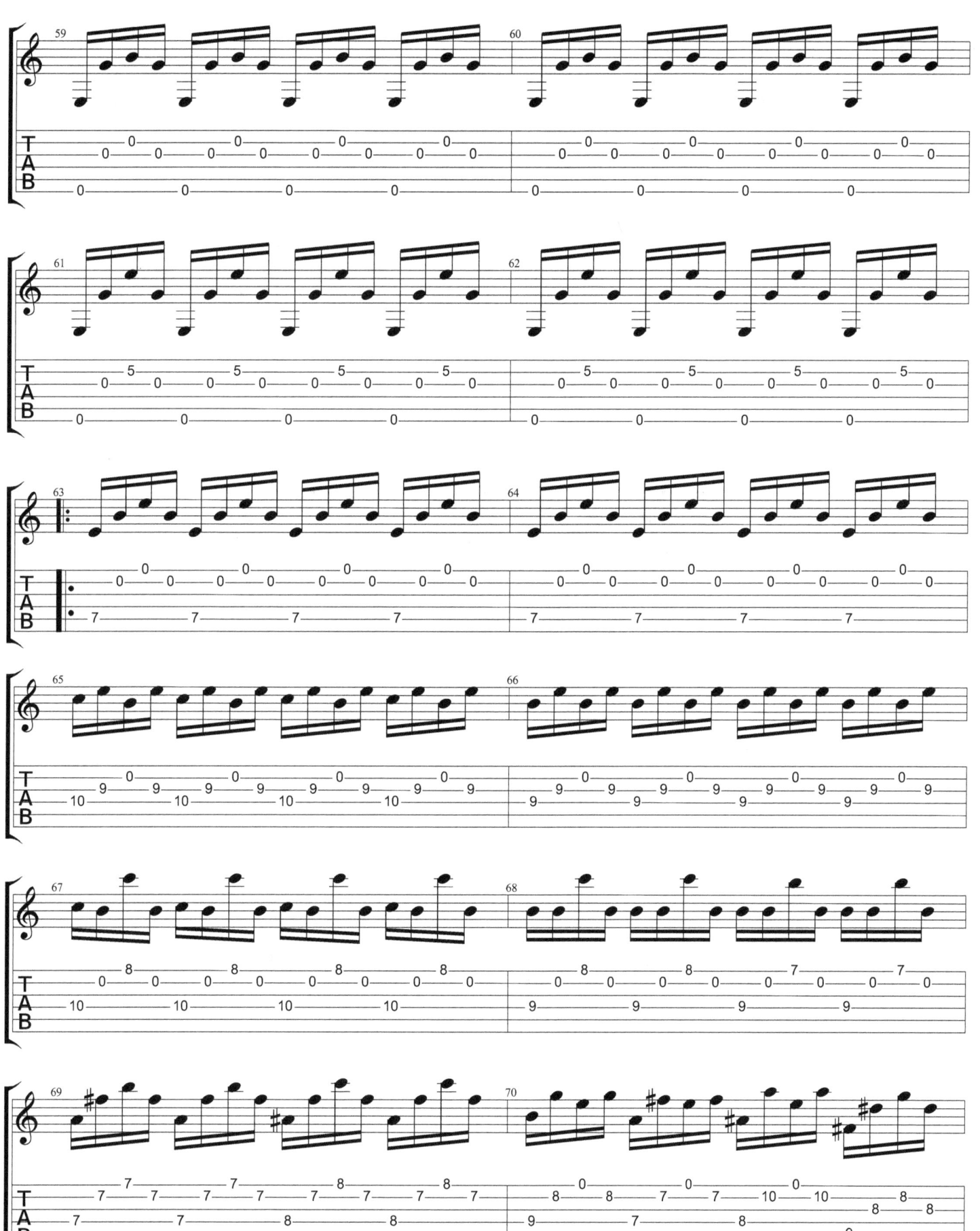

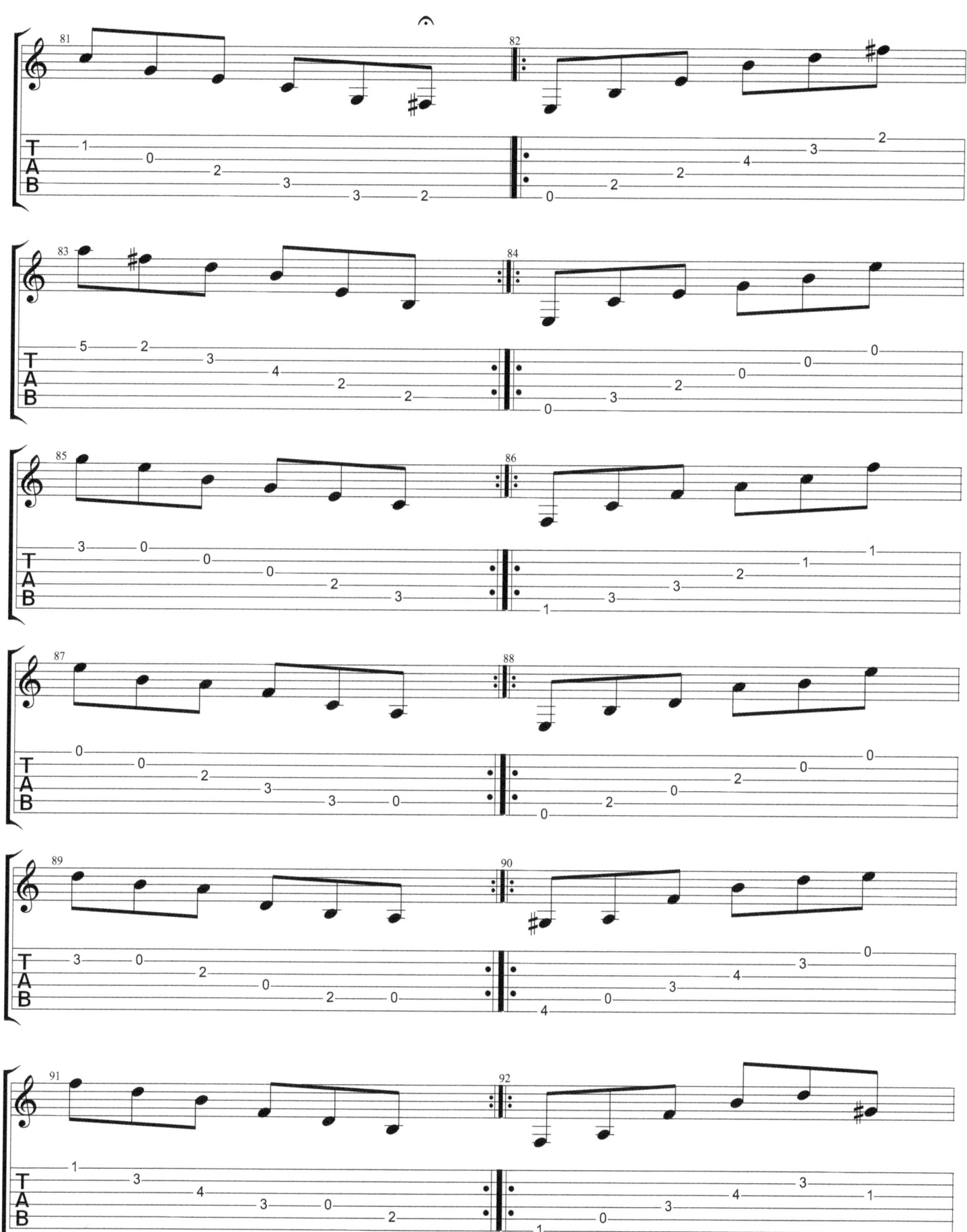

Malagueñas
for Classical Guitar
Joe Hartnett

52.

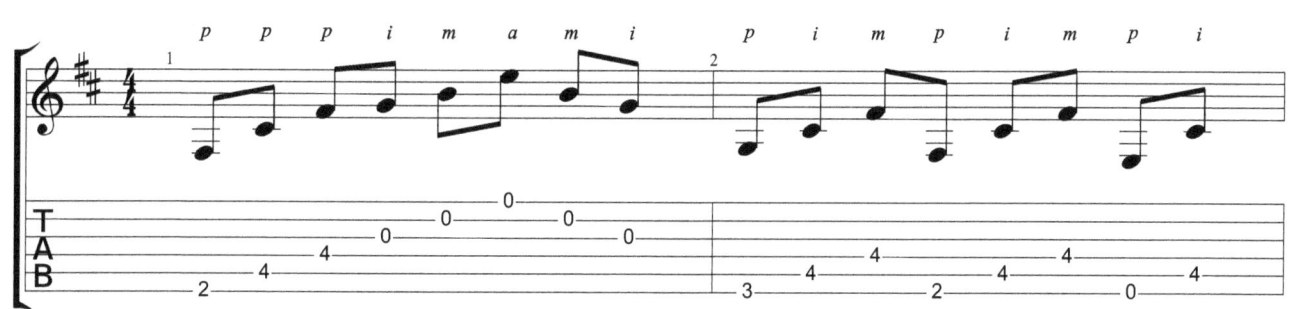
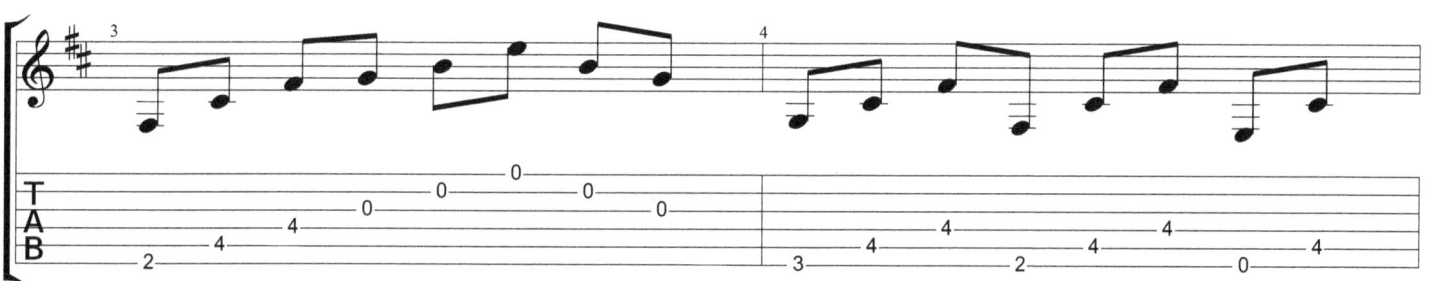

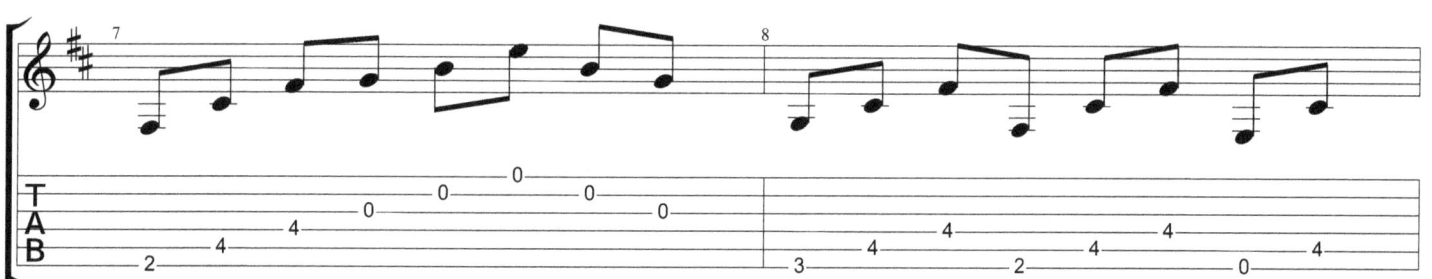

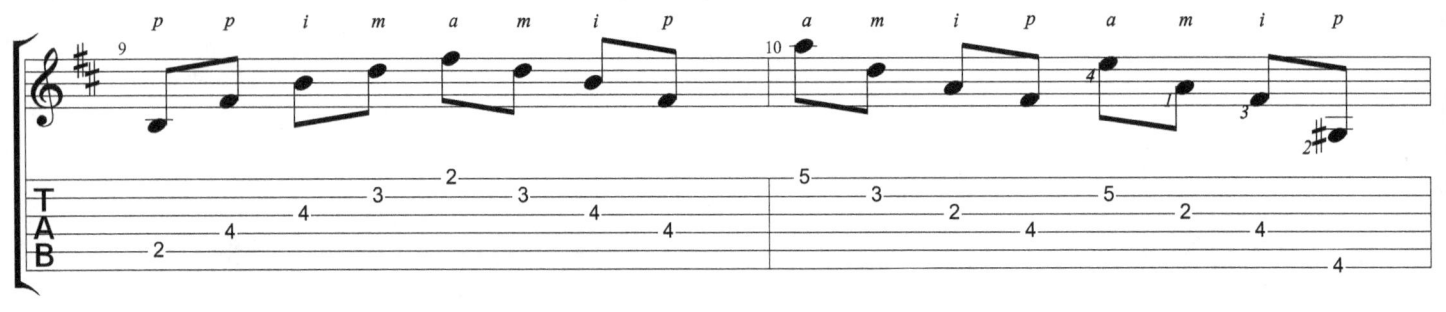
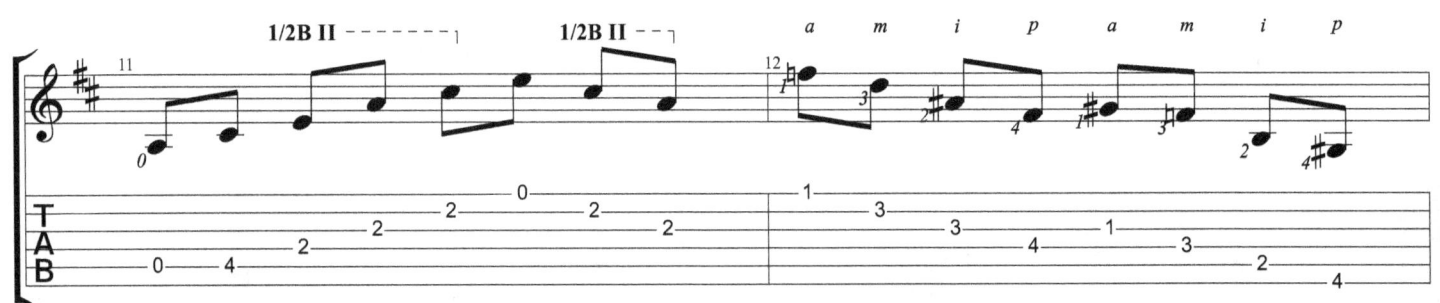
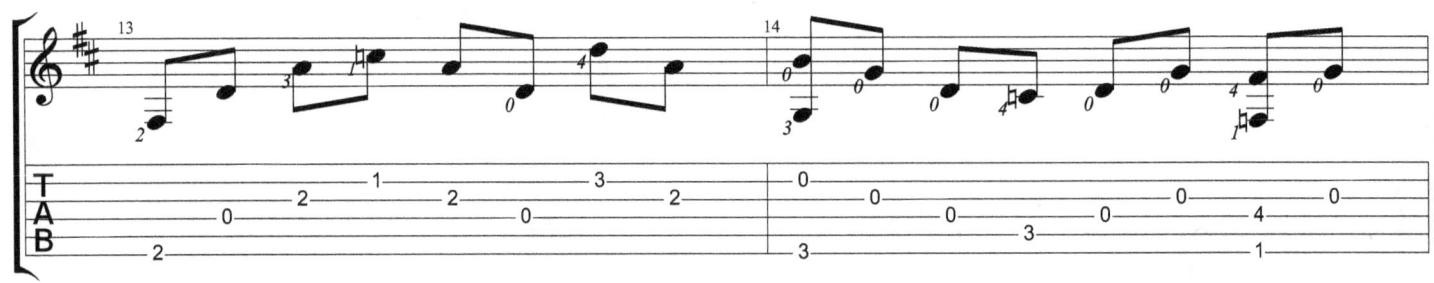
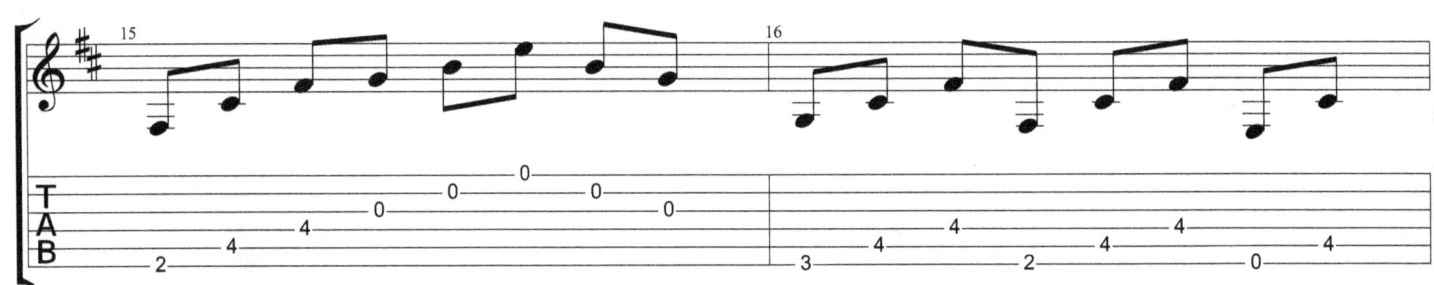
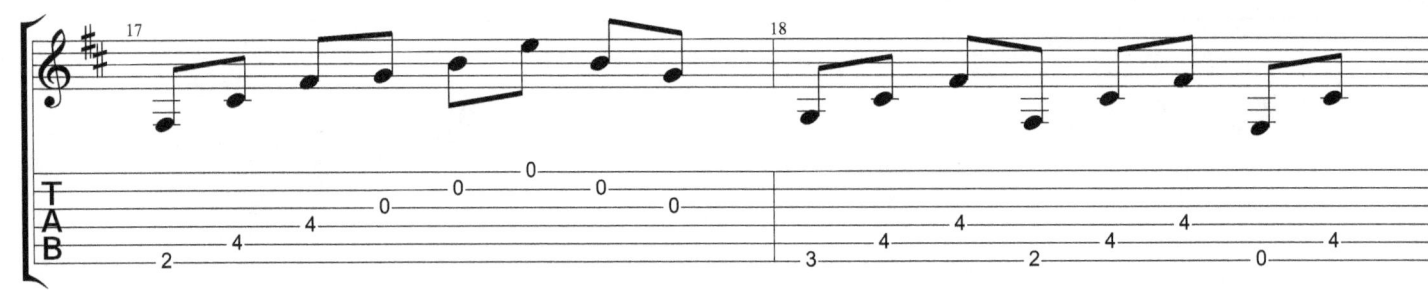

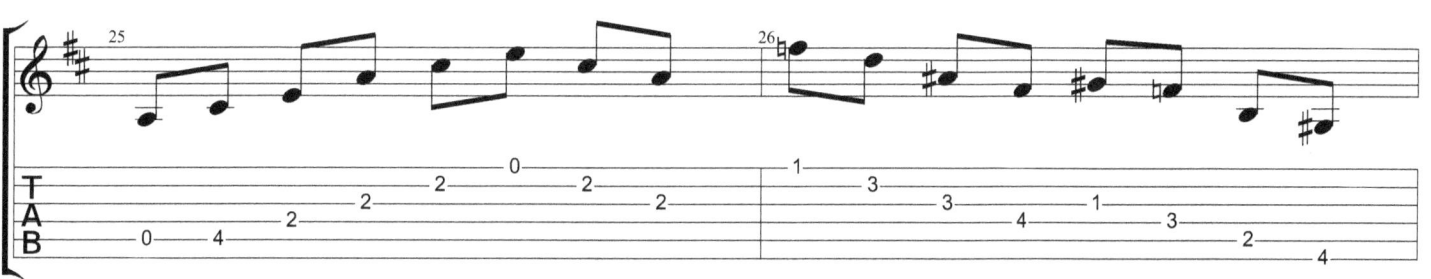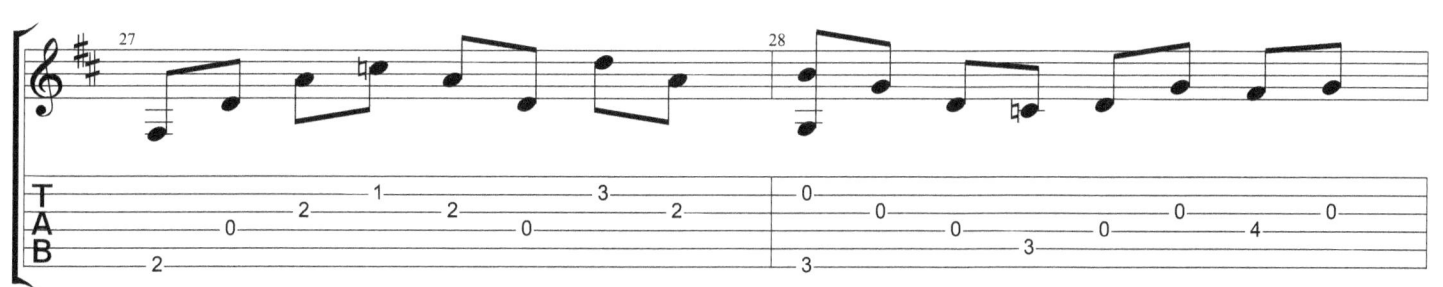

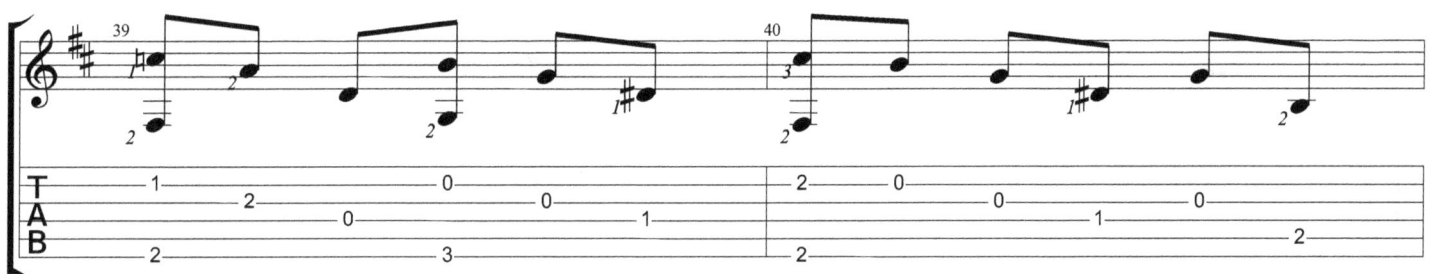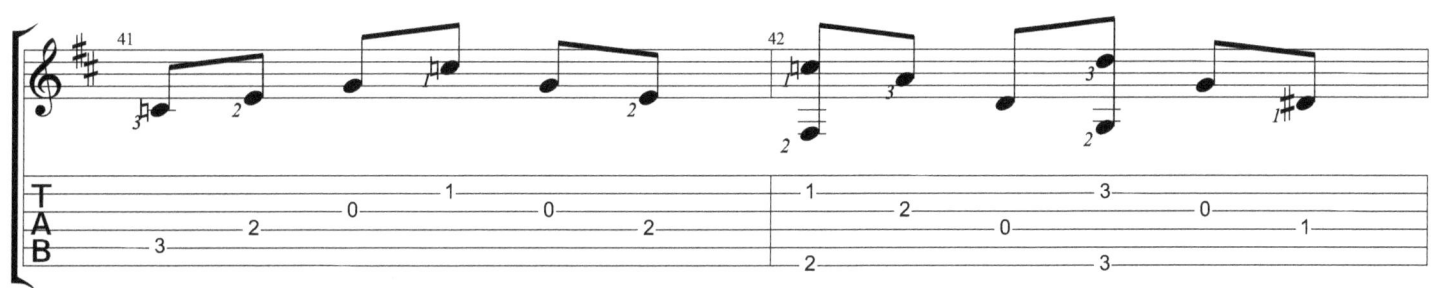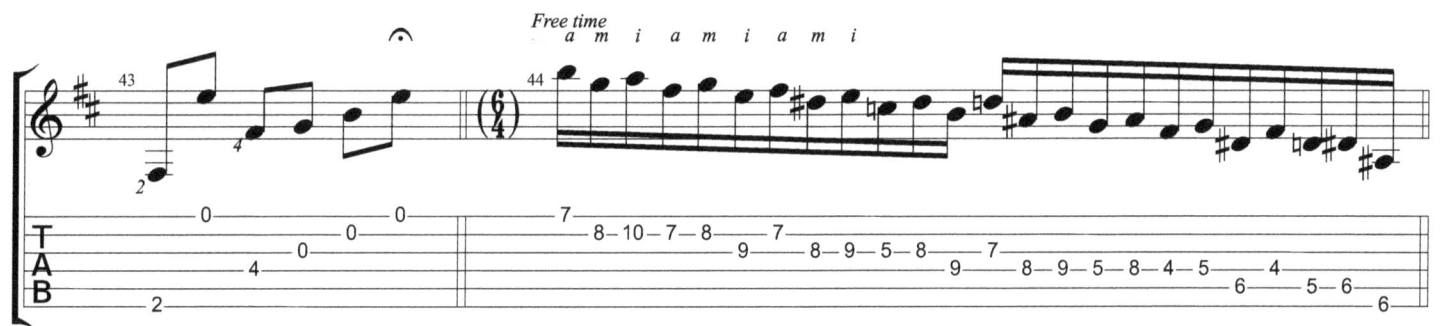

Alternate Right-Hand Fingering

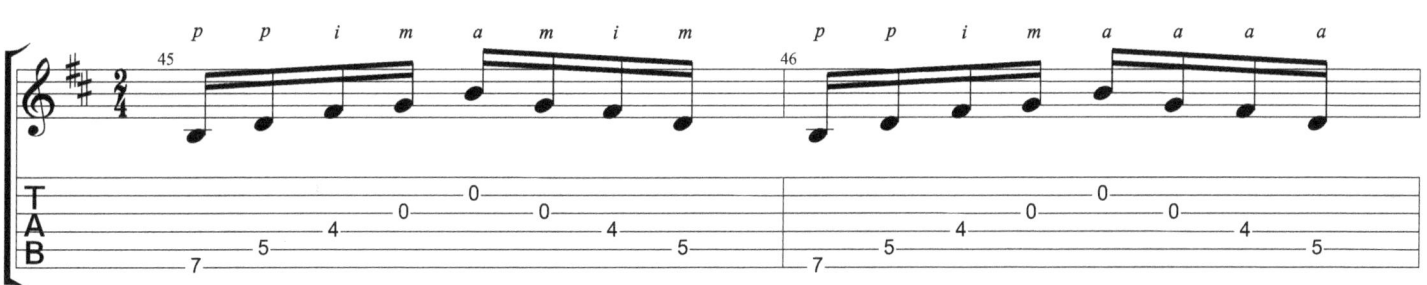

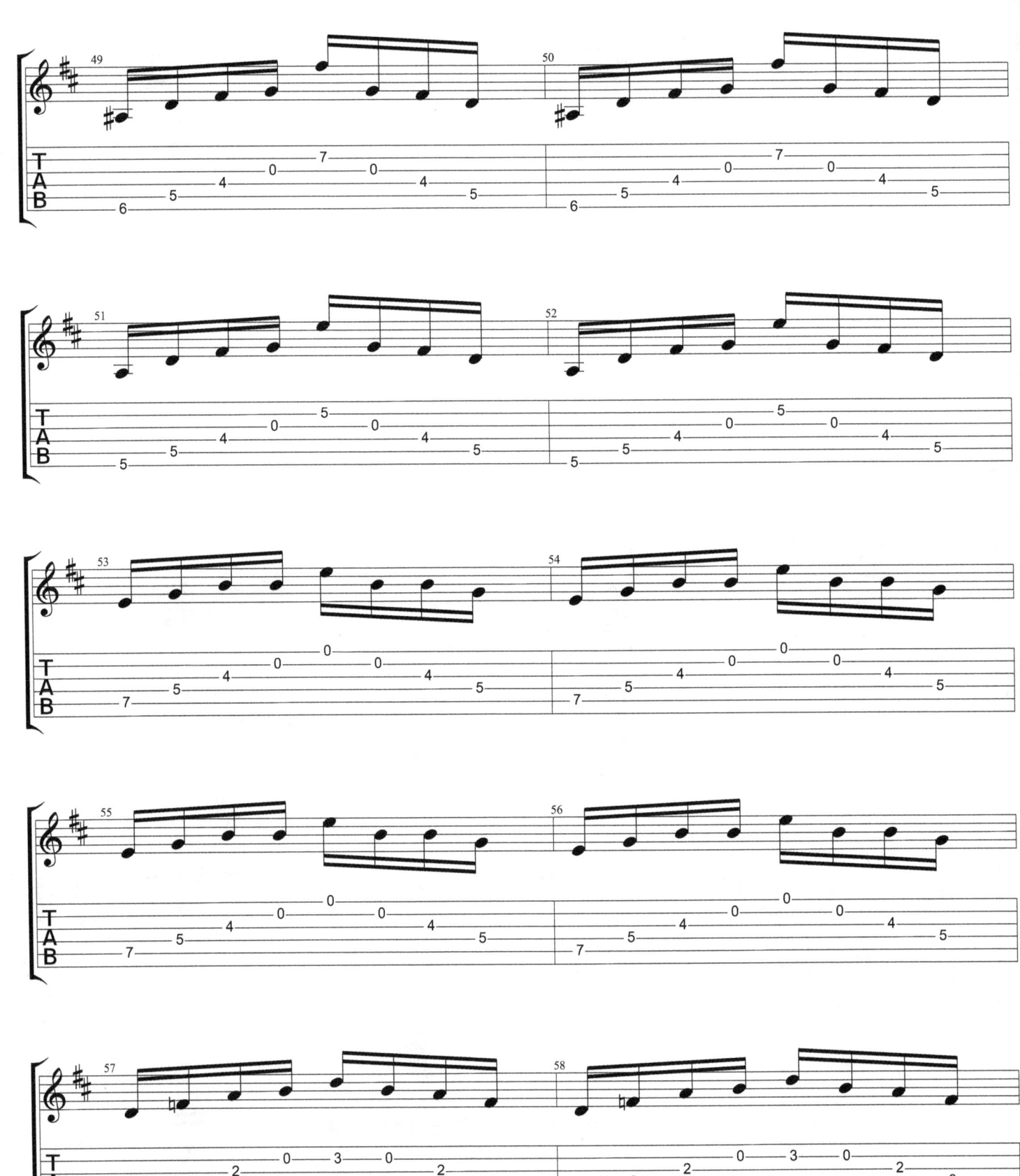

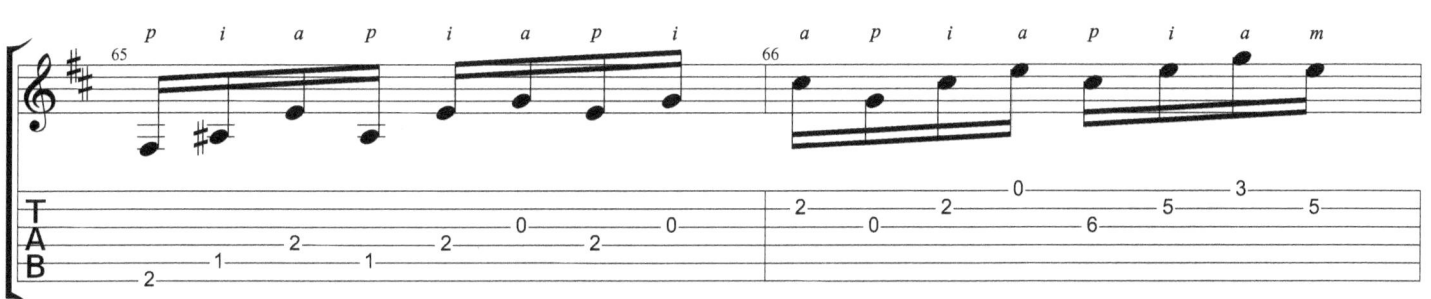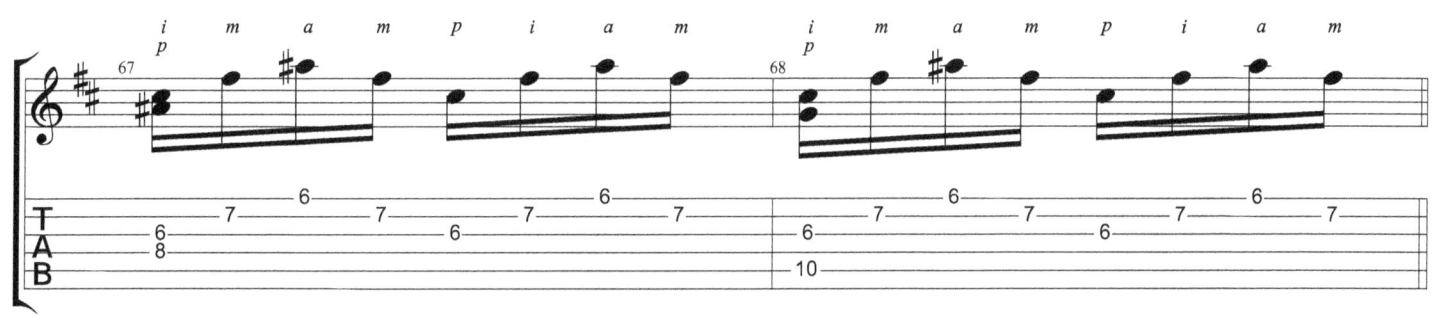

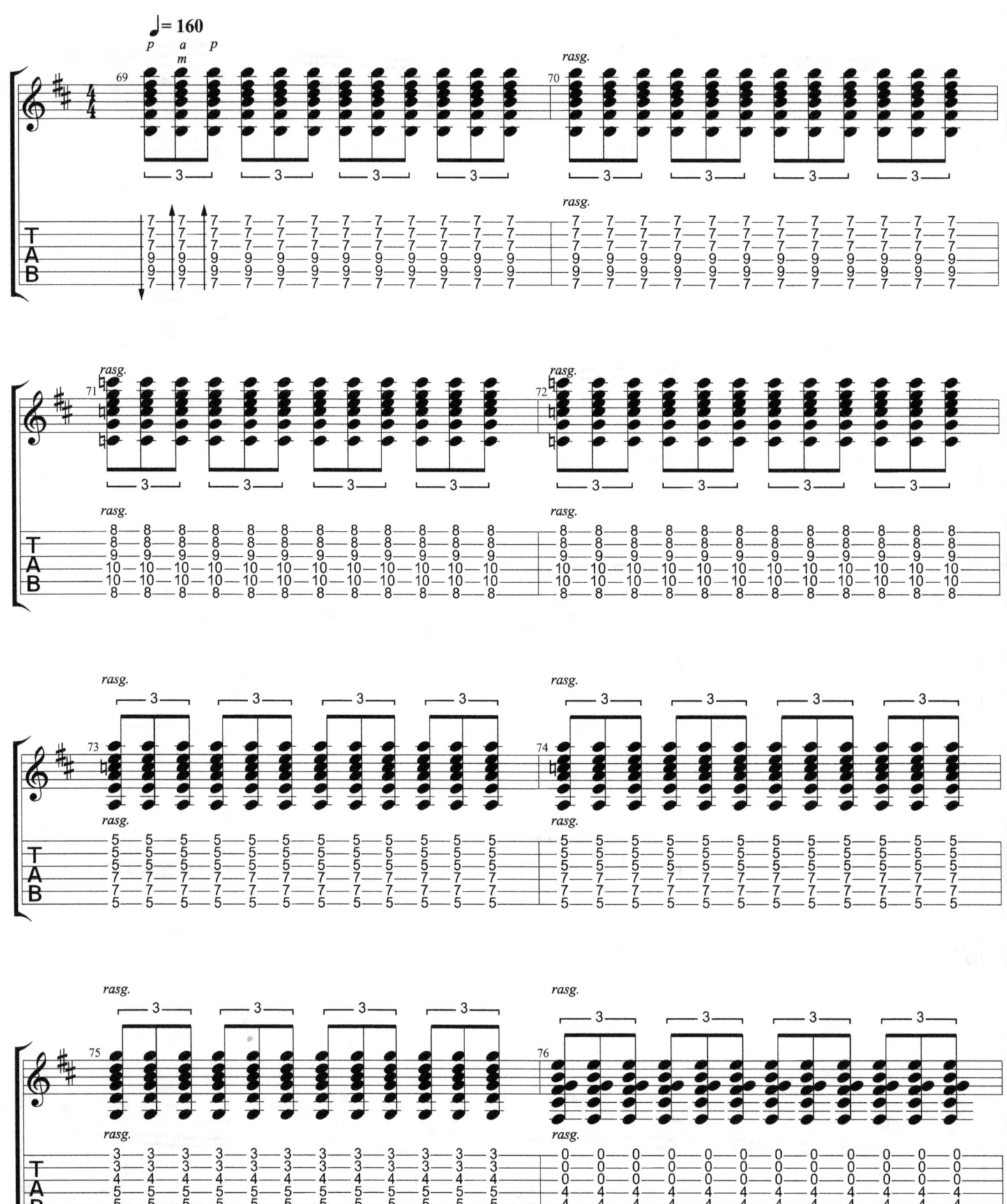

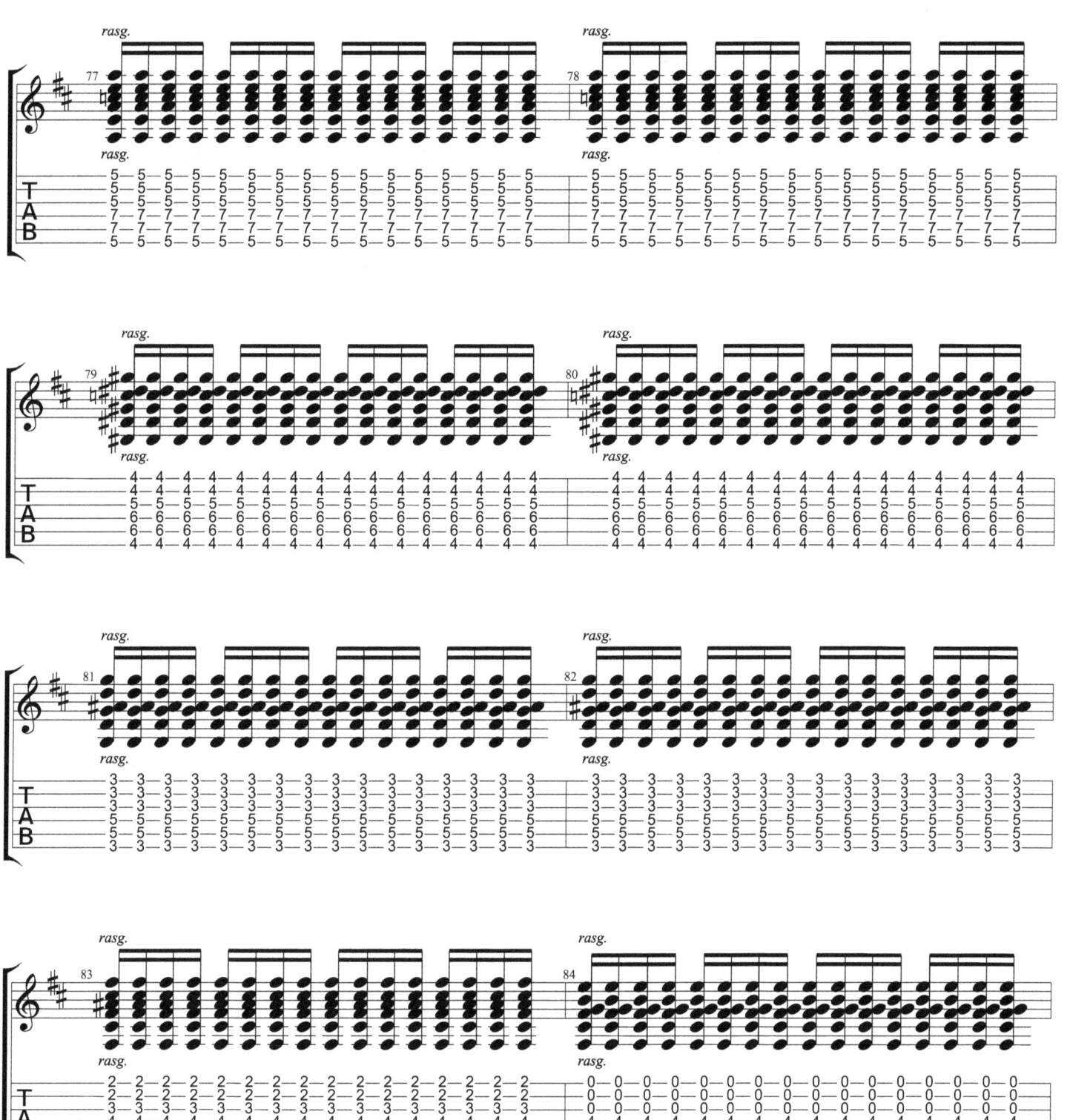

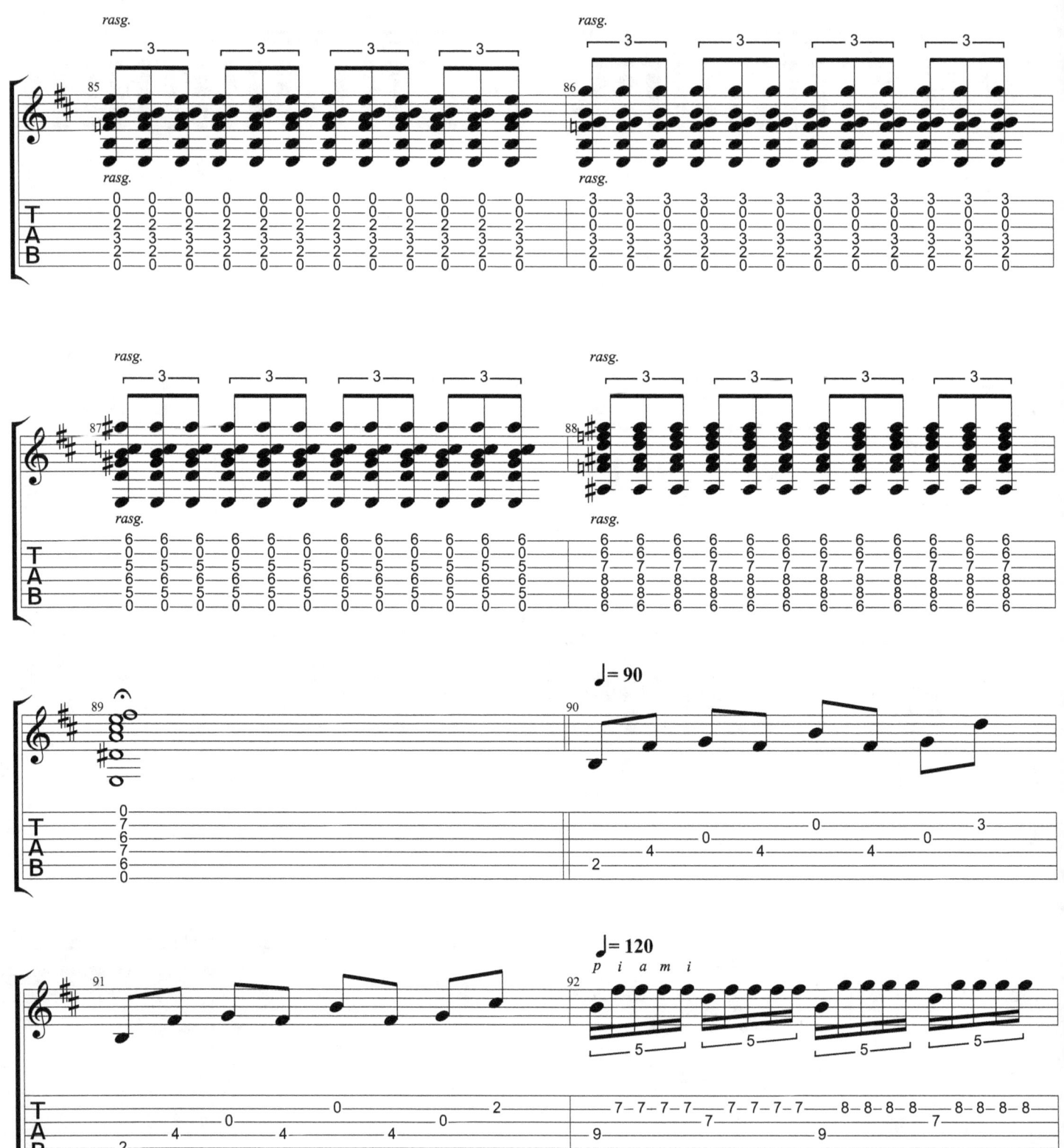

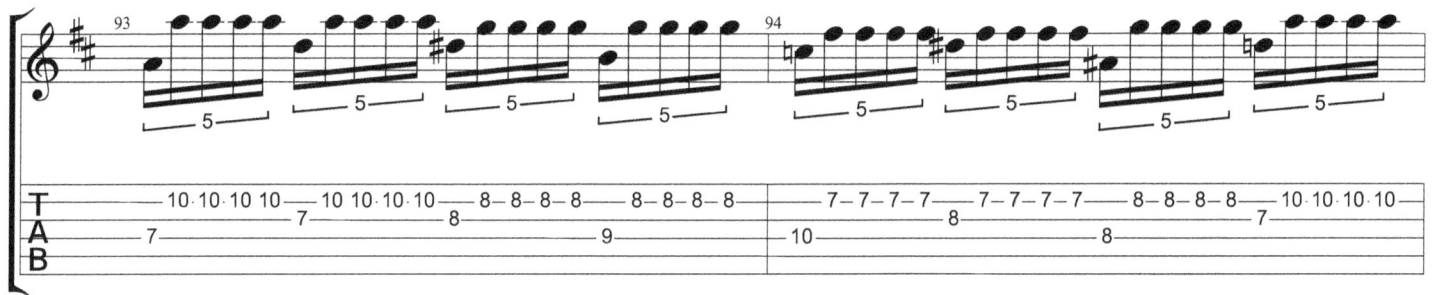
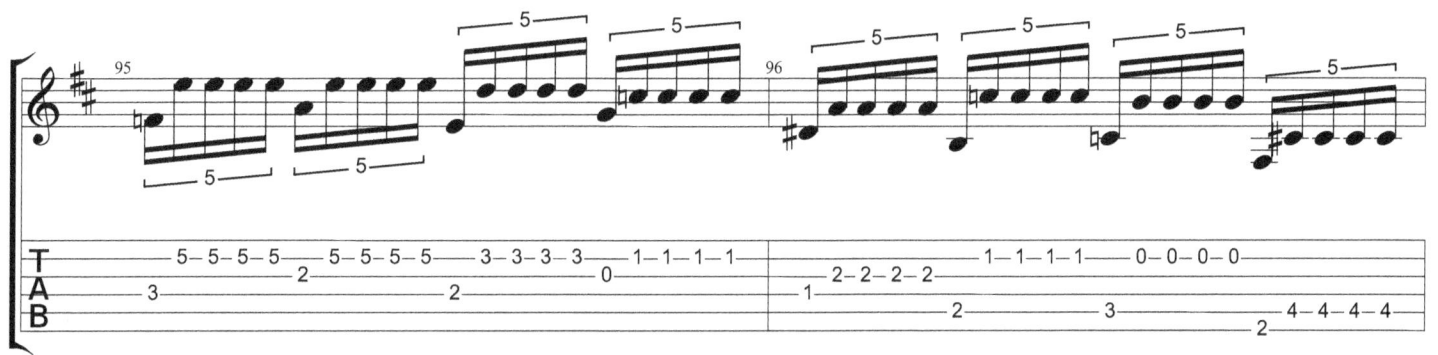

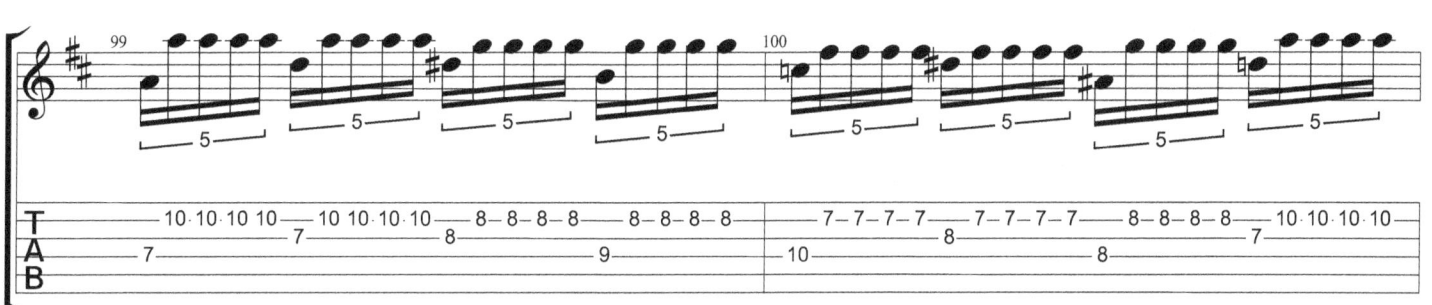

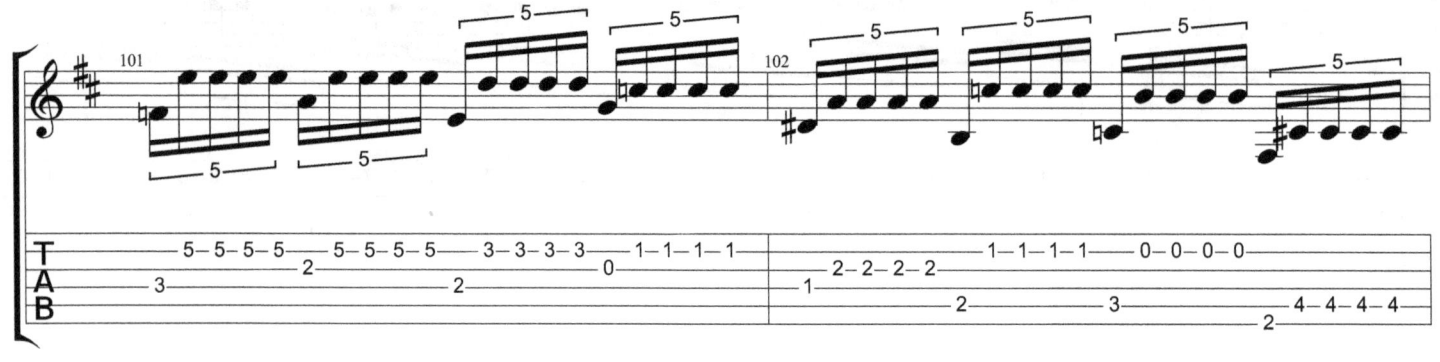
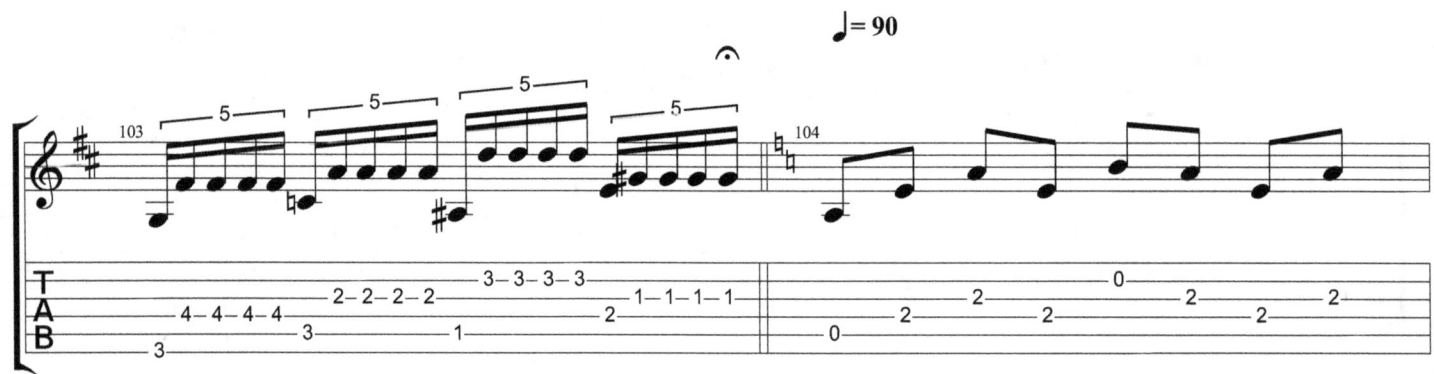
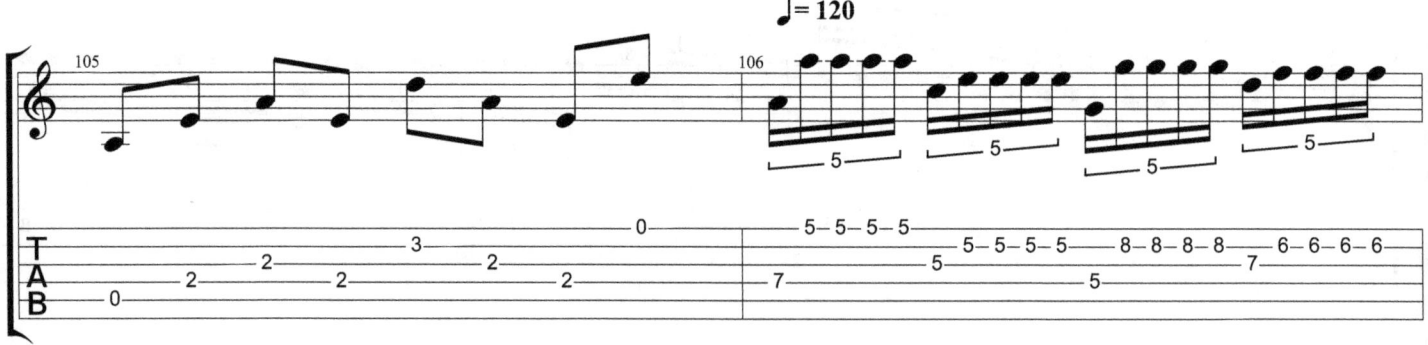
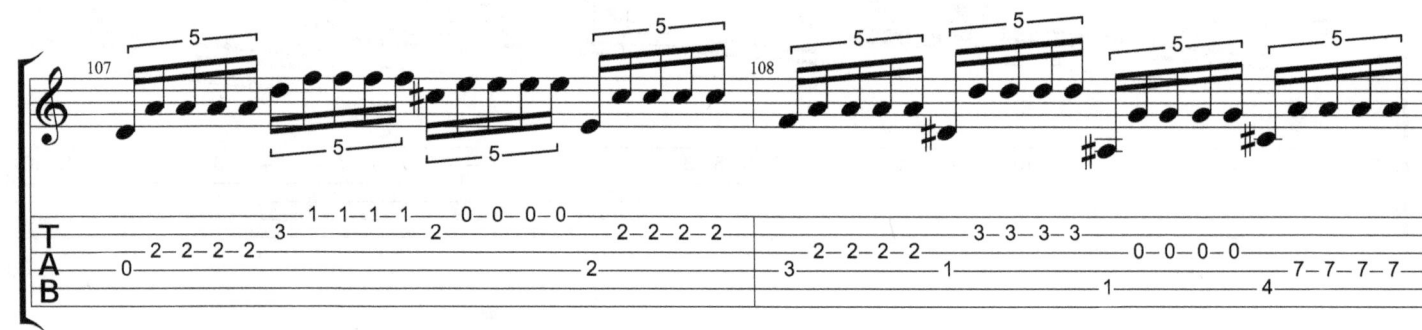

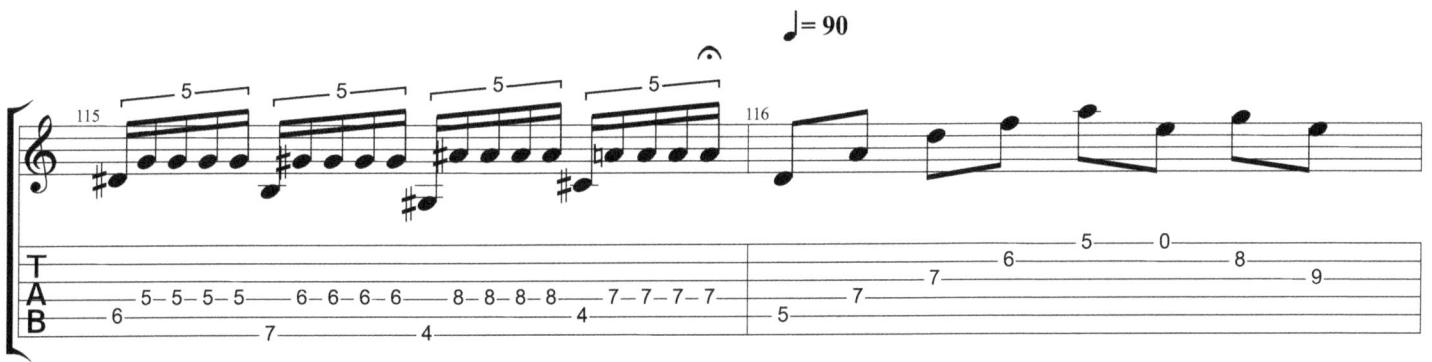

BWV 1002 Sarabande
Arranged for Guitar by Joe Hartnett
Johann Sebastian Bach, 1685-1750

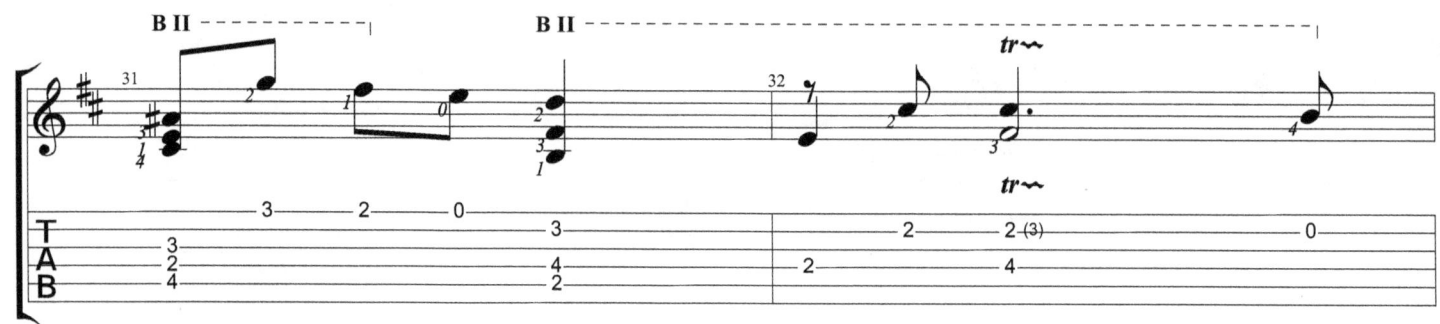

BWV 1003 Allegro

Arranged for Guitar by Joe Hartnett
Johann Sebastian Bach, 1685-1750

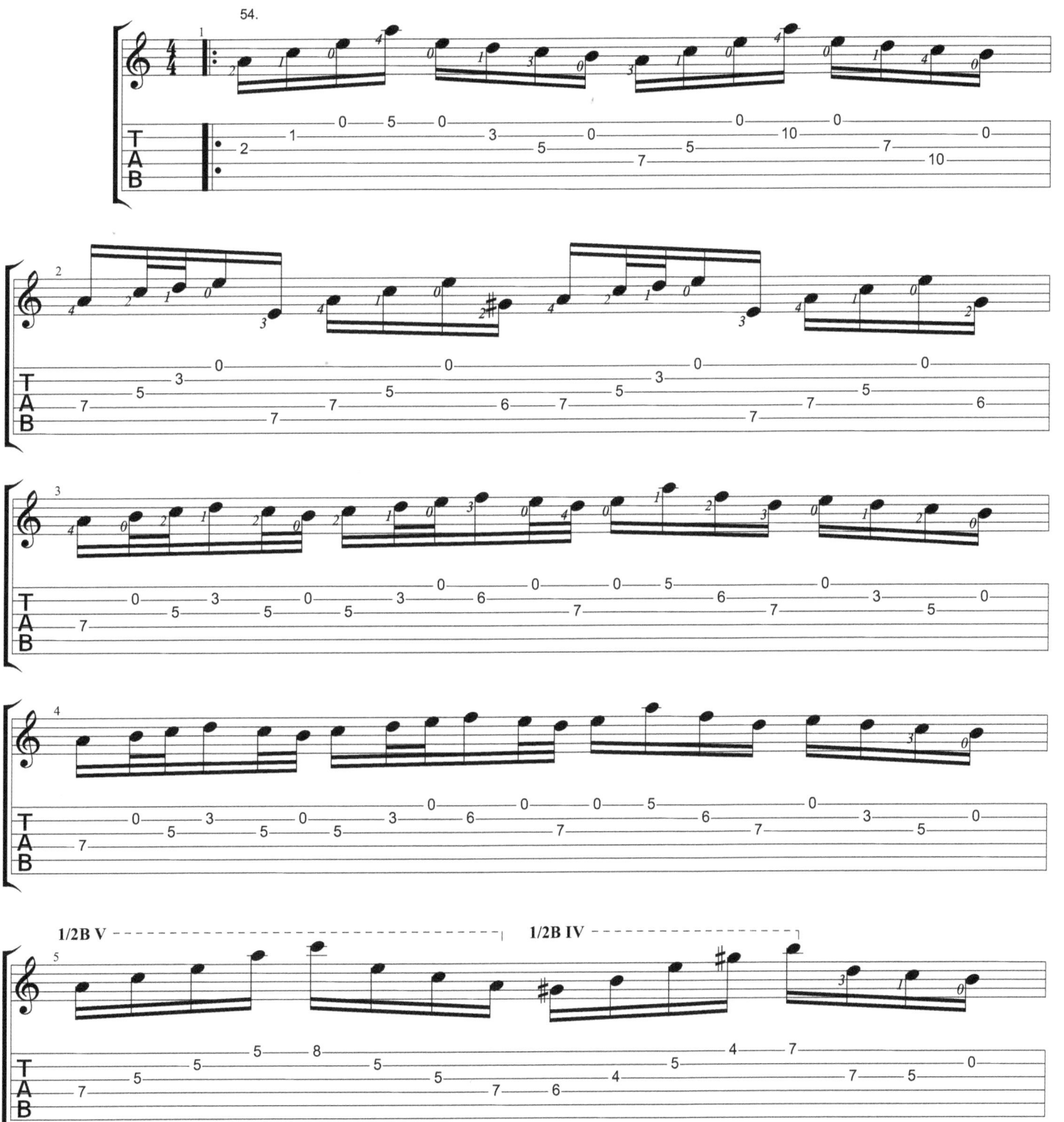

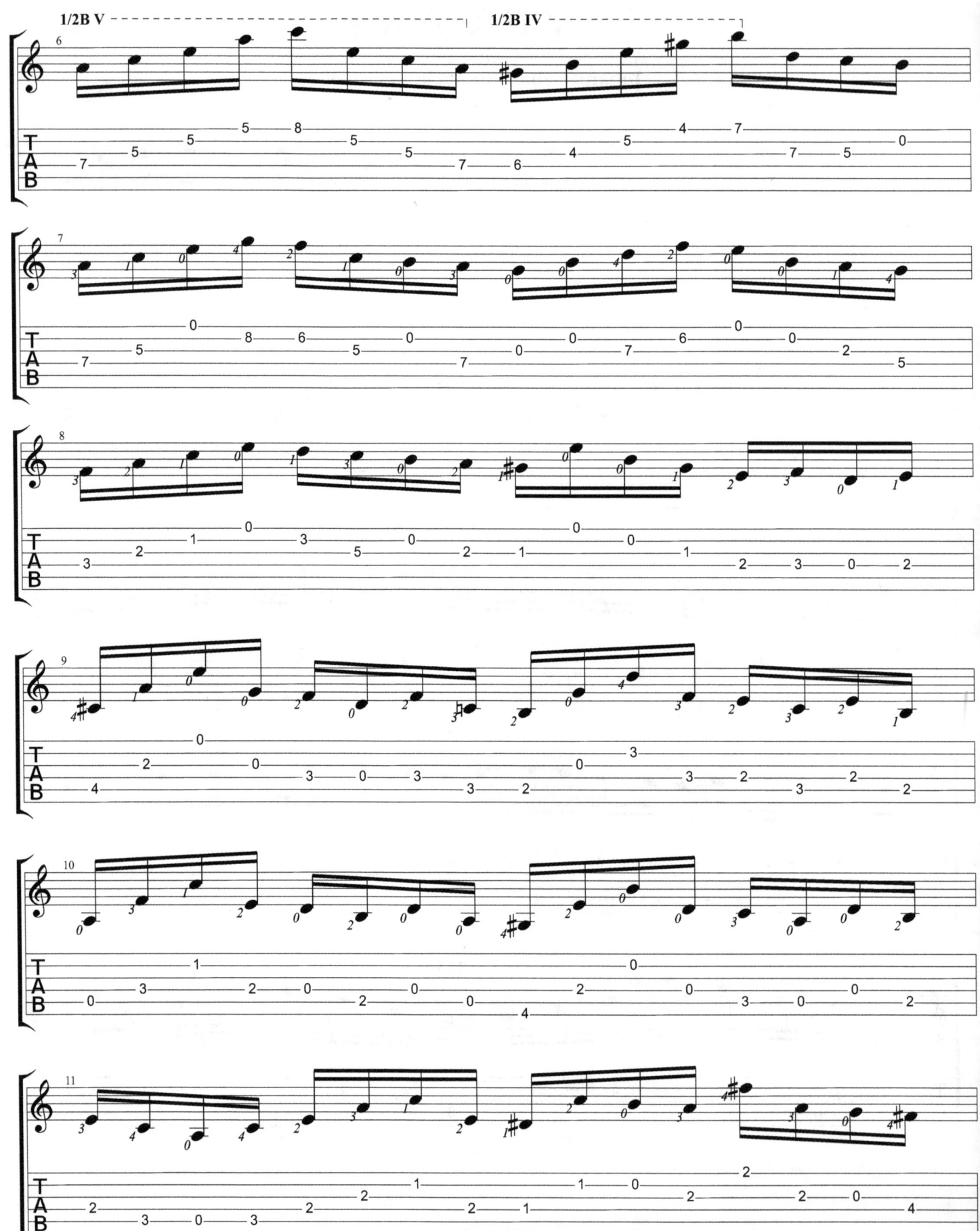

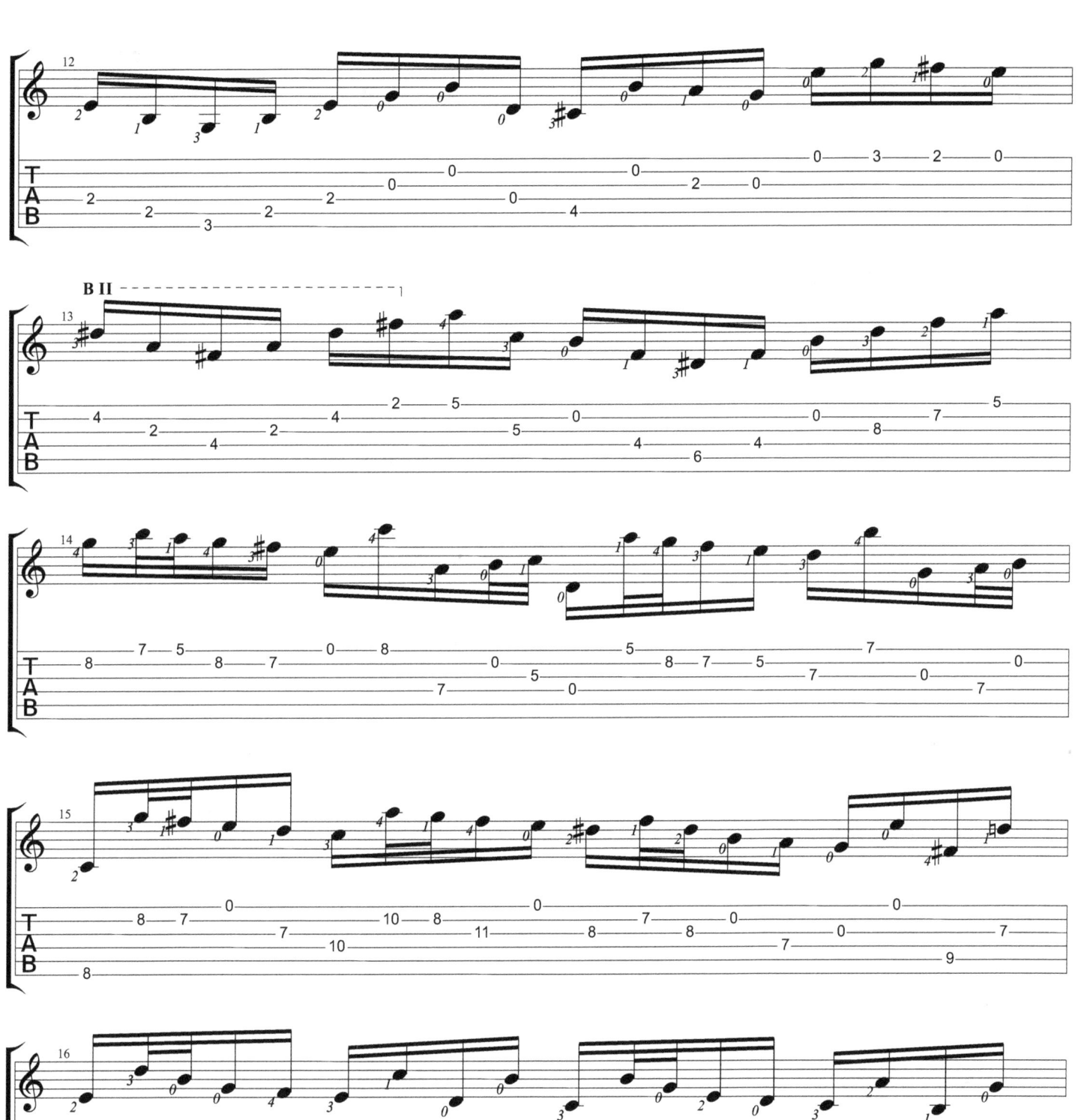

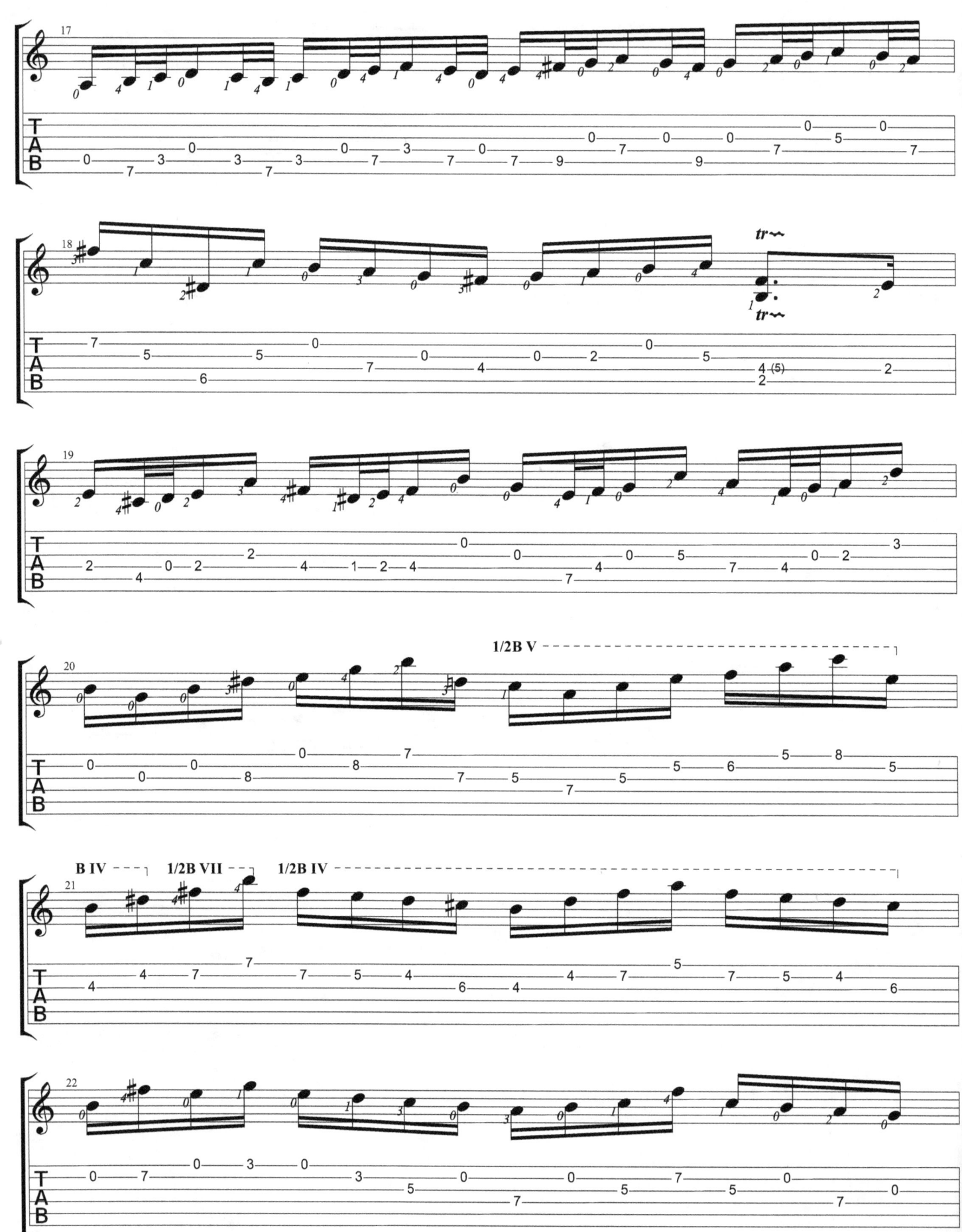

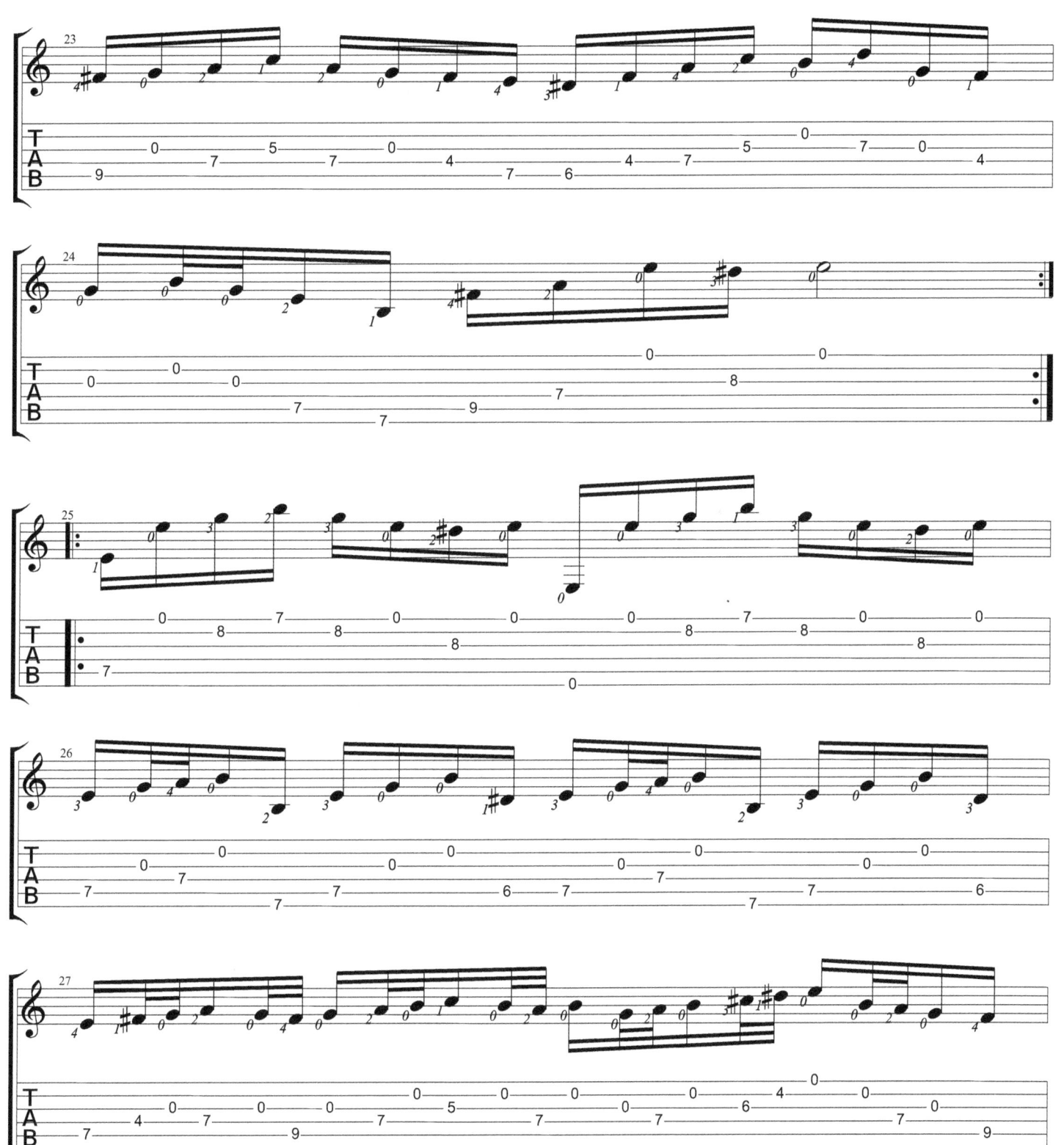

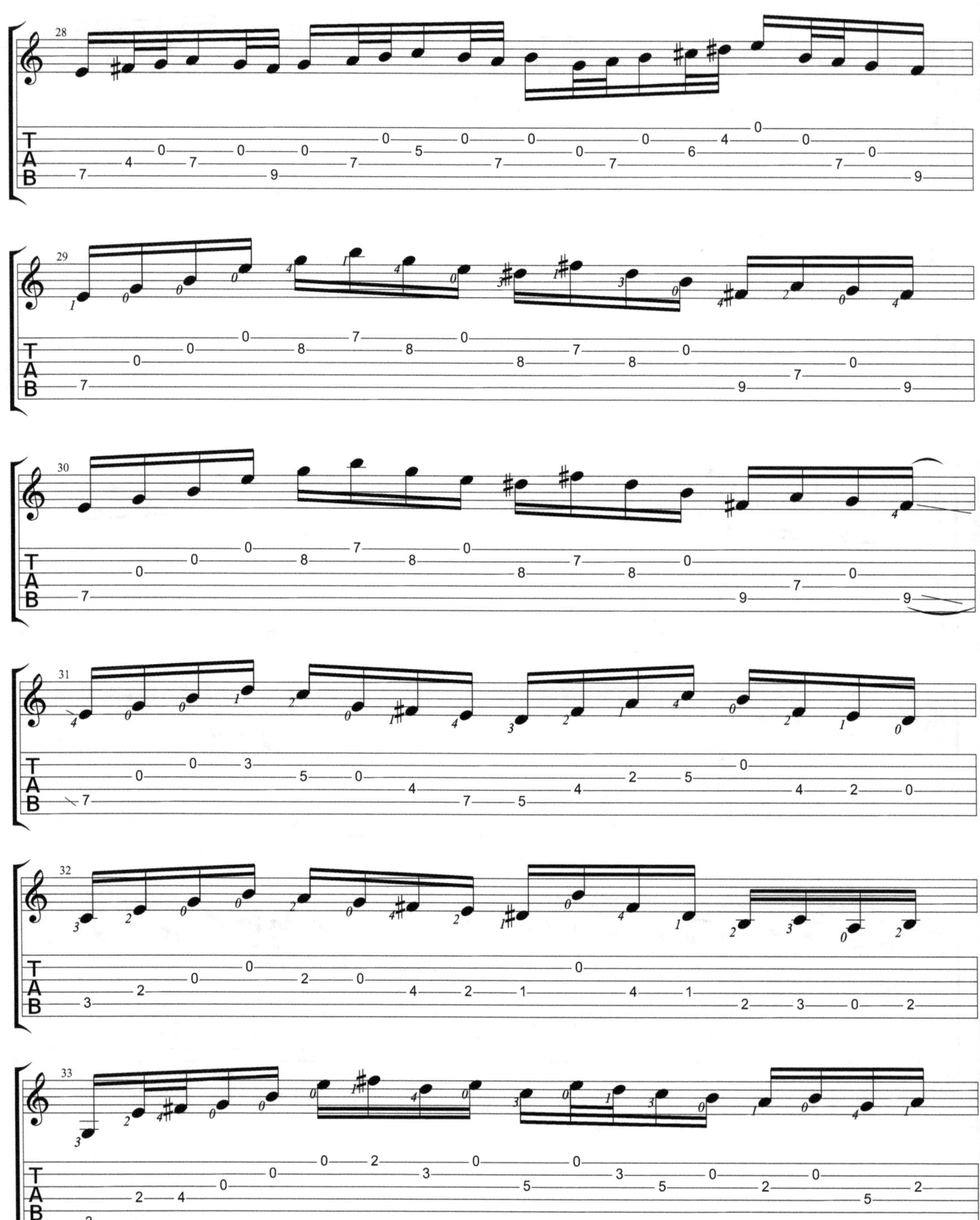

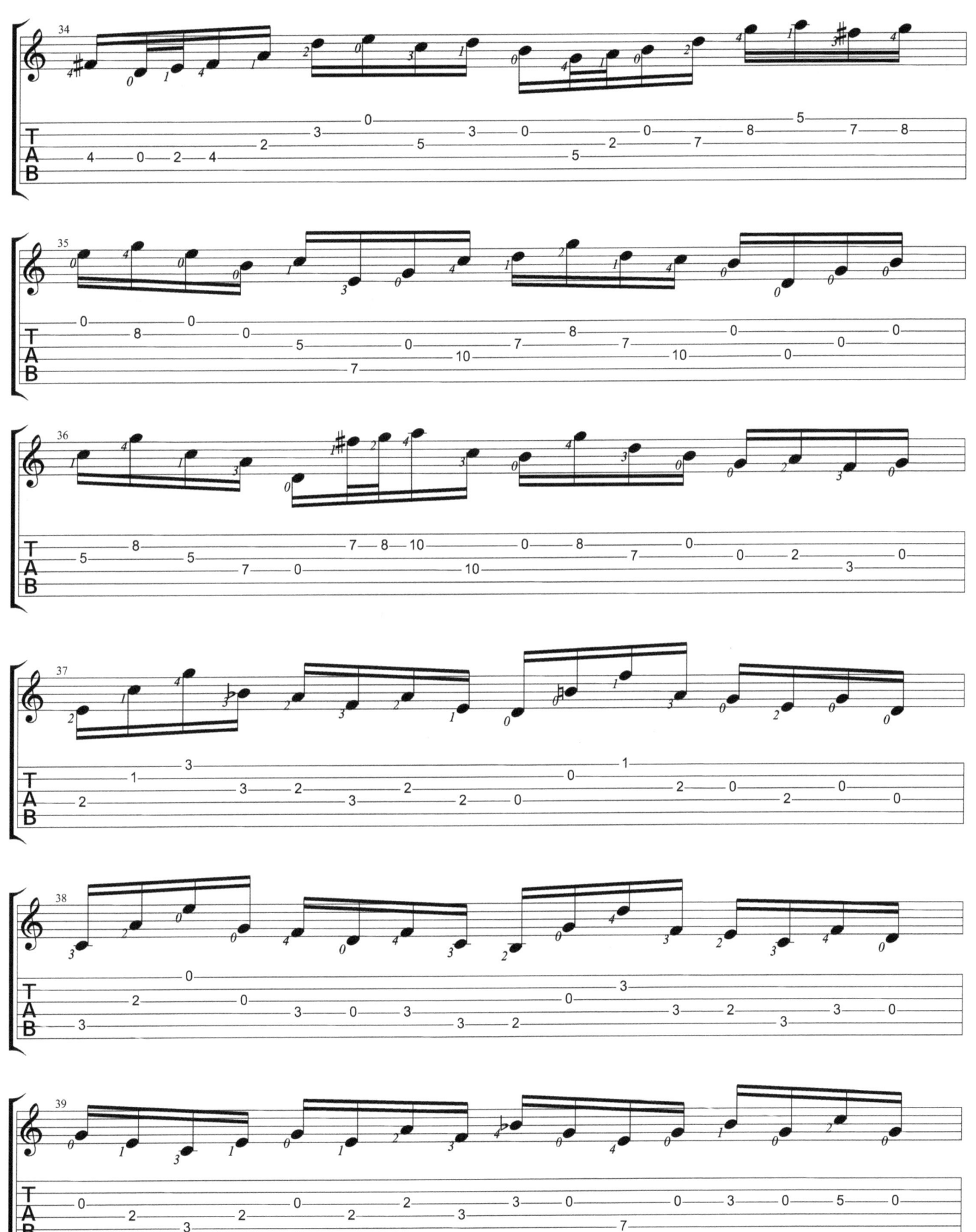

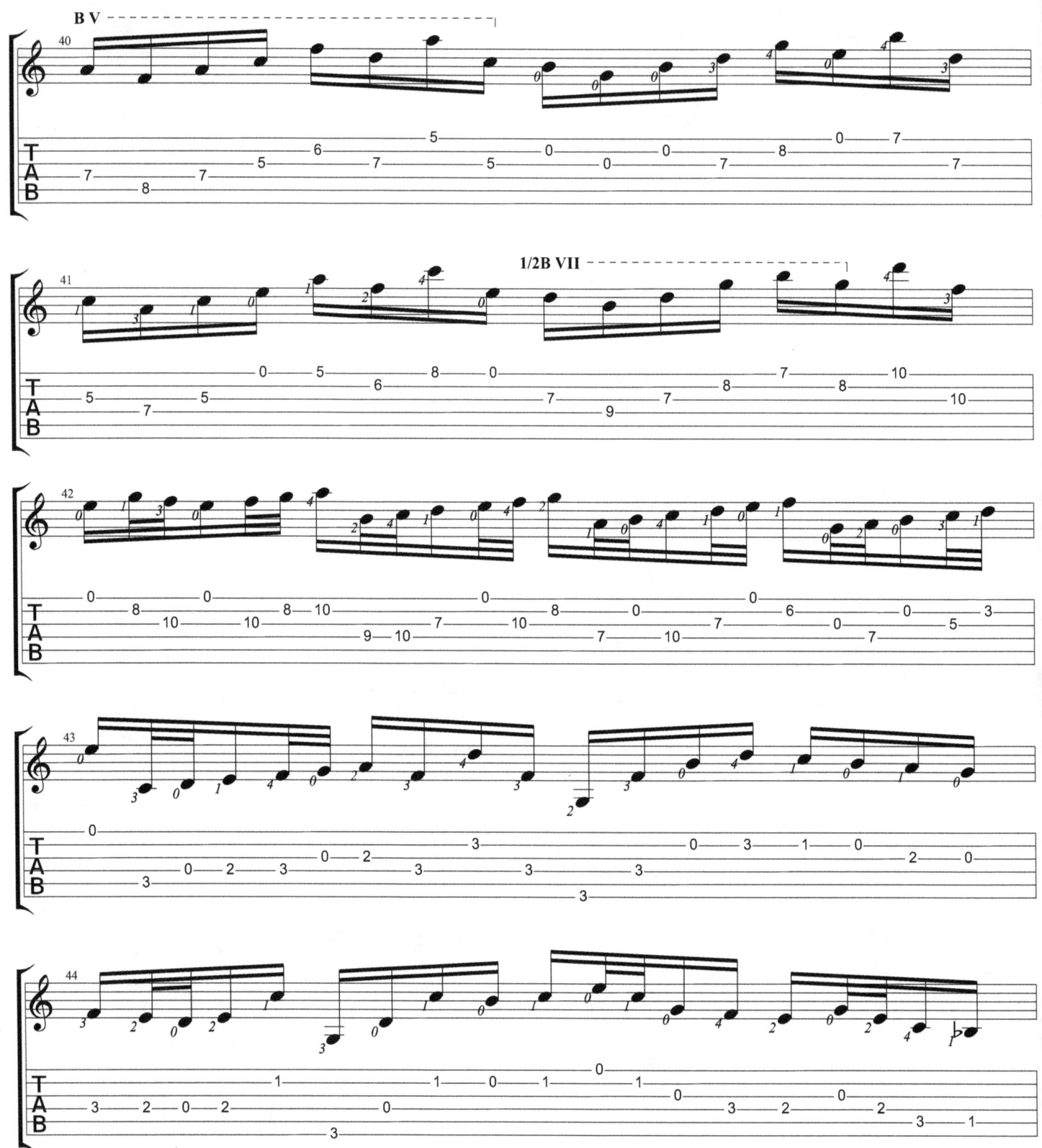

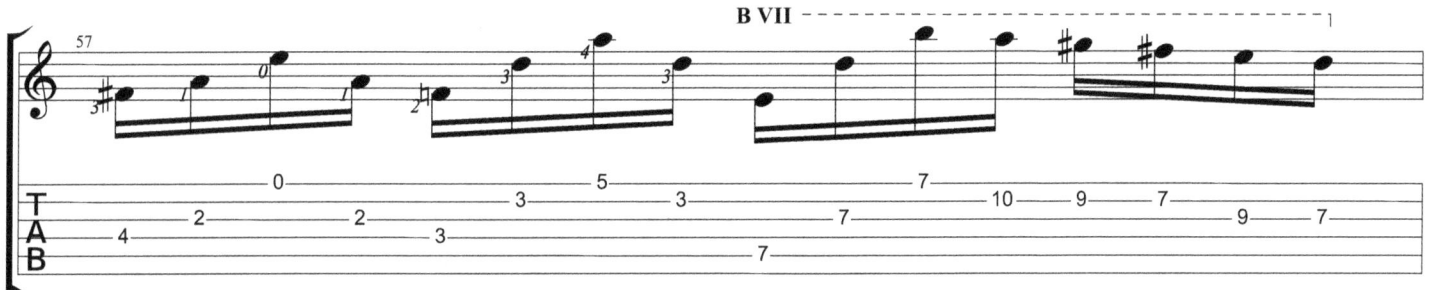
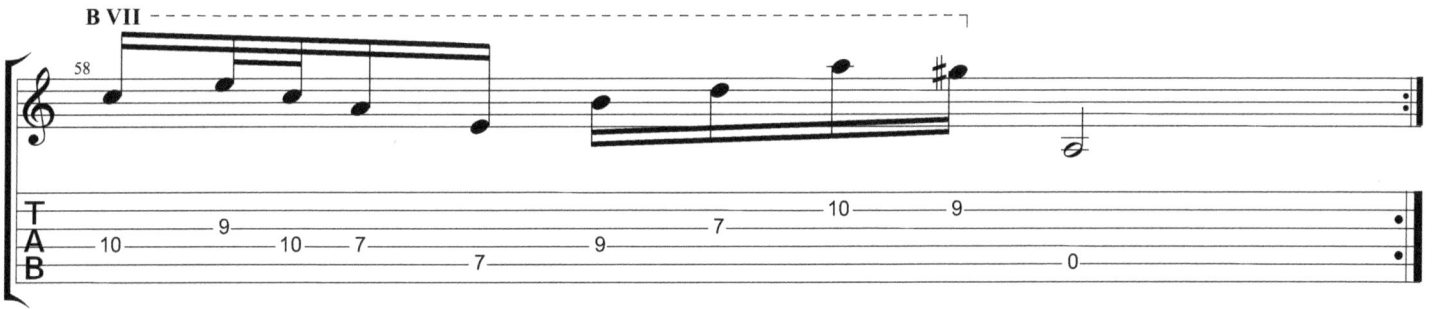

BWV 1004 Sarabande
Arranged for Guitar by Joe Hartnett
Johann Sebastian Bach, 1685-1750

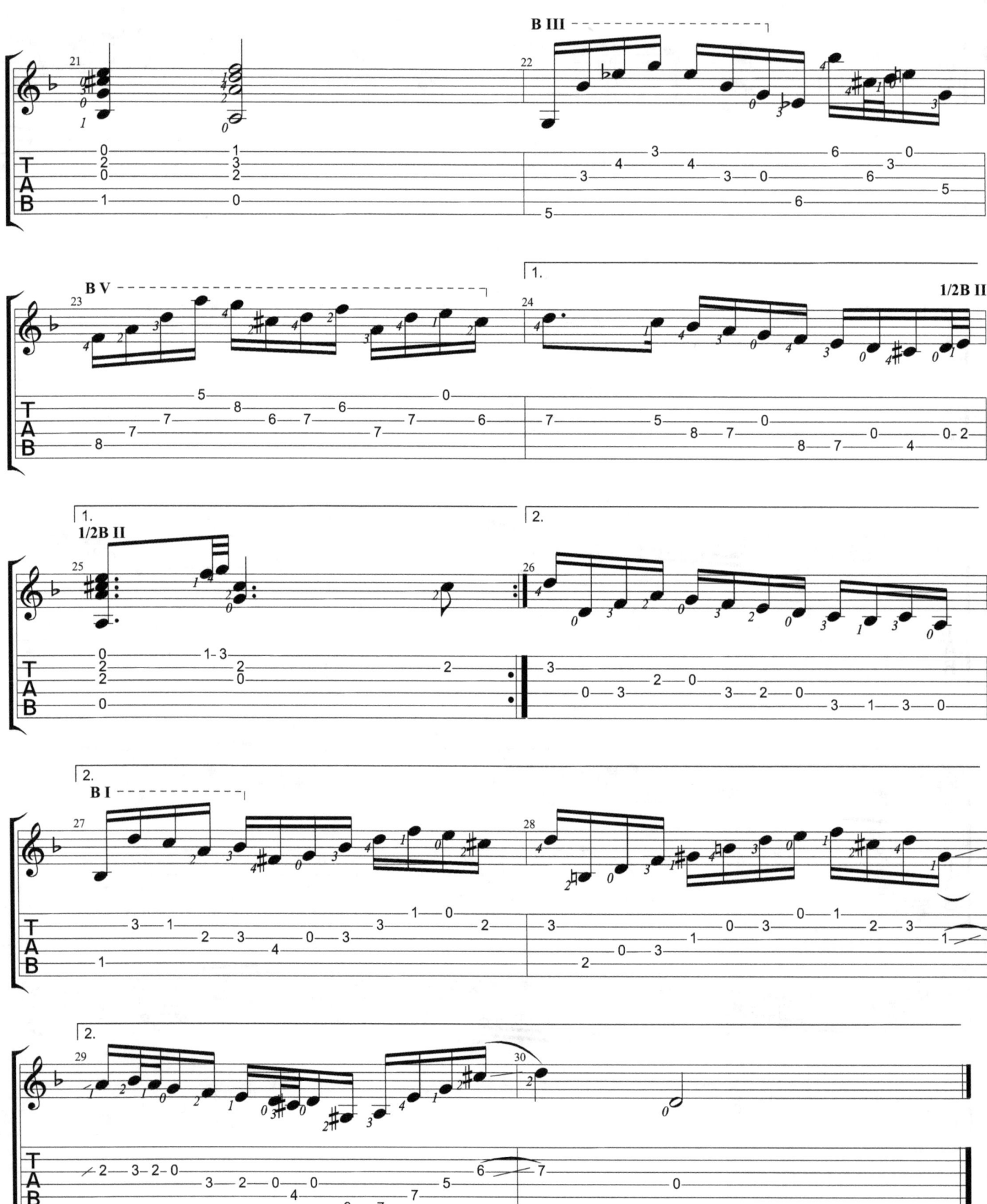

BWV 1006 Prelude
Arranged for Guitar by Joe Hartnett
Johann Sebastian Bach, 1685-1750

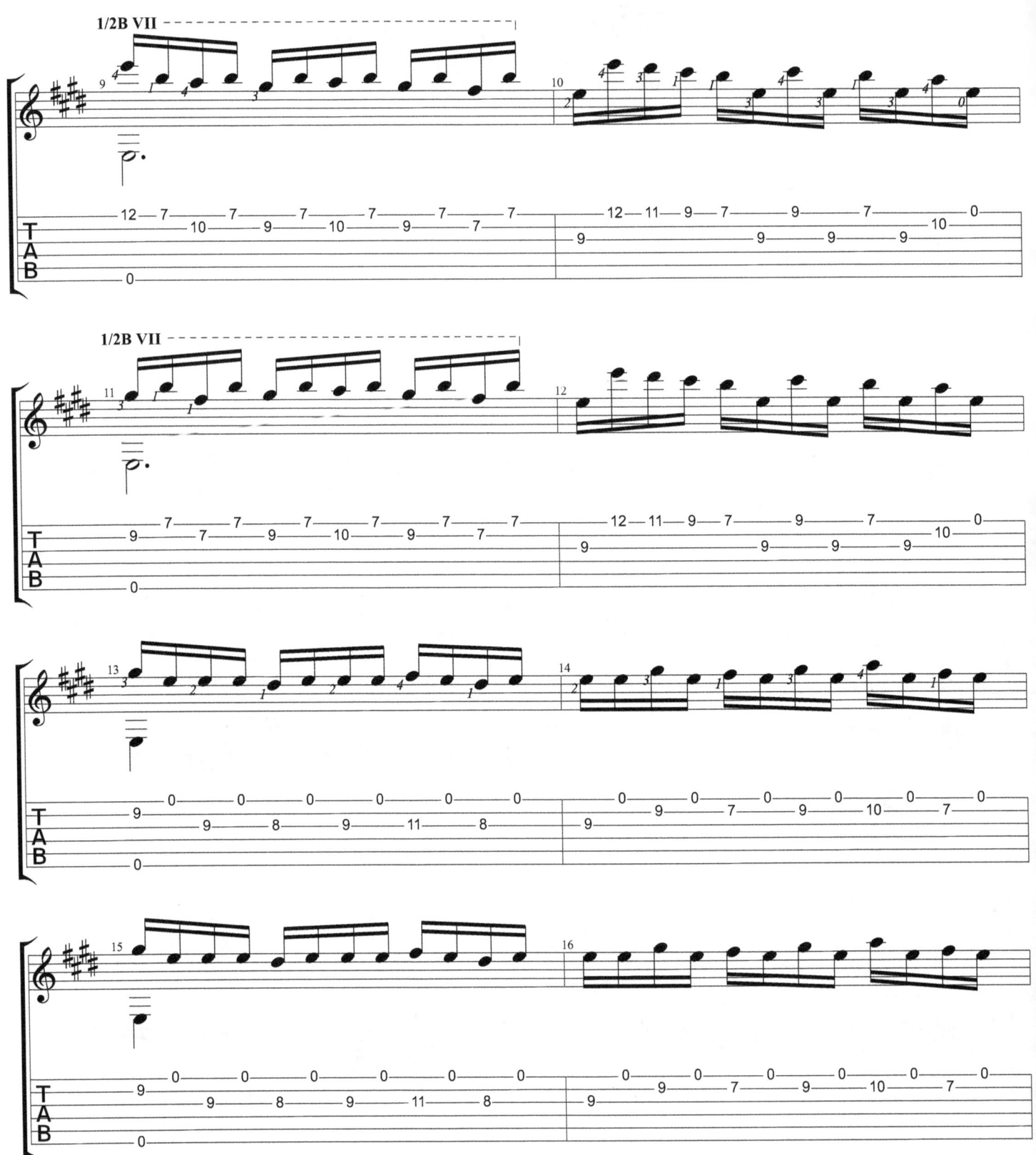

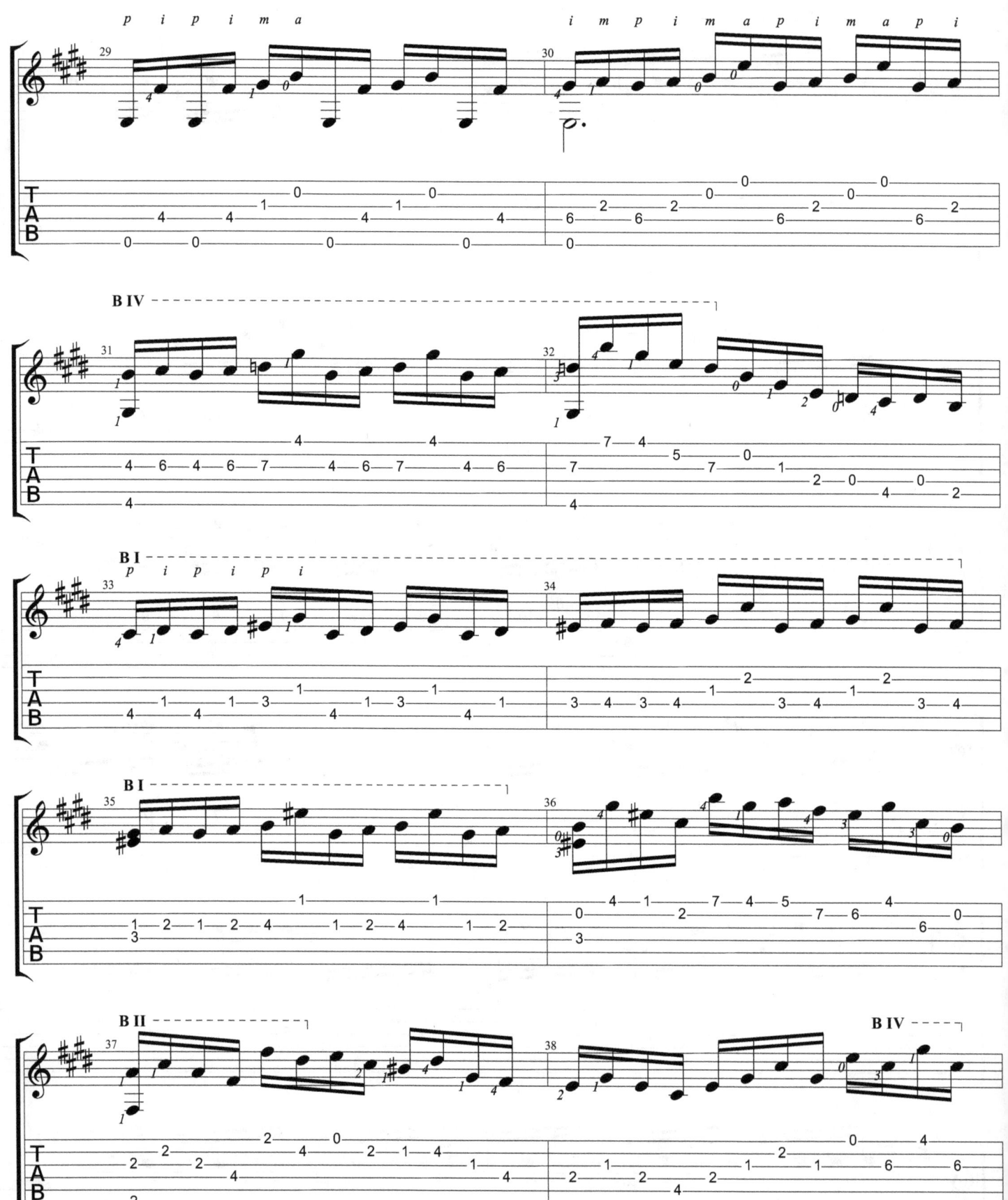

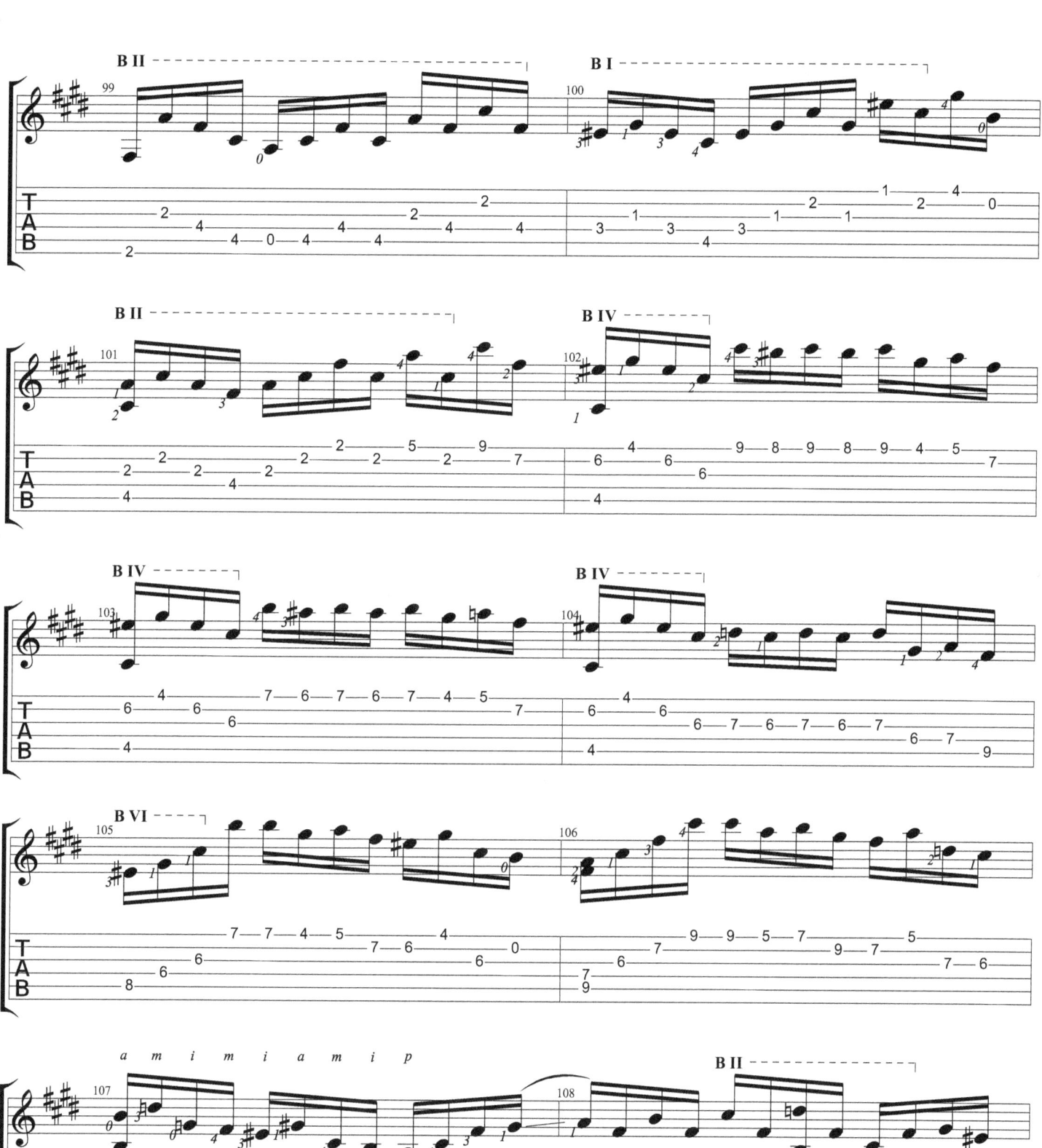

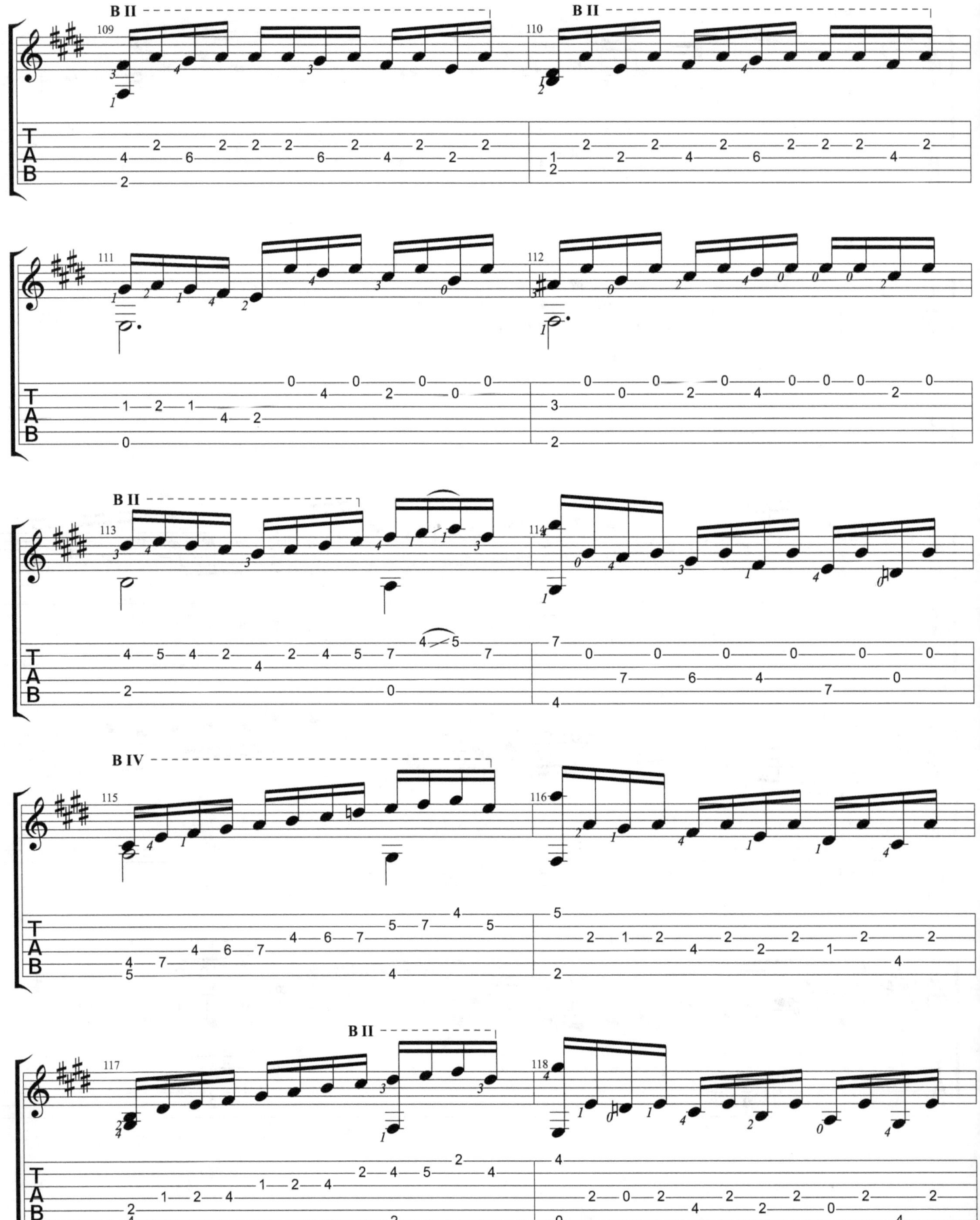

BWV 988 Aria
Arranged for Guitar by Joe Hartnett
Johann Sebastian Bach, 1685-1750

The Incendiary Guitar Lick
for Classical Guitar
Joe Hartnett

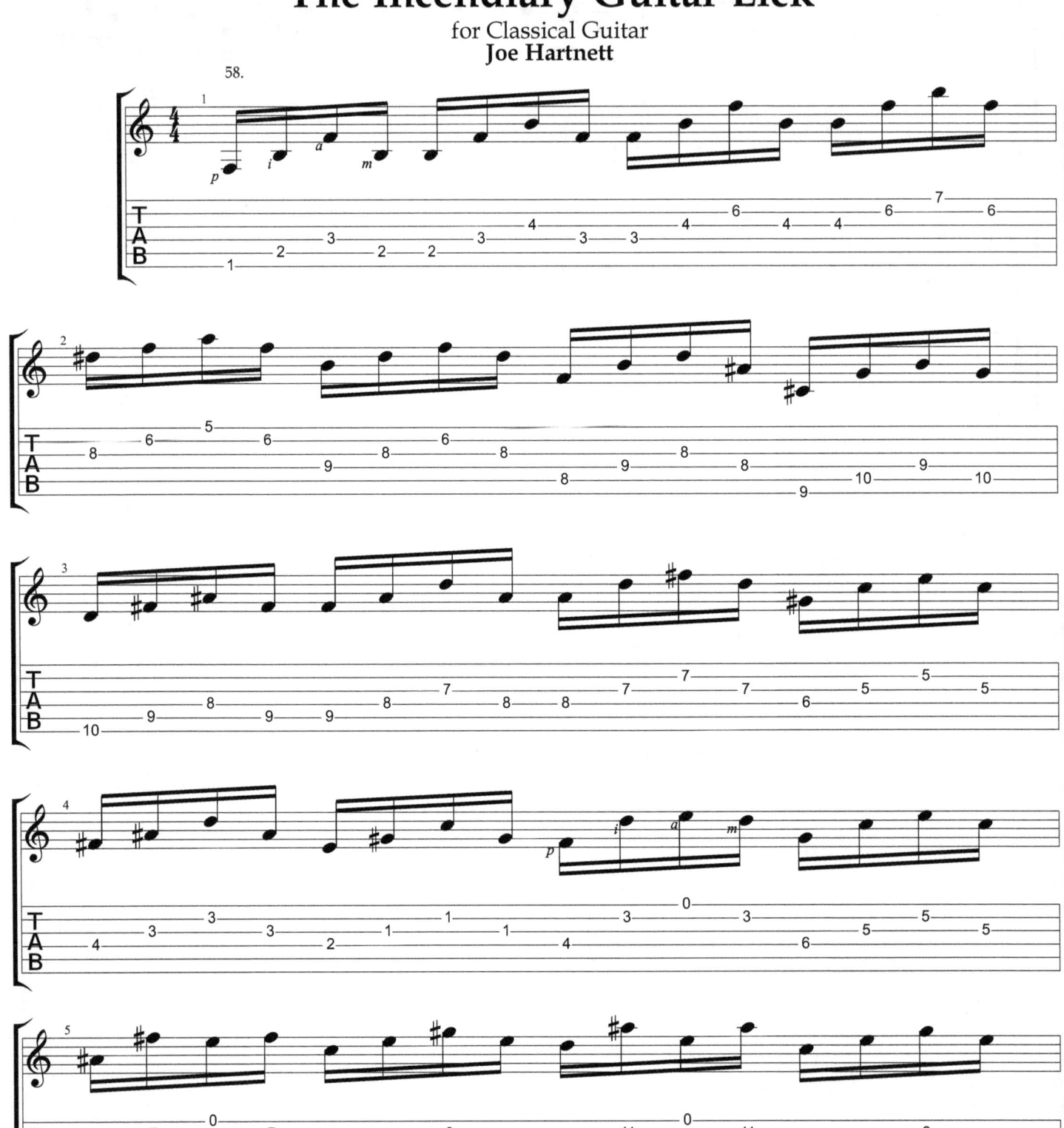

The Formidable Guitar Lick
for Classical Guitar
Joe Hartnett

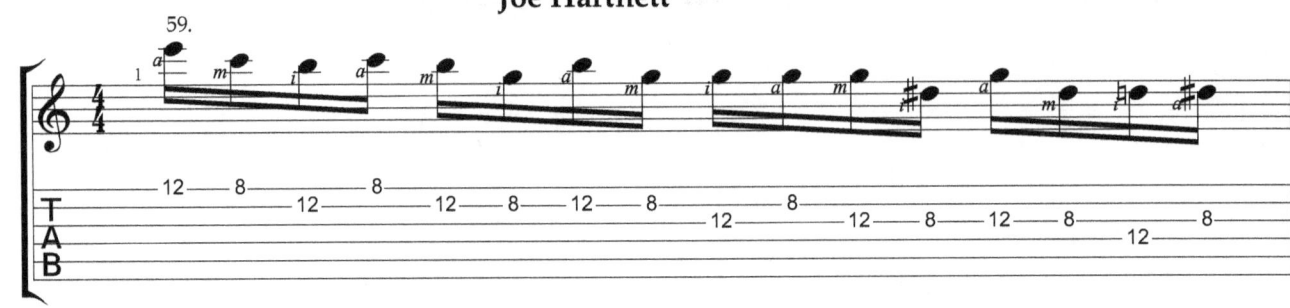

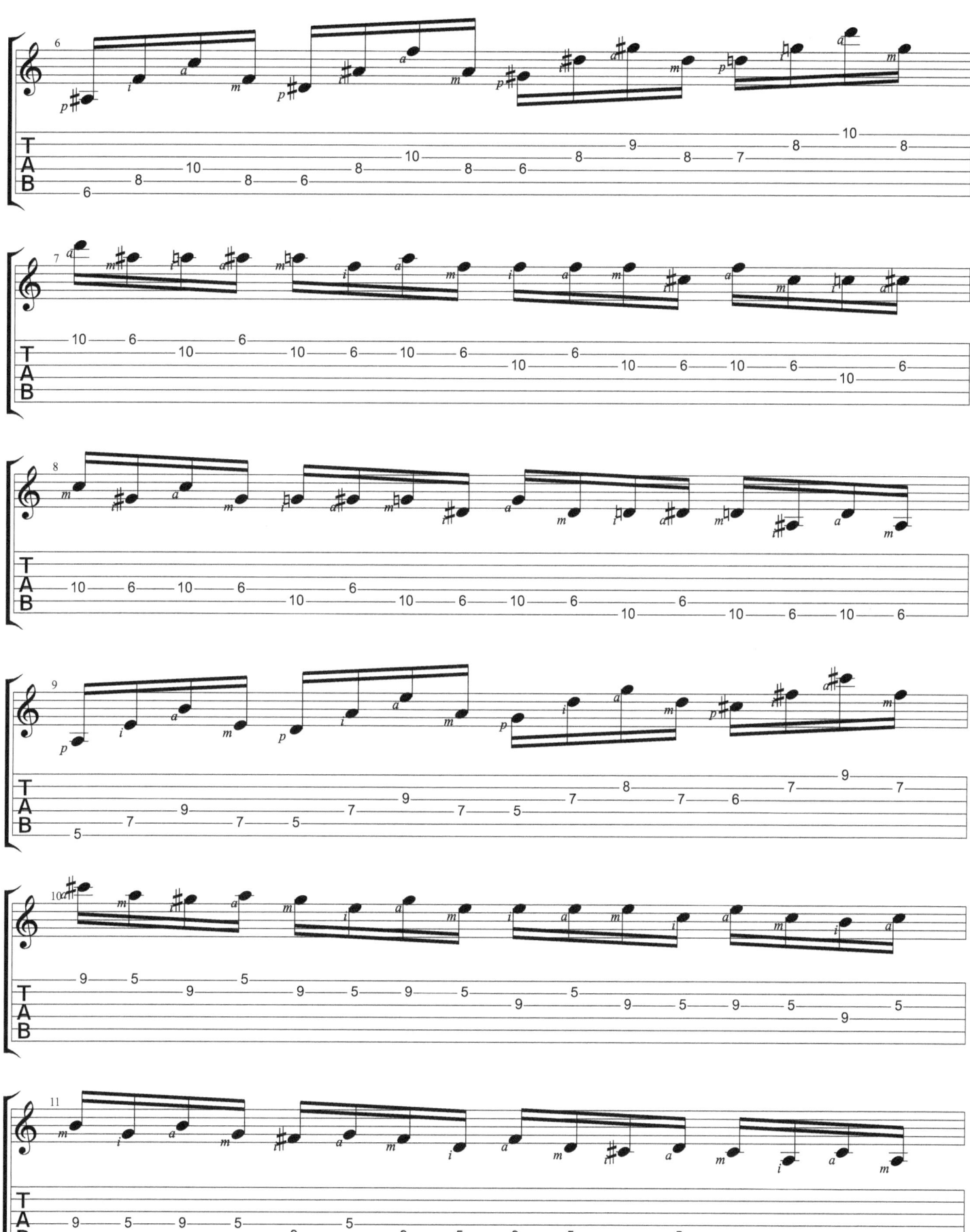

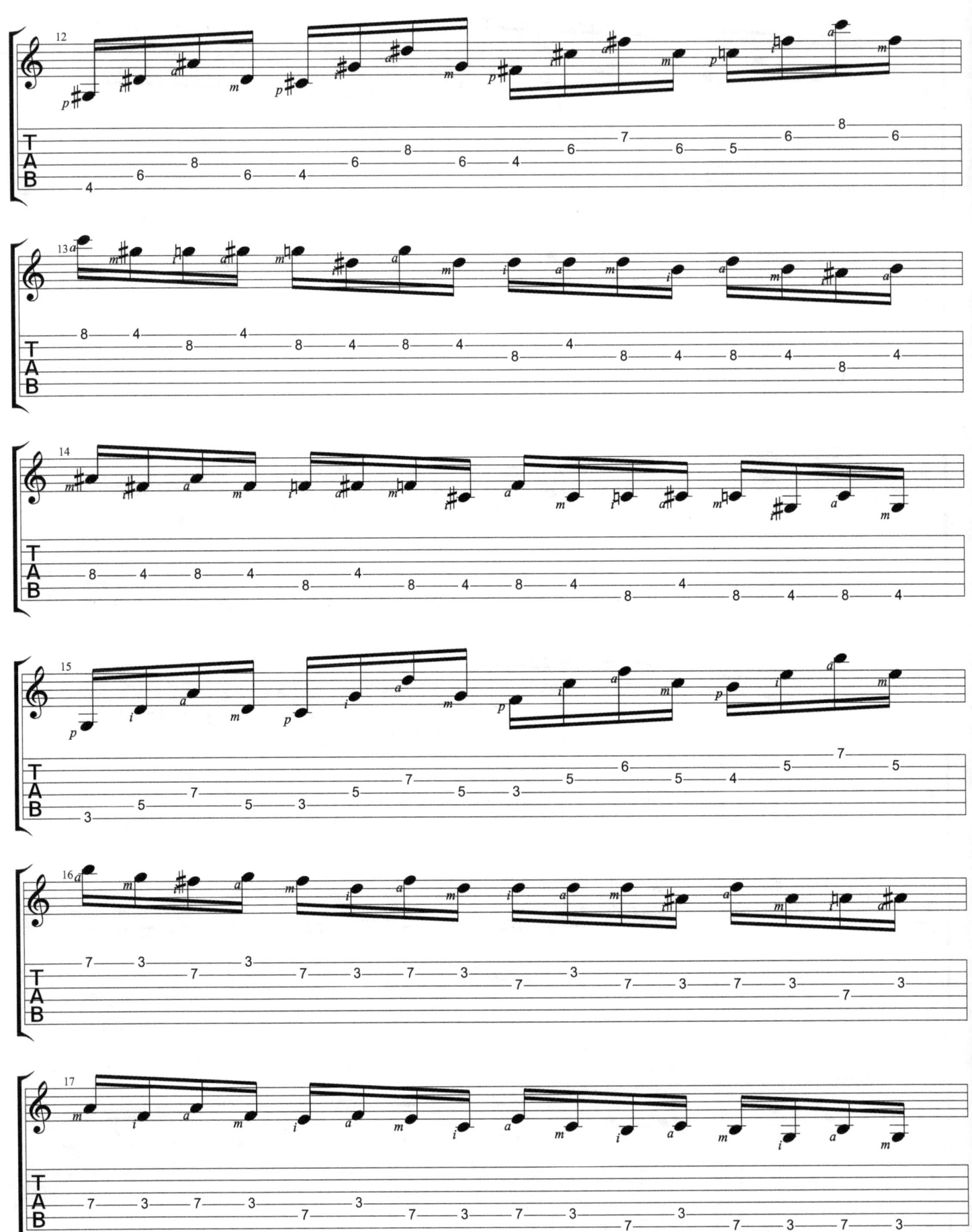

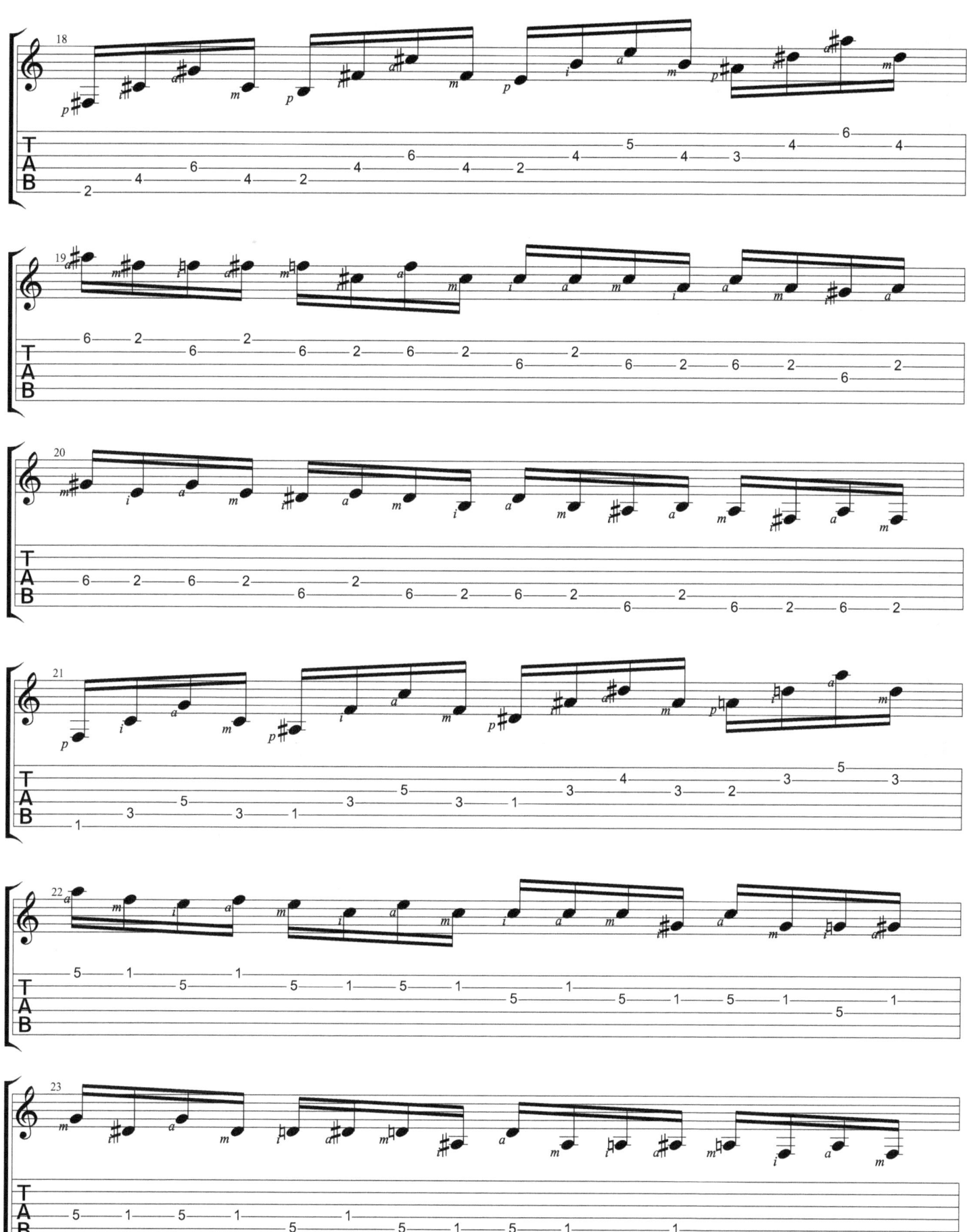

233

Reflection
for Classical Guitar
Joe Hartnett

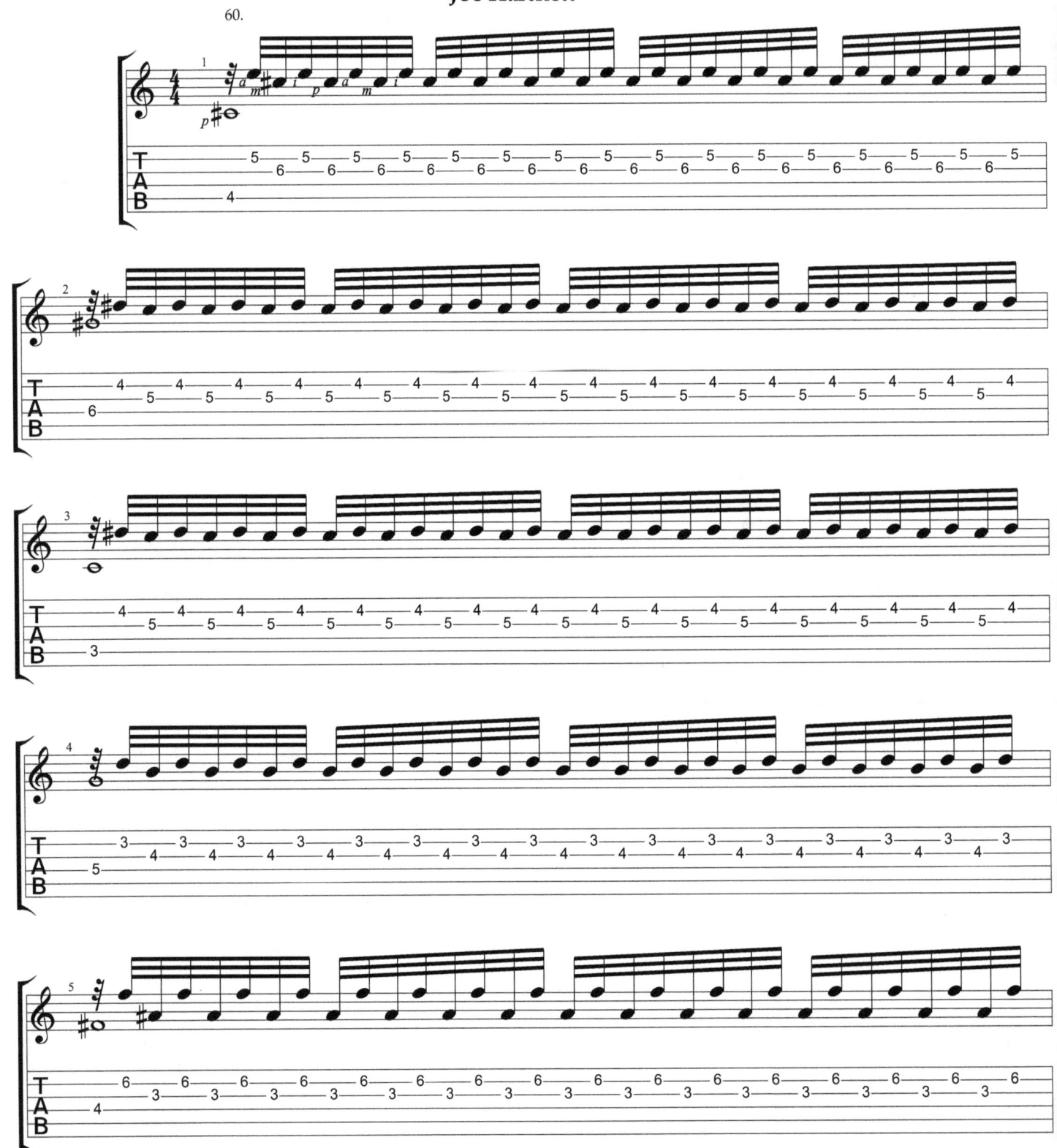

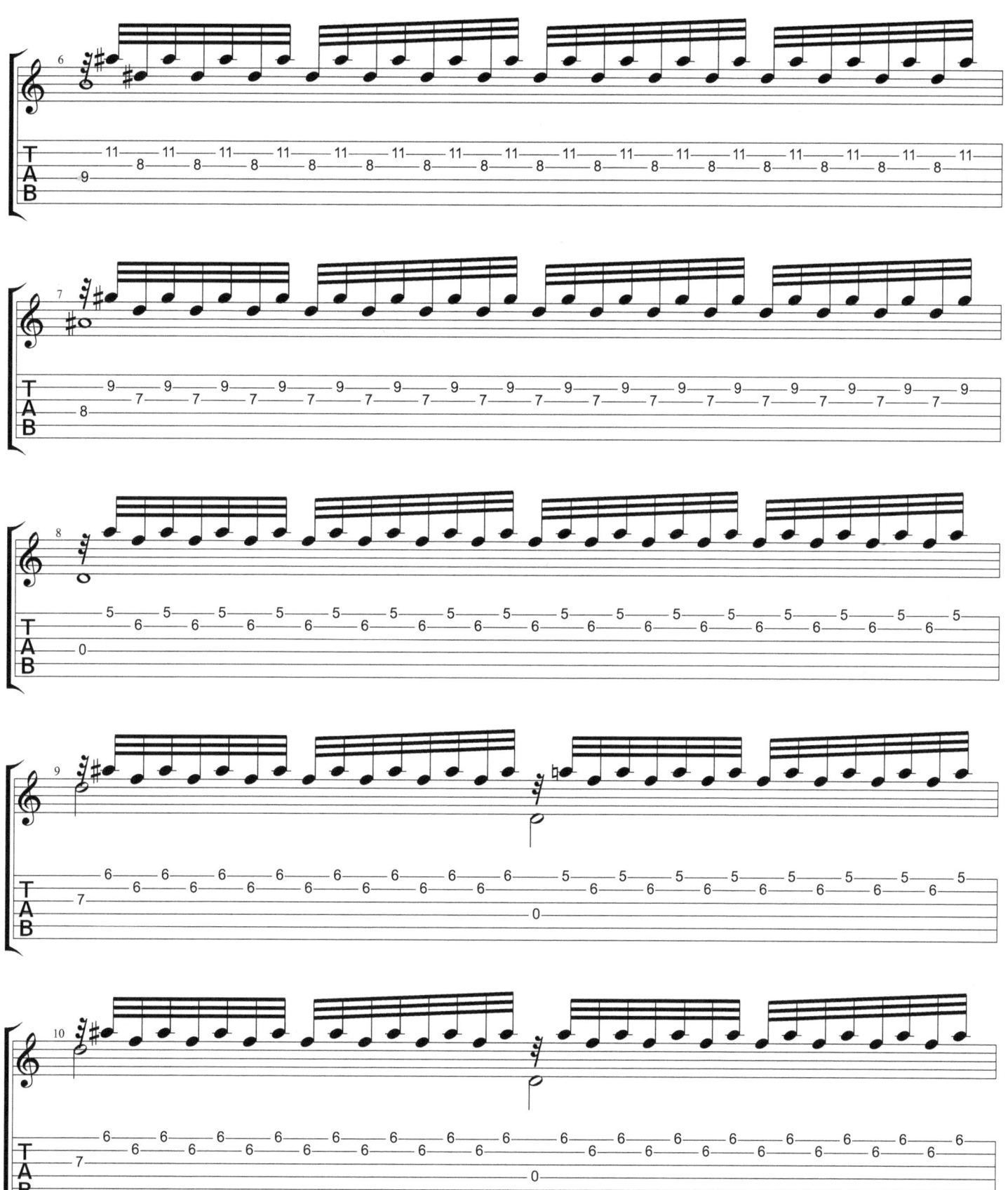

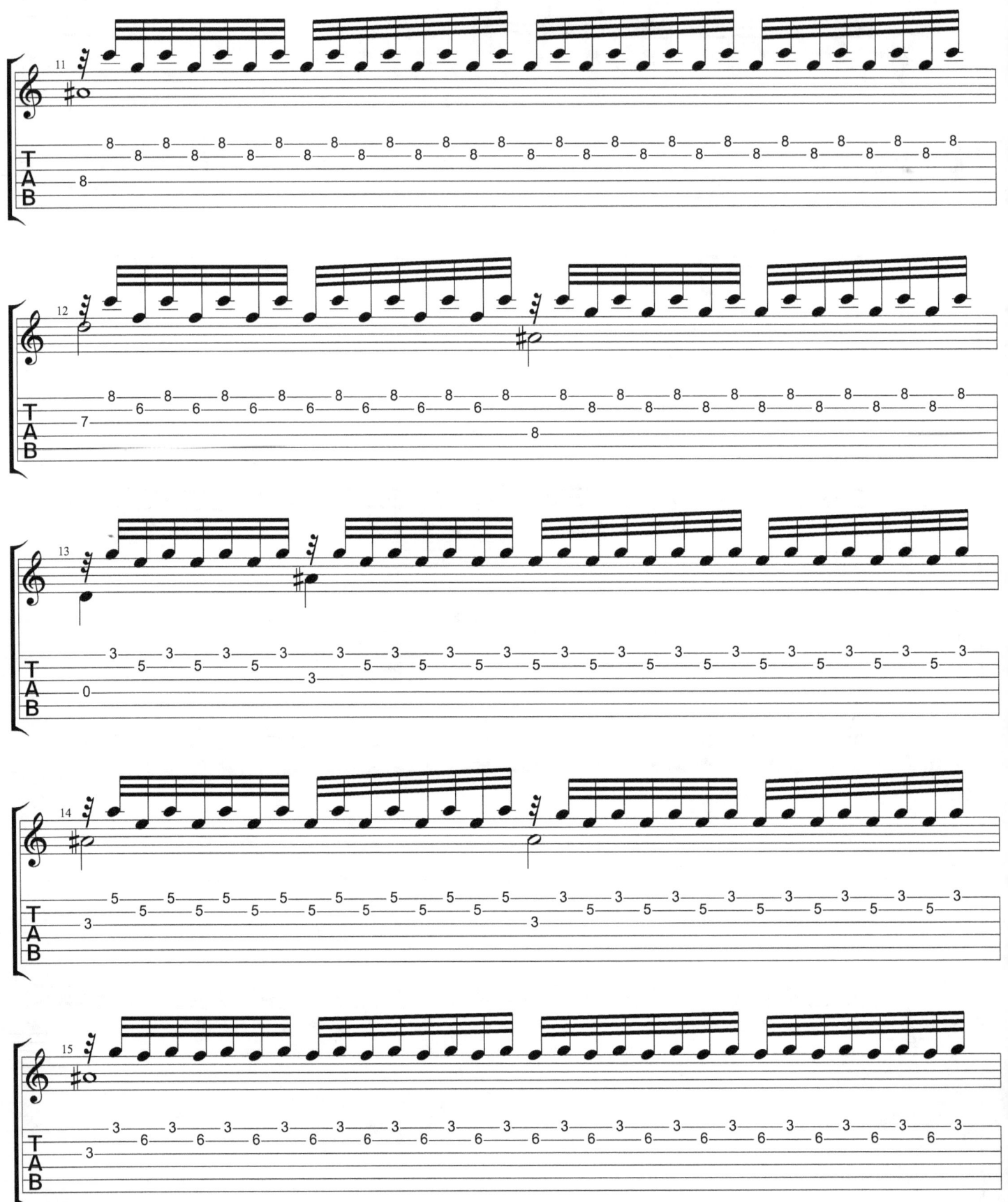

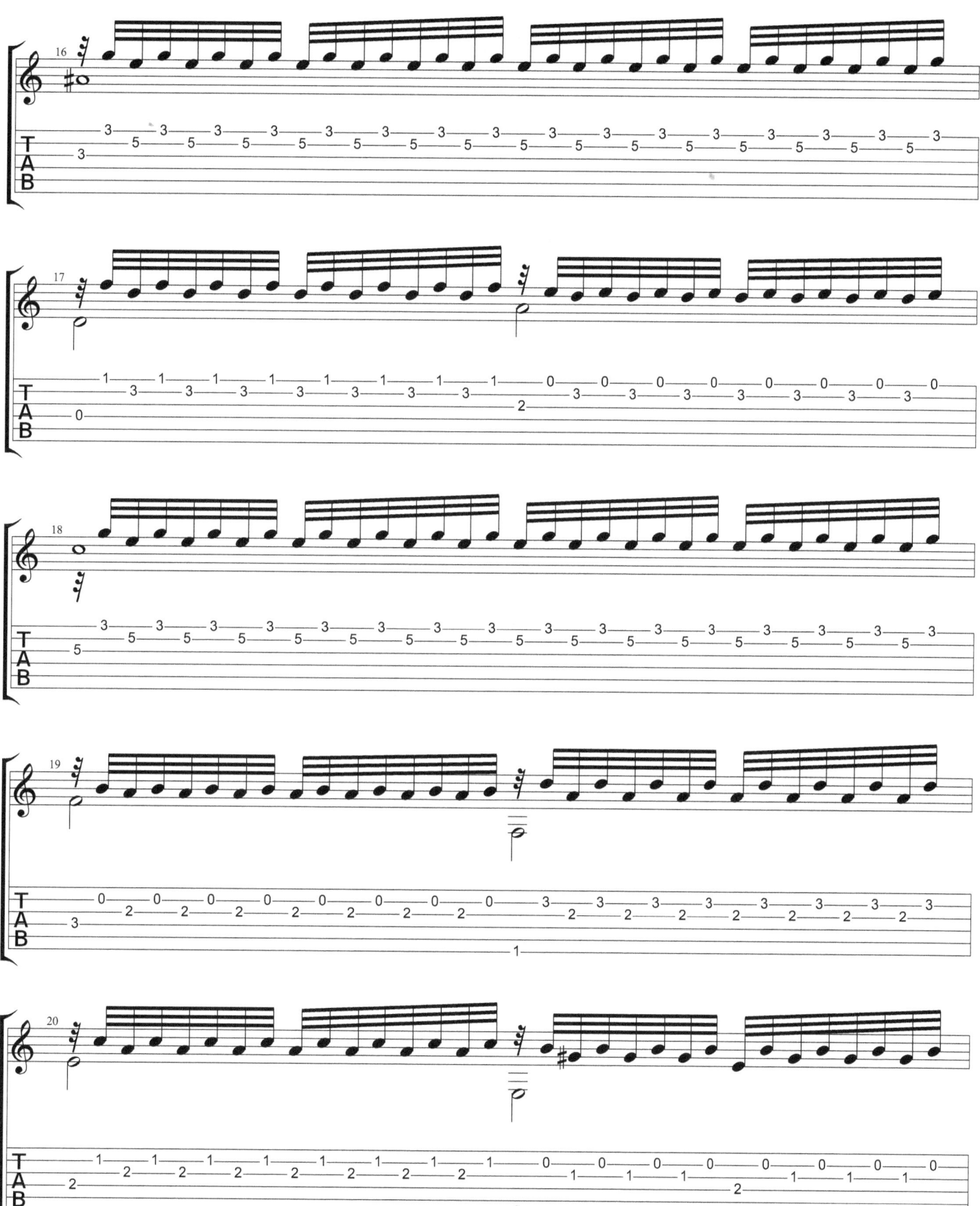

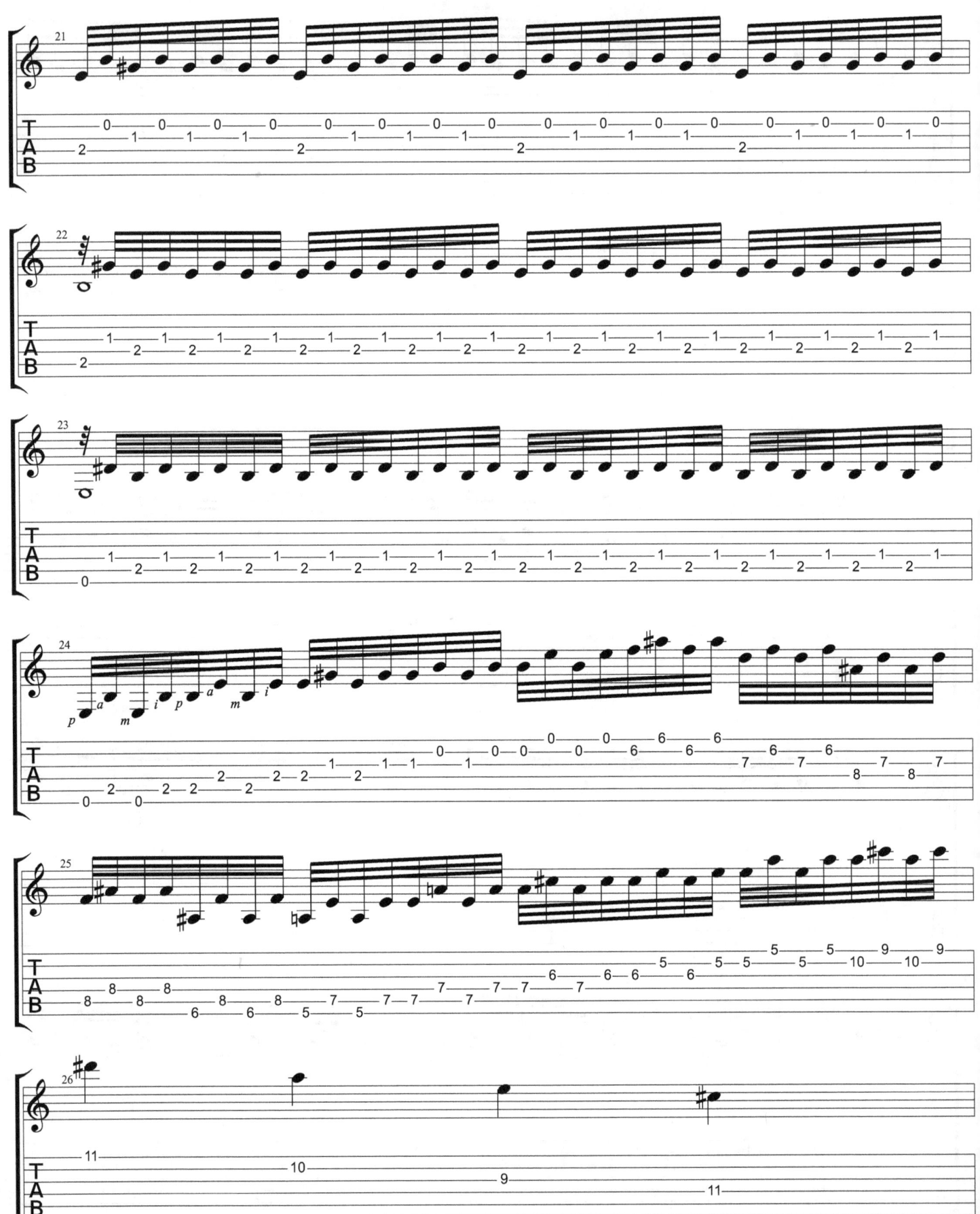

VII. Author Biography

I began teaching myself how to play the electric guitar just before my High School years. I was heavily influenced and inspired by heavy-metal lead guitarists as well as more improvisational guitarists. After my High School years, I put all of my practice into the Classical Guitar. I began teaching myself and developing my right-hand technique with various technical method books and a metronome. I soon realized I would need to read music on the guitar to someday be able to play the music that inspired me. I decided to study music and classical guitar at Keene State College in Keene, New Hampshire. A few years later, I completed my Master of Music degree in Classical Guitar Performance at Austin Peay State University in Clarksville, Tennessee.

-Joe Hartnett, June of 2016

www.ingramcontent.com/pod-product-compliance
Lightning Source LLC
Chambersburg PA
CBHW080939040426
42444CB00015B/3376